6/22

DO YOU HAVE
MONEY DEMONS?

Are conflicts over money undermining your love relationship or your life?

- Do you go on spending sprees when you get depressed
  or angry?
- Do you feel guilty or anxious when you spend money
  on yourself?
- Do you pick up dinner checks, lend people money, or
  buy expensive gifts because you believe people will love
  or admire you more?
- Has debting become a habit you can't break?
- Do you repeatedly rescue or cover up for a financially
  irresponsible partner?
- Do you think having money makes you threatening to
  men?
- Do you long for your partner or your parents to rescue
  you from money problems?

*Most money conflicts can't be resolved by financial
advice—because they're really about deeper issues. If you
answered yes to even one of these questions, Susan
Forward's new book may change your life.*

Other Bantam Books by Susan Forward

MEN WHO HATE WOMEN AND THE WOMEN
WHO LOVE THEM

OBSESSIVE LOVE

TOXIC PARENTS: OVERCOMING THEIR HURTFUL
LEGACY AND RECLAIMING YOUR LIFE

MONEY DEMONS

Keep Them From Sabotaging Your Relationships— and Your Life

DR. SUSAN FORWARD
and Craig Buck

BANTAM BOOKS
NEW YORK • TORONTO • LONDON • SYDNEY • AUCKLAND

MONEY DEMONS

A Bantam Book

PUBLISHING HISTORY

Bantam hardcover edition published June 1994
Bantam mass market edition / May 1995

ISBN 0-553-56938-4

Published simultaneously in the United States and Canada

PRINTED IN THE UNITED STATES OF AMERICA

OPM   0 9 8 7 6 5 4 3 2 1

Contents

7 Enabling a Money–Reckless Man 221

Epilogue: LIVING WITHOUT MONEY

Introduction

We fight about money all the time. And we have the same fights over and over and over It's so infuriating, so frustrating. We both end up totally drained and depressed, but nothing ever changes, nothing ever gets resolved. It's driving me crazy! I can't concentrate at work. I go to lunch with girlfriends and spend the whole time crying. I wake up in the middle of the night in a sweat. We'll go for days hardly speaking. . . . I don't know how long we can keep doing this to each other.

— *Sarah*

Love and money. What is it about these two that make for such an explosive mix? Few fights between men and women are as bitter, as infuriating, as painful as fights about money. No matter how small the amount you're battling about, money fights have an awful tendency to escalate far beyond the boundaries of rationality.

These fights may be about irresponsible spending, or unpaid bills, or losing a job, or not trying hard enough to find a new one, or using money to control a partner, or to punish. Whatever the details, money fights can erupt like emotional volcanos, spewing clouds of frustration and rage.

If you're afraid that the incendiary combination of money and love is destroying your relationship, or if you've had this problem in the past and are concerned for future relationships, this book is for you.

Money Fights

Millions of marriages and intimate relationships have been torn apart by money fights. Couples split up over money more often than they do over anything else, including children, sex, and in-laws.

What is it that makes conflicts over money so devastating to love relationships? After all, money is just a thing—it's paper, it's metal, it represents goods and services that can be bought and sold. Yet fights about money touch our most sensitive nerves. Clearly the intensity, the frequency, and the emotional cruelty of money battles are fueled by factors much more powerful than mere dollars and cents.

An Emotional Diverter Valve

Sarah, whose quote opened this introduction, was married to Greg, the kind of man who needs to be in control all the time. This aspect of his nature often led him to treat Sarah like a child in their relationship. Sarah, who hated confrontation, put up with his unilateral decisions and occasional rantings instead of standing up for herself.

At times when Sarah felt especially powerless and frustrated, she would try to make herself feel better by spending money she didn't have. This was also her way of telling Greg that she resented his telling her what to do.

Once, for example, after he blew up at her for going out with some women friends without clearing it with him first, she rebelled by splurging in a gold necklace with her portion of the rent money. Of course, this led to a fight. Sarah defended herself by insisting that she had a right to spend her own money. She didn't mention to Greg that what was really bothering her was how little and helpless he made her feel.

For his part, Greg accused Sarah of being extravagant and irresponsible. Like Sarah, he didn't get into what was probably really bothering him: his fear that if he didn't control her, she might leave him.

Tearful scenes or shouting matches over things like bills, spending, and financial priorities often serve as protective buffers between us and our deepest, darkest inner fears and insecurities. Money fights serve as emotional diverter valves, allowing us to ventilate a good deal of emotional baggage indirectly, when our feelings are too inaccessible or frightening for us to put them directly into words. It doesn't take any introspection or understanding of our unconscious struggles to fight about money.

Another client, Karen, repeatedly fought with her live-in boyfriend, Max, over the fact that he was not aggressively pursuing a raise at work. Max made significantly less money than Karen, and this was problematic for both of them. As with Sarah and Greg, there were some very deep-seated feelings underneath Karen and Max's battles, fears they were unable to express.

If Karen could have articulated what was really bothering her, she might have said: "I'm scared to death that you're going to leave me because you resent my success so much."

By the same token, Max might have said: "I feel like a failure, and I'm scared that the more successful you get, the less you'll love and respect me."

Without realizing it, these couples were using money as many of us do—as something tangible with which to act out our less accessible conflicts. These conflicts may be between us and our partner, or they may be internal conflicts within ourselves, conflicts that we bring with us into all of our relationships.

Either way, fighting about money is a convenient way to act

out these disturbing conflicts when they are too nebulous to put into words. Money is concrete, it is easy to grasp, and it is easy to hang a conflict on.

You may find it hard to believe that the two thousand dollars your partner blew on a new stereo system, or the overtime you accepted despite his vacation plans, is not what you're really fighting about. In the heat of battle, money issues really do seem to be *the* central issues.

But if you can release your tension and anger by fighting about how much you've spent, you have no driving need to face up to the fact that what you're really fighting about is how much you hurt. The truth is, when you fight about money, you are hardly ever fighting *just* about money. And if you want the fighting to stop, you've got to start by figuring out what you're really fighting about.

A Book for Women

I wrote this book for and about women. Though you will see couples locked in the draining patterns of money fights throughout this book, you will also meet women whose troubles with money exist outside of their love relationships. You don't need a partner to find techniques and exercises in this book that can help you deal with emotional struggles around spending, debting, dealing with success, or being attracted to financially inadequate or irresponsible men. In fact every woman needs to be in a healthy and loving relationship with herself before she can hope to make a relationship work with anyone else.

If you are in a relationship, you may wonder why it is *your* job to do all this figuring and then to do something about what you discover. You may not believe you are even partially responsible for what's going on. After all, money fights are a two-way street. But if you're reading this book, you probably want your relationship to change. And the most effective way to change a relationship is to change your *own* behavior within it, no matter who is primarily at fault.

Relationships are like motors with a multitude of intricately interlocking parts. If you readjust any one of these parts, the others are forced to adapt. Even if the conflicts within your relationship are largely the result of your *partner's* behavior around money, you still have it within *your* power to either get things unstuck or to make some tough decisions about your relationship from a much clearer perspective.

I certainly don't mean to imply that it's a woman's responsibility to do all the fixing in a relationship. But the unfortunate fact is that women are often the only ones willing to do the emotional work needed for effective changes to take place.

Facing the Truth

I was inspired to write this book, in part, by struggles and victories in my own life. The subject cuts very close to the bone for me, not only as a therapist but as a woman.

As with so many women, the role of money in my love relationships—not to mention my unhealthy relationship to money itself—has caused me more pain than I care to admit.

I've had a difficult and confusing relationship with money throughout much of my adult life. For years, I couldn't buy myself the simplest dress or pair of shoes without being assailed by feelings of guilt and anxiety, as if I were doing something "bad."

When I *did* buy something for myself, or someone else bought something for me, nine times out of ten my disturbing feelings would drive me to return it.

My inability to give to myself or to receive gifts from others was a powerful statement about my self-image, a strong indication that I didn't think very much of myself.

I found ways to deprive myself in relationships as well. I fell madly in love with and married a man who had a history of financial recklessness. I believed with all my heart that he would change. He didn't. We were almost always in serious financial trouble, and we fought about money constantly. Though his behavior around money was clearly central to our fights, my anger was also fueled by feelings I was unable to articulate— anxiety about his financial *and* emotional stability, frustration over his inability to keep his promises to change, and fear that I'd made a terrible mistake in marrying him.

While it was very easy for me to point the finger of blame at the man in my life, particularly since he was the one who was acting out destructively around money, there was a difficult truth that only years of therapy would later reveal to me. This truth was that our money fights were not just statements about him but about *me* as well.

Though I was not responsible for his behavior, *I* was the one who chose him, *I* was the one who covered up for him, *I* was the one who bailed him out when he got into trouble, and *I* was the one whose failure to set limits gave him permission to continue his reckless spending.

In retrospect it's clear that between my self-defeating choice of a partner and my self-defeating behavior around money, I was acting out my own unfinished emotional business. Yet at the time, my own role in the emotional and financial chaos of my relationship was invisible to me.

Other Women, Other Behaviors

In my years as a therapist, I've met hundreds of women who, like me, unknowingly acted out their own inner demons around money.

You will meet many of these women in this book—women who struggled with deprivation, as I did, and others who compulsively spent too *much* money on themselves, often money they didn't have; women who used money to put an emotional wall between themselves and their partners; women who sabotaged their own careers to make themselves appear less threatening to men; women who used money, often recklessly, to try to buy the approval of someone they loved; women who just couldn't hold on to money, who lived in perpetual financial chaos; and women who used money to repeatedly rescue financially inadequate or irresponsible men.

Some of these women knew what they were doing but couldn't stop, no matter how desperately they tried, while others were blind to what they were doing, lost in denial.

But they all had one thing in common: They felt trapped in an emotional and behavioral rut that was undermining their relationships and their lives, over and over again.

Repeating Patterns

My particular rut was a frustratingly repetitive pattern of self-deprivation. Though my marriage eventually ended, even after my divorce I continued to find myself attracted to men who were drowning in money troubles.

If I were invited to a party full of successful people, without fail I would be drawn to the one guy who couldn't make a living. "You're a doctor? You're a lawyer? Sorry, you're not my type. But what about you? The attractive man with the flashing smile and the dimples? You're fifty, you're thinking of going back to school, you're an unemployed actor, and you can't afford to put tires on your car? Would you like to come to dinner Saturday night?"

Money and love seemed to be all mixed up in my head, and that confusion was somehow controlling my attractions to men. Why did I keep doing this to myself? If I wanted to get off the treadmill, I needed to find out what this confusion was all about.

The Confusion of Money and Love

My search for some answers took me back to my youth, for it is in our families that most of our attitudes and behaviors around money are formed.

I don't remember money being much of an issue when I was a child, but as a teenager and even as a young adult, I believed I wasn't "good" enough to have money. This was primarily because my father made that point very clear to me, both through his words and through his actions.

Despite his success in business, my father was an incredibly insecure and unhappy man. As a result his moods were unpredictable and his behavior was often cruel, especially when it came to money.

He used money to control me, to punish me, and to hurt me. He would invariably humiliate me when I asked for money, whether it was for going out with my friends or for basic necessities like schoolbooks. He would tell me I was being greedy, selfish, and demanding.

My father used money to deprive me. This hurt me terribly, but not because I wasn't getting a new blouse. It hurt because I felt unloved. He wasn't just withholding money—he was withholding love as well.

On those few occasions when he did give me money or gifts, he was also generous with his attention and affection. I experienced these infrequent moments of generosity as expressions of the love I so desperately wanted from my father. It became increasingly difficult for me to distinguish between money and love. These two were becoming inseparably enmeshed in my mind.

If your parents used money in any kind of consistently unhealthy way—whether they lavished it on you or withheld it from you, whether they were irresponsible with money or hoarded money, whether they rewarded you with money or used it to punish you—you probably grew into adulthood confusing money and love just as I did.

A Window to the Inner Self

By digging into the source of my own attitudes and beliefs about money, I was finally able to uncover the reasons for my adult self-deprivation. I was living out the messages of my childhood, still using money to reinforce my feeling that I was unworthy of being loved. Only now it wasn't my father depriving me, it was myself. I had taken up where he left off.

In depriving myself both materially and emotionally, in not being able to buy anything for myself, and in choosing men who had little to give me, I could temporarily dampen the echo of my father's critical words. If I deprived myself, I couldn't be selfish, I couldn't be greedy, I couldn't be a "bad girl." And in this way I could momentarily assuage my terrible fears of being unworthy and unlovable.

My behavior around money revealed who I felt I was. It was a metaphor for my approach to love and to living. This is true for all of us:

Your behavior around money is not some disembodied psychological oddity. It is a reflection of your whole personality style, especially your style of loving.

If you feel unworthy of having money, you probably feel unworthy of love. If you are stingy with money, you are probably stingy with expressions of love. And if you have a chaotic relationship with money, you probably have chaotic love relationships as well.

Your self-defeating behavior around money can be a window to the very core of your being. And if you take the time to look through that window, you can discover many of the inner demons that are causing you so much trouble.

Money Demons

When we get into a pattern of money fights or when we use money in excessive, destructive, and distorted ways (or support a man who does), we are being driven by unconscious conflicts and emotions that I call *money demons*.

Money demons are hungers, yearnings, fears, guilts, and anxieties. They are feelings of emptiness, of shame, of anger, of inadequacy, or of loneliness. They may stem from painful experiences in adulthood, or they may be related to unfinished psychological business from childhood. But no matter what their source, they are the driving force that fans rational discussions about money into blazing arguments, that overwhelms us with guilt when we consider making even a modest purchase, that pushes us to spend wildly beyond our means, or that powers the magnet that draws us to financially irresponsible men.

Do You Have Money Demons?

The following questions can help you clarify whether you or your partner have money demons of your own to grapple with. Some of these questions may be tough for you to think about— it's always hard to confront our own fears or insecurities. Because of this, your first impulse may be to deny that an unsettling question applies to you. While denial may help you fend off uncomfortable feelings, it also prevents growth and change. Let your discomfort guide you—not deter you. It's a sure sign you're digging in the right spot.

- Do you go on spending sprees when you get depressed or angry?
- Do you feel guilty or anxious when you spend money on yourself, even though you may spend generously on others?
- Are you terrified of losing everything you have, even though you've got a steady source of income?

- Are you unwilling to leave a bad relationship primarily because you're afraid you can't take care of yourself financially?
- Do you regularly insist on picking up dinner checks, lending people money, or buying expensive gifts, because you believe it will make people love and admire you more?
- If you make more money than your partner, does it cause a great deal of stress in your relationship?
- Does your partner use money to control you?
- Do you use money to control your partner?
- Do you repeatedly rescue or cover up for a financially irresponsible partner?
- Are you continually in debt, even though you make enough money to cover your basic living expenses?
- Do you expect your partner (or your parents) to rescue you from money problems that you have created?
- Is your confidence undermined by the fear that having money makes you threatening to men?

If you answered yes to *any* of these questions, you can be sure that your money conflicts are being complicated by emotional or psychological conflicts. You either have money demons of your own, or you are involved with a man whose money demons are having a negative effect on your life.

You may find that you bounce back and forth between some of these behaviors. Or you may have discovered that some of these questions apply to you now, while others refer to things you've done in the past. Money demons can drive you to act out around money in sometimes contradictory ways depending on your circumstances and the nature of your relationship.

At various times in my life I have been a self-depriver, at other times something of a spendaholic. Both of these behaviors stemmed from the same personal demons, but under different circumstances they rose to the surface in different ways. When I was at that stage in my life when I yearned for clothes I could afford but couldn't bring myself to buy, I would have scoffed at anyone who told me that a few years later I would be topping off my credit cards with frenzied shopping binges.

But for me, these two seemingly opposite behaviors were really two sides of the same coin. In my deprivation phase, I was reenacting familiar feelings from my past. In my spending phase, I was overcompensating for those same feelings—all the while setting myself up to relive them again, through debt.

I don't mean to imply that because you have money demons your money fights aren't rooted in real financial disagreements or troubles. Sometimes money conflicts *are* just money conflicts. Modern financial pressures can be tremendous, and that sort of stress can be hard on any relationship. But you can't assume that you *don't* have money demons just because your financial problems are real. The two often go hand in hand. By identifying and dealing with your money demons, you have a much better chance of finding ways to weather hard times with your love relationship intact.

The Inner Backlash

As if all of these psychological forces weren't complicated enough, we women also have to overcome some very powerful social and cultural messages about money.

Women's roles and self-images have always been strongly affected by the messages we got from parents, lovers, peers, teachers, jobs, advertisements, and various forms of entertainment.

Some of the most powerful of these messages involved professional women or women who worked by choice rather than financial need. These women were typically stereotyped as hard, cold—and lonely.

A woman didn't have to read too deeply between the lines to understand that she wasn't supposed to pursue her career "like a man" if she wanted to be loved by one. And if she wanted a man to think she was "feminine," she was supposed to act passive, dependent, self-sacrificing, and all-giving.

In the past few decades the messages have changed—at least on the surface—encouraging us to overthrow the old, restrictive images and take our power, be the best we can, "just go for it."

And money was supposed to be our great liberator. Having our own money was supposed to free us spiritually as well as economically. We would become independent, we would be confident, we would feel safe. Money was supposed to empower us, open up new options and opportunities for us. It was supposed to give us new wellsprings of self-worth and self-sufficiency.

Unfortunately, many of us haven't allowed ourselves to enjoy these gains. We've done a much better job of freeing ourselves intellectually from old beliefs than we have of freeing ourselves emotionally. On the outside we may seem self-assured and competent, but on the inside a lot of us still have an internal war going on—a struggle with our deep-seated anxieties about how independent and prosperous we're allowed to become and how we're supposed to act to be desirable to men. We still wrestle with a fundamental question: "Can I be powerful and successful and still be loved?"

I call this dilemma, and the ambivalence and fears it creates, the *inner backlash*. This backlash is a reaction to the emotional cost of trying to exorcise old stereotypes that are still deeply ingrained. On the one hand, we strive to move up the ladder, while on the other, we worry that we're undermining our relationships by doing so. Far too many women respond to this backlash by sabotaging their careers or their finances, becoming martyrs for love.

How This Book Can Help You

I wrote this book to help you figure out not only what's really going on between you and your partner when you fight about money, but also what's really going on inside of *you*. By using the dramatic experiences that the women in this book have been generous enough to share, you can discover how your personal money demons are controlling you and how you can learn to manage them.

As we cut through the confusion together, I will give you specific behavioral strategies and exercises that you can put into practice immediately to help you put the brakes on the negative money-related patterns that are tripping you up or fueling fights in your relationship.

When Differences Are Misleading

At first glance some of the situations we'll look at in this book may not seem to apply to you. I urge you to take a closer look.

Your behavior may be different, but you may very well share the same money demons or a similar history of romantic troubles with many of the women in this book.

The money demons that haunt self-deprivers, for example, might drive other women to spend uncontrollably or to make bad relationship choices.

Or you may not be involved with a money-reckless man, but the limit-setting techniques I describe in Chapter 7 can be just as effective if you are living with a financially controlling man. If you are a compulsive debtor or gambler, you can use them effectively to change your own behavior.

None of the cases in this book shows a complete course of therapy—each case could fill a book of its own if I were to attempt that. Instead, I have chosen to use one or two primary cases to demonstrate just a few exercises in each chapter, hoping that by the time you finish this book, you will have a good all-around grasp of the ways in which you can use these techniques in your own life.

Money Management Is Not Enough

Some authors insist that the solution to money problems in a relationship is sound financial management. But it's rarely that simple. Financial solutions, as anxiety-reducing as they may temporarily be, simply cannot resolve emotional and psychological problems.

Women who can recite all the principles of good money management—or even run a tight financial ship at the office— are still often bewildered and frustrated by their inability to put those principles to work in their personal lives. Even when your financial solutions are clear, it can be difficult if not impossible to implement them before you come to terms with your money demons.

For example, if you are a compulsive debtor, you may find it fairly easy to set up a reasonable budget for yourself, but money demons can still drive you to cheat on that budget. This will not only undermine your determination to work toward a solution but aggravate your feelings of frustration and helplessness.

Or if your partner is using money to control you (or if you are using money to control your partner), financial solutions will do nothing to deal with the fears that are driving the need to control or the resentments that have built up between you.

Until you deal with the inner issues that are really driving your money fights, sound money management can offer only a Band-Aid solution.

We all use money to express our deepest fears, tensions, fantasies, self-worth issues, and emotional wounds. But if you use money as a window to your inner self—as I was ultimately able to do—you will gain the insight to expose these money demons. This will finally give you the power to do something about the money fights your demons inflame and the behaviors that they drive.

I wrote this book to show you how.

1

Emotional Barricades

I really love him, and I know he loves me, but there's this thing called money that keeps getting in the way. We fight about it all the time because I won't move into his place with him, and that pisses him off. It's not that I don't want to—it's just that I can't afford it. So he says he'll pay the rent, but I can't handle that. I don't like being dependent on a guy—they always turn it on you.

—A.G., age 28

It's like I'm terrified of having him be there for me because, what if he leaves me? I have this horrible fear that if I get too used to him being there for me today, I won't be there for *myself* tomorrow. So I find ways to push him away.

—P.B., age 34

In God I trust, but not in joint accounts. They just scare me. He gets really upset about it because it's a commitment thing for him. But every time he brings it up, it just pushes my buttons and we end up fighting about it.

—R.L., age 45

Rita had been feeling slightly uneasy all morning. But as she and her boyfriend Stan drove to the electronics store, her anxiety began to build. Rita wasn't ready to buy the TV.

This was going to be their first major joint purchase. They'd been living together for three years, yet Rita still felt the need to keep sepa-

rate bank accounts and to split their expenses. She really didn't want to buy the TV.

She had felt this same anxiety a week earlier, when Stan had brought up marriage again. "We're not getting any younger," he'd said, which hadn't exactly thrilled her since she'd been trying to avoid the thought of her upcoming forty-fifth birthday. "And it's not like we don't know what we're getting into. I mean, we've been together a long time."

As they pulled into the parking lot, she felt a tightening in her chest. "Are you sure we should be doing this?"

"I thought we already settled it." His voice sounded irritated, as if he'd been expecting this reaction from her.

"You're the one who wants it," she said. "I don't see why I have to pay for half of it."

"What are you talking about? You're the one who came up with the idea of getting a bigger TV in the first place. If you were so luke-warm about the idea, why did you wait till we got to the store before you brought it up?"

"Because I knew you'd get defensive about it," she said.

"It's only three hundred dollars apiece, for God's sake. We're both making good money. What's the big deal?"

Rita felt like crying. The "big deal" was that these fights were becoming a habit.

Symbols of Commitment

The depth of Rita's anxiety and the intensity of her fight with Stan were way out of proportion to the mundane event that had triggered the conflict.

The cost of the television was not a major factor—she made a good living running her own independent bookkeeping business, and he was doing well teaching tennis.

Still, when they pulled into that parking lot, that six hundred dollars might just as well have been six thousand, to her. Rita was overreacting.

The line between healthy emotional expression and emotional overreaction is vague; the concept is difficult to pin down. But at least in retrospect, most of us know an overreaction when we see one—or experience one.

Overreaction can come in the form of a tantrum, a depression, a physical outburst, or even an illness. I had a dear friend who once broke out in hives because her bank called to tell her she was overdrawn. She seemed very calm on the outside, yet her emotional response precipitated a physical symptom.

Obviously, emotional overreactions are easily identified when they're extreme. Still, even if your behavior is outrageous, you're often unaware of it while you're doing it. It's easy to be blinded—as Rita was—by your own emotional responses when they're especially powerful.

Symbols of Danger

Rita and Stan ended up buying the TV, but that did nothing to lower her general state of anxiety. Their money fights became increasingly bitter as Stan pressured her to "stop keeping score" and combine their finances. Rita's elaborate bookkeeping to maintain their separate accounts was a constant annoyance to him.

RITA

We've been together three years, and I can still go through our house and say, "This is mine, that's his." He pays for certain things, I pay for certain things, and we put all our receipts in this fishbowl in the kitchen. Then at the end of the month I tally it up on the computer, and whoever owes who, we pay it down. To the penny. He really hates it.

SUSAN

Why is it important to you to keep everything separate?

RITA

I guess it's like, "God if we own the TV set together, what
if he leaves?" I mean, it frightened me. Like, "Does he really love me?" I need him to tell me that . . . that he loves
me. To tell me he's never leaving. So the things become
symbols of a permanence: "Let's keep everything separate,
so if you have to leave, you can leave. You know who be-
longs to what."

Rita's logic was hard to follow. In fact, it seemed self-contra-
dicting. If she was afraid Stan might leave her, why didn't she
welcome the symbol of commitment that a relatively large joint
purchase might represent? Instead, she saw it as a symbol of
danger. The very thing she should have embraced triggered her
to panic.

I'm not suggesting that there is anything unhealthy as such
about choosing to keep independent finances in a relationship.
But such choices need to be made from a position of free will
and an honest assessment of the issues and the alternatives. Rita's decision was based, instead, on fear and denial. She'd be
more likely to make a healthy decision by flipping a coin.

The Vulnerability of Dependence

Rita was struggling with the same painful paradox that many
contemporary women struggle with in modern love relationships—we want someone to share the weight of our fears, our
anxieties, and our day-to-day responsibilities, but we don't
want to be dependent.

As we become intimate, we often fear that we're sacrificing
our independence. On the other hand, if we guard our independence too fiercely, we may end up withdrawing emotionally. A
healthy balance between personal autonomy and intimacy is an
elusive thing.

Unfortunately, instead of facing this challenge head on,

many women heed the call of fear and erect emotional walls in an attempt to avoid becoming too dependent.

This is what Rita was doing. The more deeply she allowed herself to be drawn into her relationship, the more fearful she became of how devastated she would feel if Stan were to leave her. The closer they became, the more threatened she felt. And the more threatened she felt, the more she unconsciously distanced herself from Stan.

In this way, Rita could push her fears of dependence back down below the surface, at least for a while.

I'm the last person in the world to suggest that women return to the dependent role we've been struggling to escape for the last few decades, or that there is something wrong with being wary of over-dependence. But there is a point at which wariness becomes self-defeating. Fear of dependence becomes counterproductive if it leads us to treat intimacy as our enemy.

All too often, we react to our healthy distaste for dependence as Rita did, by unconsciously pushing a loving partner away. In Rita's relationship, this need for separation came into play in other ways as well.

RITA

Every time he mentions marriage, I can feel myself freezing up. I start hemming and hawing, I make stupid jokes, I start an argument . . . anything to change the subject. I just can't bring myself to talk about it, even though I feel awful about what it does to him. It's so important to him that we trust each other . . . he gets this look on his face that makes me want to cry. . . . I can see how much this is hurting him . . . but I get so scared.

Money was not the only thing Rita was keeping separate from Stan. She was keeping her heart separate as well. And I was pretty sure I knew why—the fear of dependence almost always has its genesis in a more primitive and universal fear.

The Fear of Abandonment

The fear of abandonment is the fear of being left devastated, helpless, and alone—of having the emotional or financial rug pulled out from under us.

We all have this fear to varying degrees. For those of us who are in proven relationships, or who feel confident that we can handle the pain of a breakup and take care of ourselves, the fear of abandonment is manageable.

But even if we have the safety net of a good relationship or a solid career, many of us lack the *feeling* of security we need to control our fear of being left alone.

The fear of abandonment is often a vague, dark terror that we don't readily identify. To protect ourselves from this fear, we erect defenses: We may become hypersensitive to any criticism or slight, interpreting it as rejection; or we may act abrasively to prove that we're not vulnerable, that we don't need anyone else to get by; or we may do or say irrational things in moments of desperation.

Unconsciously, we often try to avoid feeling vulnerable to abandonment by finding ways to push our partner away.

Lost in the Shuffle

Rita was fixated on the possibility that Stan would leave her, even though she had no reason to suspect that this was a real threat. In fact, when Rita talked about Stan, she always portrayed him as an honest, decent man who wanted very much to make their relationship work.

In light of her disproportionate fear, I thought it likely that she was unconsciously using Stan to symbolize someone else in her life, someone important who may have abandoned her in the past. I asked Rita if she had any idea who that person might be.

RITA

It's got to be my mother. My first day of kindergarten, she sent me off to school, and when I came home, she was gone. It turned out she'd checked into a hospital with they didn't know what. They never figured it out either. In those days—it was 1952, 1953—I remember looking at her through a window from the outside of the hospital, and that was as close as I could get for six months. So, yeah, there's a lot of abandonment. Partly through just the way life dealt the cards. See, my folks were separated at the time, so I stayed with an aunt—I guess I felt abandoned by my dad, too. I have a lot of childhood memories about feeling like that.

What a horrible experience for a five-year-old! Rita lost her mother for six months on the one day that symbolizes for so many children their first regular separation from their parents—the first day of school.

In addition, Rita had already lost her father to the mysterious realm of parental separation. And when her mother was hospitalized, she was never told why her father sent her to an aunt instead of taking her in himself. No wonder she had so little faith in the security of relationships.

RITA

Nothing lasts forever, right? I just feel like relationships are transient. I've been divorced, my folks were divorced . . . and when you have that kind of experience, that kind of attitude, you want to keep your life easily separable from anyone else's.

When Stan wanted to purchase a TV with Rita, her pattern of keeping things separate was threatened. This brought on a flood of the very fear that had been instilled in Rita so well, both in childhood and in her own marriage, the fear she was still trying to avoid—the fear of being dependent on someone she couldn't depend on.

Money as a Weapon in Divorce

Clearly, the fears that drive us are often rooted in childhood, but childhood is not their only source. While Rita's fear of dependence had its genesis in childhood events, it was also painfully compounded in her adulthood by an extremely bitter divorce.

RITA

Larry was a real control freak. Even though I was working, he took my paycheck every week and doled out the money as if it were some big favor. I felt like a little kid, and as time went on, it only got worse. So I finally left him. He went nuts. All I wanted was out, but he just wouldn't let me go without making me suffer. So he went after everything we had with a vengeance. It was a real shock. I mean, I had to fight for stuff he didn't even like. . . . This crystal vase my grandmother gave us as a first anniversary present? When we were married he wouldn't even let me put it out, but now all of a sudden he wouldn't let it go, even though it wasn't worth more than a hundred dollars. Every little thing became a battleground for him—our CD collection, my jewelry, even my car—just because he wanted to punish me. The whole process was really degrading. He made everything as painful as he could.

Faced with this sort of humiliating and spiteful confrontation, many women capitulate, settling for far less than their equal share, despite the advice of their lawyers. The desire to escape the emotional battering of a bitter divorce frequently causes women to lose sight of their financial interests.

Women get a cold dose of reality when they find themselves fighting over possessions that once symbolized their hopes for a lasting relationship. But money (and the things it can buy) is all too often a vindictive husband's weapon of choice for acting out feelings of hurt or anger when a relationship breaks up.

Rita ultimately stood up for herself in her divorce proceedings and got a basically fair settlement. But this didn't stop her from coming away from the proceedings feeling as if she'd been run over by a train.

With her childhood experiences of abandonment reinforced by the emotional brutality and betrayal of a man she'd once loved, it was almost inevitable that she would develop a problem trusting men in subsequent relationships.

Repairing Trust

We all need a basic ability to trust in order to make relationships work. And that ability is something that must be formed in childhood through the predictable presence of our caretakers.

But parents have to go to work, and sometimes they get divorced. Most children can adjust to these situations as long as they have some idea where and when they will see their parents (or parent) again, whether it is at the end of the day or the end of the week.

Rita's experience of discovering her mother gone without explanation had to have been devastating. Still, she might have viewed it as an unusual circumstance and not come away traumatized. Unfortunately, she had already lost her daddy to divorce, and on top of that, her trust had been shaken before.

RITA

When my folks were still together—I guess I was about three or four—I remember waking up one night and calling for my mother. Nobody answered. I figured they were downstairs, so I got out of bed and went down, but they weren't there either. That's when I started getting scared. I went outside. . . . It was really freezing, but I didn't care. I just stood there in the dark, crying hysterically, screaming for my mother at the top of my lungs. Finally, she came running from the house next door. They'd gone over to play cards, figuring I'd just sleep through the night as I usually did.

Rita's mother's hospitalization was not just a shock, it was a trigger for feelings of terror that had been planted by an earlier scare. To Rita's mother, the card game incident may have seemed like a momentary crisis, but to the little girl screaming in the snow, it was an experience that would eat away at her ability to trust well into adulthood.

Writing to the Frightened Child Within

If Rita wanted to stop putting distance between herself and Stan, she had to start learning to trust, not only in Stan but, more important, in herself. She needed to have trust in the fact that she was an adult who was fully capable of weathering emotional storms. And to do that, she had to relieve the fears of that part of her that still felt helpless, small, and dependent—the part of her unconscious that still reacted like a frightened little girl locked within her.

As part of her work in therapy, I asked Rita to write a letter to that little girl—reassure her that she would not be abandoned again.

RITA

I have to tell you I think that "inner child" stuff is a lot of horseshit. I just don't buy it, I don't feel it, I don't believe it.

SUSAN

Look, if you don't like the idea of an inner child, write a letter to the child you used to be, or pretend you have a daughter who's going through the same thing, and write the letter to her.

It still sounds too touchy-feely to me.

Despite her resistance, I persuaded Rita to give the exercise a try. The following week she brought in this letter. I asked her to read it out loud.

Before I start, I just want you to know that I cried when I wrote this. I couldn't believe it, but I did.

"Dear Little Rita,

"I'm writing this letter because I want you to know that you don't have to be afraid anymore. You learned to be afraid when you had to depend on people who wound up leaving you, but I'm taking care of you now, and I can't leave you, because we share the same body. We're together now, and we've got to stop being afraid because that's what's hurting us.

"Stan isn't Daddy, and he isn't Mommy, and he isn't Larry [Rita's first husband]. He says he loves me, and he acts like he loves me, so I think we should both try to believe him and start acting like it.

"Even if he does leave, we're strong enough now to pull through it, because even though we love him, we can survive without him. We've got each other and we can make it together. So no more fear, no more mistrust, no more pushing him away. It's time to open up and take our chances.

"I'll always love you,

"Me."

I knew that the letter sounded a lot braver than Rita really felt. Her fears had been digging in for a lifetime; they wouldn't go away overnight. But the letter established important emotional and behavioral goals for her, goals she could expect to reach if she was willing to do some work in therapy and to take some emotional risks.

The Inner Monologue

Along with her letter-writing, I gave Rita some behavioral exercises to do. The first was very specific: Go on weekly shopping trips with Stan to make joint purchases, even if these purchases were small—pots and pans, an answering machine, CDs, whatever. This was a way of desensitizing Rita to the threat that "symbols of commitment" presented to her. In buying small things with Stan and seeing that the sky didn't fall in, Rita could chip away at her fears.

I also gave Rita a more general anxiety-reducing technique—a little inner monologue to repeat if she started to panic while shopping:

This is my anxiety. It has no business being in my life. It is a relic from the past. It can only hurt me, so I don't need it and I don't want it.

Though this may seem simplistic, inner monologues like this one can be very effective. They allow you to respond to the present *in* the present, instead of falling back into past patterns. They anchor you in reality and force you to think about why you're doing what you're doing. You can no longer react automatically to your money demons. Instead, you must make conscious choices about how you're going to behave.

Using her inner monologue, Rita was able to calm a lot of her anxiety.

RITA

I think one of the things I realized in therapy and talking to other people was that what I was doing wasn't normal. That people that live together—whether they're man and wife or not—tend to share a lot more than Stan and I did. And I guess it felt so natural to me to keep it separate that it never had occurred to me at that point that in a way there was a wall around our intimacy. But now, I'm very slowly trying to find ways to share. We're actually starting to buy things together.

As Rita and Stan began to share more of their possessions, she began to feel more comfortable sharing her emotions. And as she opened up emotionally, she discovered that their new levels of intimacy were slowly drawing him closer. Rita's fear of abandonment didn't evaporate overnight, but she was gradually gaining the upper hand.

The Fear of Engulfment

Abandonment has a flip side: engulfment.

While the fear of abandonment is the fear that you will be left alone by someone you love and need, the fear of engulfment is the fear that you will lose your *self*. You're afraid that you will somehow be consumed by your partner, that your identity will become indistinguishable from his, that he will overrun your boundaries, dominate you, disempower you.

With a controlling or emotionally abusive man, this is a perfectly realistic, healthy fear. Men who are controlling and/or abusive feel threatened by a partner's emotional or financial independence, and they try to smother it with possessive, domineering behavior. There is nothing wrong with being afraid of a relationship like this.

But many women operate from a deep unconscious fear of engulfment that bears no relation to their partner's behavior or attitudes. These women will project their fears onto even the most benign, respectful, supportive man, putting tremendous roadblocks in the path of intimacy.

The Comfort of Distance

Carrie heard the front door open, and her heart sank. She had wanted everything to be perfect for their first anniversary dinner, but the chicken had taken longer to prepare than she'd expected, so she was running twenty minutes late. And now Mario was home early.

He walked into the kitchen with a bottle of champagne in his hand. "Happy anniversary, Care."

"You're home early."

"I couldn't wait."

She smiled. He put his arms around her and gave her a lingering kiss. She melted into his warm embrace. But at the same time she felt the familiar butterflies starting up in her stomach. She tried to ignore them, and to her relief, they seemed to go away.

Mario popped open the champagne and poured them each a glass. "To us." They clinked glasses.

As Carrie took a sip, something caught her eye—something lodged in the neck of her champagne flute. "What's this?"

She stuck her pinky in her glass and fished out a teardrop diamond on a gold chain. She felt the tears rush to her eyes. "Oh, Mario . . . it's beautiful." She threw her arms around him and hugged him tight.

"You like it?" he asked.

"I love it . . . but it must have been so expensive."

"Let me worry about that."

She held the diamond up to the light and watched rainbows dance across the facets. She felt incredibly lucky to have such a loving husband. . . . Then the butterflies started up again.

"I love you." He took her in his arms and kissed her again.

She wanted to let herself go, to become lost in his kiss. But those damned butterflies . . . her mood began to sour. Mario's kiss began to make her feel uncomfortable. She felt as if she were outside of herself watching herself going through the motions of kissing him in a fake, mechanical way. She had an urge to push him away, but she didn't want to hurt his feelings. She couldn't understand why she felt this way, but it just kept getting worse.

Finally, she pulled back. "I've got to check the chicken," she mumbled, knowing full well that it would be another twenty minutes before it was done. "Why don't you go relax while I get dinner ready?"

"Can I help?"

"Just give me a couple minutes, okay?"

He left the room, leaving her feeling confused. Why was it that she felt so mixed up about the man she loved? Just because he tried to love her back?

It's always bewildering when the emotional response you have to a situation is completely different from the response you would expect—and even want—to have. But it's not unusual. When you experience a seemingly positive event in a negative way, you've imbued that event with a symbolic meaning, and it is that symbol that you're reacting to.

In some cases, a negative reaction to a positive event may be justified. For example, it's perfectly reasonable to become angry about a gift that your partner gives you as a bribe to try to get you to forgive him for some inexcusable behavior.

But this was not the case with Mario's gift, and Carrie knew it.

CARRIE

I felt really bitchy for the rest of the evening, but I just kept stuffing it, trying to be romantic when I didn't feel like it, trying to be cheerful when I didn't feel like it . . . and I kept feeling phonier and phonier. Finally, I just couldn't keep it in anymore, and he asked me what was wrong. I didn't know what to say because I really didn't know, so I told him I didn't think we should be spending money on diamonds just now. He made some joke about letting *him* worry about the money since he's the one with the MBA . . . and I told him not to patronize me . . . and he accused me of PMS . . . and we were off and running. I ended up locking myself in the bedroom in tears.

As with so many money fights, the content of Carrie's and Mario's fight was almost irrelevant. Carrie admitted that she knew there was no substance to her professed financial concerns. Mario's salary as a bank vice-president was sufficient to support the two of them. In fact, she had been able to quit a job she hated and devote herself to various political causes close to her heart. Money was not a real issue in her relationship, but it *did* provide a convenient outlet for venting her anxiety.

CARRIE

Later that night, when he came to bed, he was really apologetic, which made me feel incredibly guilty because I felt like it was all my fault. And then—this is really hard for me to talk about—he started to make love to me, and . . . well, I felt like my insides were cramping up when he touched me. I didn't know what to think. That had never happened before. But I was so afraid of hurting him . . . so I faked it. And the whole time I felt . . . smothered, totally smothered.

No matter what Mario's role may have been in making Carrie react as she did, she clearly had plenty of her own issues to work on. Their anniversary was not the first time Carrie had found herself inciting fights or withdrawing emotionally. It seemed to happen whenever Mario was being loving and romantic, whenever he tried to give to her materially or get close to her sexually.

Carrie seemed to have an emotional predisposition against getting too close. On several occasions she had almost backed out of their engagement. When Mario had finally pressed her to make wedding plans, she found reasons to veto a half dozen caterers before he finally put his foot down and insisted she make a choice. On their honeymoon she was plagued with doubts because his constant attention felt oppressive to her.

Something within Carrie was preventing her from enjoying the pleasures of intimacy.

Filling in the Blanks

In order to get a better handle on Carrie's anxiety, I asked her to do a simple sentence-completion exercise. I would give her the first half of a sentence, and she was to finish it in her own words.

I emphasized that this was in no way a traditional free-association exercise—she did not have to give me the first words that came into her head. Rather, I wanted her to give each sentence completion as much thought as she needed.

Here are a few examples:

SUSAN

If I let Mario get too close to me, I will . . .

CARRIE

Rely on him too much. I'll lose my identity. . . . I'll be an appendage.

SUSAN

If I let Mario get too close to me, *he* will . . .

CARRIE

Smother me—smother me with love.

SUSAN

I'm afraid Mario will smother me because . . .

CARRIE

Men always do that. That's what men do.

Carrie's choice of phrases like "rely on him," "be an appendage," and "smother me with love" indicated a strong fear of engulfment. She was afraid that somehow, if she were to let down her defenses and allow herself to be vulnerable with Mario, her identity would melt down and blend into his. Ironically, it was not Mario but her own fear of engulfment that was engulfing her.

The Struggle for Individuality

Fears like Carrie's are never spontaneous. She must have learned them from someone. And as I worked with her, it became clear that that someone was her father.

CARRIE

I couldn't just get an allowance. I had to make up these
"budgets" whenever I wanted money, and he'd always
quiz me on them. It was like he made me do it so he could
get into my private stuff. He wanted to know where all the
money was going because he didn't want me to do anything he didn't know about. He opened my mail, he lis-
tened in on my phone calls. . . . I complained about it
once, and he told me as long as he paid the phone bill, it
was his right. I felt like I couldn't breathe without him
counting the breaths. My way around it was, I just stopped
asking him for money. And I hated it when he'd give me
presents because they always felt like they had all these
strings attached. So I'd buy an apple at school for twenty-
five cents, and that was all I'd have for lunch. That way I
could hoard the rest of my lunch money—like a buck fifty
a day. And I started sewing all my own clothes. I got a job
at sixteen, as soon as I could get a permit.

It's certainly reasonable for parents to want to know where
their children are spending their money, but Carrie's father
took his parental prerogative to an extreme. He used parental
concern as an excuse to keep his daughter under his thumb.
Carrie felt understandably overwhelmed by his constant, invasive presence.

As a result, she began to find ways to separate herself financially from her father at a very young age. In this way, Carrie
tried to gain some control over her life.

CARRIE

I didn't want to be dependent on my father. Because my
father . . . to be dependent on my father meant this complete loss of self. To everybody we knew, I was "Hal's
daughter," even after I grew up. That was my claim to
fame. So part of my struggle was to have my own money

and not to take anything from him, and that's how I could have an identity separate from him.

Carrie learned early from her father's example that men would use money to invade her privacy and overrun her life. It never occurred to her that she was making an unfair generalization based on a sample of one. She just assumed, as most children do, that her father was representative of all men.

Now, whenever Mario tried to give her something, his gesture evoked the same invasive, controlling associations that she had once attached to her father's gifts and loans. She felt the same old anxiety that her father used to make her feel, and she tried to protect herself in the same way she had as an adolescent—by asserting her independence.

Her old fear of engulfment came rushing back to transform a loving gesture into a threat.

There is nothing unhealthy about treasuring your self-definition. Every woman has the right to her own individual thoughts, feelings, opinions, and activities, and this right is worth protecting. But Carrie was defending her individuality against shadow assailants. She was erecting barricades against an enemy who didn't exist. She was projecting her leftover childhood fears onto Mario, and this was eating away at their relationship like an acid.

Avoiding Repetition

We psychotherapists hit bumps in the emotional road just as our clients do, and like our clients, we have to dig deep within to rebuild. Being a therapist is no guarantee of emotional self-knowledge, as Erica—my client and colleague—discovered.

ERICA
I put in fourteen-, fifteen-hour days, and then when I go home I write evaluations. I can understand why Luke gets upset—he gets tired of sitting watching TV alone every

night. And we fight about it a lot. But I've worked so hard to get where I am, and I love what I do. I just can't bring myself to slow down. It's like I'm attached to a Mack truck, and it just keeps driving, driving, driving. I never planned for it to work out this way, but I've got no life, I never have any fun, I haven't gone out or seen friends in months, I've got no time for Luke. . . . He's always saying he might as well be living alone, and it's true. The thing of it is, I know that if I ease up a little, nothing's going to happen. I'd still make good money, and even if I didn't, Luke makes good money. But when he asks me to drop some clients, I just can't handle it. I feel like he's trying to trap me into being dependent on him, and I just don't want to do that.

Erica's intellectual understanding of her situation just wasn't trickling down to her feelings. She may have *known* that she was working more than she had to, and that her schedule was driving a wedge between her husband and herself, but something more powerful than insight was preventing her from changing the way she chose to spend her time and energy.

I'm very sympathetic to the fact that career pressures, the realities of competition, or financial pressures often demand excessive hours. I've faced those pressures plenty of times myself.

But Erica could well afford to cut back on her practice. She was established and respected in her field—she did not have to see every client who came her way. Unlike many women, she had no supervisor or employer to answer to or to impress. She was also in the enviable position of being able to cut back without jeopardizing her livelihood or her lifestyle.

Not everyone who works too hard and too long is a workaholic. But Erica was.

Afraid of Turning into Mother

I asked Erica why she was afraid that if she cut back she would become dependent on Luke, when she knew that she would still

be making good money and could always get new clients if she
had to.

ERICA

I know it doesn't make sense, but I'm so scared of this. . . .
I've seen so many dependent women go down the tubes,
including my mother. My father used to treat her like crap.
I mean, he used to scream at her all the time. He didn't
even pretend to love her—she was just like his slave. I remember coming home from school, and she'd be crying in
the kitchen, and I'd ask her why we didn't just leave him,
but she said she couldn't. She had to stay with him for
us—for my brother and me. She said she couldn't support
us herself. But then one day he took off, just disappeared,
and left us with nothing. It was hand-to-mouth from there
on in. Welfare, odd jobs, whatever. I swore to myself that
I'd never do what she did—I'd never, ever be forced to
count on a man as she was. Any man.

Erica had long since insured her own economic self-sufficiency, but the fear of dependence has a way of taking on a life
of its own. Her fear was not based on her adult understanding
of her situation; it was based on the emotional perspective of
the confused little girl she had once been. That little girl had
never gotten over seeing her mother being controlled and de-
meaned by a man who derived most of his power from his
command of the family's finances.

As an adult, Erica's fear had motivated her to get a professional education and to work hard building a practice. This gave
her real financial security. But no matter how much she earned,
it was never enough to make her feel safe.

Erica couldn't stop running as fast as she could from the
prospect of repeating her mother's helplessness. Most workaholic women are running from something, often a stressful
relationship. Though money is often the apparent motivation
for workaholism, it is rarely the only one.

Balancing Your Life

In order for Erica to get out of the self-defeating rut she'd worked herself into, she needed to do some childhood work, similar to Rita's, to deal with her fear of dependence. At the same time she needed to do some specific behavioral exercises to deal with the fights in her relationship and her patterns of avoidance.

But before she could do either of these things, she needed to relieve some of the pressure of her draining work schedule. The first thing I asked her to do was to stop taking on new clients.

ERICA

I can't just turn people away when they're hurting. That would be like abandoning them.

SUSAN

I hate to break this to you, Erica, but you're not the only therapist in the world. You're so concerned about taking care of everybody else that you're not taking care of yourself, not to mention your marriage.

Her resistance was tenacious. She was panicked by the idea of not working every available moment, or of not making as much money as she possibly could. Money had become her symbol of independence, and she wasn't about to give it up easily. But she understood her need to do so. It took a lot of wrangling, but we finally compromised on a plan for her to form a therapy group with six or seven clients she had been seeing individually, and this freed up several hours a week for her.

In addition, she agreed—again, with some reluctance—to phase out, within thirty days, her consulting position at a local hospital.

And finally, she rearranged her remaining clients so that she was no longer working after seven in the evening or on Saturdays.

At first Erica found her new-found freedom very stressful. She had no idea what to do with her unstructured time. She had spent so many years devoting herself to other people's needs that she, like so many women, had given up many of the recreational activities she used to enjoy herself.

Eventually she was able to revive her interest in many of these activities—concerts, plays, movies, tennis, romance—but it took quite a bit of work for her to be able to allot both the time and the energy to herself.

The enormous strides that Erica made in her lifestyle, however, had only a modest impact on her marriage. Free time alone was merely a prelude to the work that she and Luke would need to do to deal with the buried resentments between them. Luke could not just turn off his pain from having felt like such a low priority in Erica's life for so long. Nor could he ignore his anger at her for associating him with her father, whom Luke despised.

As Erica advanced through therapy, she discovered that she and Luke had forgotten how to talk to each other. They had become so entrenched in arguing or ignoring each other that normal conversation had slipped out of their repertoire. So Erica and Luke agreed to make the reversal of this trend their starting point. They approached their marriage as if it were a new relationship, and in a sense she and Luke began to get to know each other all over again. They're still in the process, but they are both dedicated to making the marriage work.

It's never easy to make meaningful change in your life when you are driven by deep-rooted fears. But as Erica began to live a more balanced life, she was able to gradually conquer the fears that were driving her to sacrifice everything else in her life for the sake of work.

Self-Help Strategies

The purpose of the "Self-Help Strategies" sections that you'll find at the end of every chapter in this book is to show you how to adapt the techniques illustrated in that chapter and make them work for you. In this chapter we have seen three basic techniques at work, all of which can be effective outside of therapy.

I think many of you will be surprised at the dramatic impact that some relatively simple behavioral changes can have both on your self-image and on your relationship.

Filling in the Blanks

This exercise will help you clarify and label your fears. If you are not in tune with your fears, you will probably want to do this exercise before attempting either of the others. You can't write to the child within you about your fear, or create a monologue about your fear, until you have some sense of what that fear actually is.

There is no limit to the use of sentence-completion exercises like this one. They are invaluable in helping you focus your thoughts, feelings, and beliefs. In this chapter, we've shown this exercise at work on engulfment issues. But you could just as easily use it to deal with any other money demon.

As an example, here are some sentences you might want to complete for the fear of abandonment:

When we fight about money, I get scared because I'm afraid he will _____ .
I'm afraid he will leave me because _____ .
If he leaves me, I'm afraid I will _____ .
I'm afraid to commingle our money because _____ .
I'm afraid of ending up like my mother (or father) because _____ .

Using these examples as a springboard, you can create sentences of your own that are relevant to your particular situation.

Writing to the Frightened Child Within

Writing a letter to the child within you not only validates and reassures that child but calms your adult self as well. Hearing the words is as important as writing them, so you might want to read the letter aloud to your partner, to a trusted friend, to a mirror, or even into a tape recorder. Letters like Rita's are simple yet powerful tools for dealing with anxiety.

Assure the child within you that you know what she was afraid of and that she has no need to be frightened anymore because you, as an adult, will protect her.

The Inner Monologue

You can use the inner monologue I gave to Rita, or you can create your own. Find some time when you can be by yourself, take the phone off the hook, and kick your shoes off. It helps to be in a calm, quiet place.

An inner monologue starts its life as an outer monologue, so you will be saying these words out loud. One way to decide what you want to say is to imagine a friend having an anxiety attack. Imagine that friend coming to you for reassurance, and say the words out loud that you might use to comfort her. You can use these same words to comfort yourself. Another approach is to imagine your anxiety as a person whom you want to banish from your life, and find some words to tell it as much.

Concentrate on reminding yourself that your anxiety is a self-defeating ghost from the past and that it will only hobble you in the present unless you control it.

2

Self-Depriving Women

I look, I long, I want, and then I say, "No, I can't."

—S.A., age 26

I'm on my second husband, and he's just as bad as my first. I
don't understand why I keep getting stuck with these tightwads.

—M.L., age 42

The hinge cracked off my glasses, but I just couldn't bring myself
to spend the money on a new pair. So I ran around for almost
three months with this ridiculous Band-Aid holding my glasses
together.

—C.J., age 51

For years, I had a recording in my head that played every
time I considered buying something for myself. The message
went like this: "You don't need it, Susan. You don't deserve it.
You can live without it." This tape would click on even if the
item I wanted to buy was inexpensive and practical.

I know now that I was not unique. For many women, this
sort of self-denial is a way of life. They just can't be good to
themselves. Some refuse to buy themselves special treats, even
occasionally. Others won't even buy themselves practical things
unless the purchase is so cheap that it's virtually guaranteed to
be damaged or low quality. And at the far end of the spectrum

are those women who are so self-depriving that they will skimp on even the most basic necessities, like medical care, heating, or food. These are all self-depriving women.

Patterns of Deprivation

Women are often stereotyped in our culture as greedy and materialistic. Books and movies are full of manipulative gold diggers and flighty spendthrifts. But though such women do exist, there are millions of women who turn the stereotype upside down. Handcuffed by powerful money demons, they are unable to spend money on themselves—even if they can well afford to—without suffering tremendous feelings of guilt and anxiety.

Bewildered by their own behavior, most of these women would describe themselves as "thrifty," "cautious," "level-headed," or "conscientious." But these adjectives don't come close to expressing the emotional toll that self-depriving women must pay. In addition to depriving themselves materially, self-depriving women almost always find ways to deny themselves love and affection.

Self-deprivation is more than a spending habit—it is an emotionally painful way to live.

An Unrewarding Cycle

Sally virtually collapsed onto the hard plastic cafeteria chair. She was already drained from her shift in the cardiac care unit, and the day was only half over. First one of the other nurses had gone home sick, leaving them short-handed. And then two patients had suffered cardiac arrests at the same time. By the time the cardiac team had gotten both patients stabilized, Sally felt as if she'd been through an aerobics workout. Lunch was a welcome respite.

Sally opened the brown bag she'd brought from home and stared at the American cheese sandwich. It still bore the imprint of the heavy clipboard that someone had dropped on her lunch bag, making the sandwich even less appetizing than usual. She smelled pasta, and her eyes drifted to the food line, where she could see steam rising from the fresh lasagna.

Sally longed to toss her sandwich and buy herself a hot lunch. After this morning's ordeal, she'd certainly earned it. But the idea of throwing away a perfectly good sandwich and spending five dollars for lunch made her feel uneasy.

Just that morning, she'd had another argument with her husband, Ward, about the money she had spent on an extra winter coat for their thirteen-year-old. He had complained, as he usually did, that their finances were way out of hand. She suspected he was exaggerating—they both had good jobs, and their expenses were not high. But he kept the books, so she had no way of knowing.

His tirade had made her defensive, so she had called him a tightwad. Then, as always, she was overcome by guilt. She knew how important it was to him to be prepared for financial setbacks. She knew that his penny-pinching was for the good of the whole family. And she really didn't mind going without, as long as her children were well taken care of.

Still, the thought of a hot lunch was tantalizing, no matter how extravagant and self-indulgent it seemed. She began to feel a gnawing guilt for even contemplating spending money on herself, despite the fact that the amount was insignificant. With a final sigh of resignation, she closed her eyes, got a grip on herself, and unwrapped her crushed cheese sandwich.

When Sally got home late that afternoon she felt more depressed than usual. Ward was already home, but he barely looked up from his work to greet her. She looked at him and was suddenly struck by an eleven-year-old memory. It had happened just a few weeks after their wedding. She had come home from work, and Ward had vaulted the couch to greet her with a kiss. It was a small moment, but a precious one—an image she would never forget.

Sally looked at him now and started to cry. At the sound of her *tears, Ward finally looked up. "You must be tired," he said. "Why don't you go to bed?"*

The next day, Sally called my office for an appointment. When she came in later that week, she told me how hard it had been for her to come in for therapy because of the expense. There were so many other things she could think of to do with the money besides spending it on herself. She conceded that her marriage was deteriorating to the point of collapse, and she was desperate to find a way to save it. I suggested that she weigh the cost against her need. She decided to make a six-week commitment to therapy and at the end of that time to reevaluate.

Sally painted a bleak picture of a "dead" marriage. Her husband was a high school teacher who lectured to students all day, but when he came home at night, he couldn't seem to find three words to say to Sally. She went to work, she came home, she cooked dinner for the family, she cleaned up, and she went to sleep. She used to be able to depend on her two children for some affection, but now they were teenagers, they were too busy with their own lives to bother with "Mom."

Sally's life had become an unrewarding cycle of loneliness and frustration.

The Receiving Valve

In a soft, tentative voice, Sally struggled to describe a tangle of personal and relationship problems, but she seemed vague about what those problems were. She was miserable, yet she couldn't pinpoint a specific crisis either in her life or in her relationship that was causing her misery.

It was when she described the cafeteria incident that the alarm bells finally went off for me. Sally's inability to buy herself a hot lunch was a tangible signpost that singaled a pattern.

I asked Sally whether she always had so much trouble spending money on things for herself.

SALLY

Just last month, I fell in love with this hat, but it was fifty dollars. So I spent about forty-five minutes in the store just looking at myself in the mirror with it on, then putting it back and looking at other stuff, then going back to it and agonizing. Finally the salesgirl talked me into buying it. But the minute I walked out of the store, I started feeling guilty. I kept thinking, "I have no right to buy this," "Ward's going to get upset," "We're going to have another fight," "I shouldn't have let that girl talk me into it." I just knew I'd made a big mistake.

Sally had a problem with what I call her "receiving valve." I use this term to describe the network of psychological, mostly unconscious feelings and beliefs about how *deserving* we are that cause us to deprive ourselves.

I think the simple image of a valve is a useful way to visualize what controls this complex range of self-depriving behaviors. But there is nothing simple about the mechanism that allows a woman to inflict so much punishment on herself by agonizing over the normal act of wanting something.

Our receiving valve controls how comfortable we feel giving to ourselves or letting others give to us. But women whose feelings of undeservedness shut down their receiving valve can still be quite generous—sometimes even extravagant—when it comes to spending money on others. The metaphorical valve may stop the flow inward without affecting the flow outward. This can be especially true when it comes to spending money on children.

Many self-depriving women live vicariously through their children, treating sons and daughters in ways that they couldn't imagine treating themselves.

And some even buy nice things for themselves—every once in a great while. Even a jammed receiving valve must open occasionally—to allow us to buy ourselves necessities, if nothing else. It is not necessary to totally deprive yourself of material goods in order to be a self-depriver. But these lapses rarely go unpunished by the unconscious.

Sally *was* able to purchase her hat. However, she was so overwhelmed by guilt that it was impossible for her to enjoy it.

SALLY

All the way home, I couldn't think of anything but how extravagant the hat was and how it would upset Ward. I just knew he was going to give me "The Look" and then a lecture about the value of money.

By the time Sally got home, she was so worked up that she couldn't even bring herself to take the hat out of the car. So she decided to take it back the next day. It wasn't worth the aggravation to her.

Ward may have been as disapproving as Sally described him. But he may just as easily have been a handy justification for her self-depriving behavior. I had a hunch that Ward was not the true cause of Sally's anxiety. Rather, her purchase was just too far out of sync with her core beliefs about who she was and how she deserved to be treated.

frugal.

The Beliefs That Define Us

When I refer to "beliefs," I mean those opinions, attitudes, and judgments about ourselves that have been evolving since our earliest childhood. These beliefs define our perceptions of our lovability, our deservedness, our competence, our talent, our intelligence, our outward appearance, our spirituality—all of those things that make up the ephemeral concept we call self-esteem. And the beliefs that mold our self-esteem determine what we feel we are entitled to, whether it be love, money, success, or peace of mind.

No one gets through any phase of life without *some* wounds

to his or her self-esteem. But many people have positive experiences that compensate for these wounds. For others, however, these wounds become dominant unconscious themes in their personalities, motivating all sorts of different self-defeating behaviors.

If we were to walk around with a constant awareness of our worst thoughts and feelings about ourselves, we might not be able to tolerate the anxiety and pain. So our unconscious acts as a kind of mental shield, attempting to protect us from our most uncomfortable feelings and attitudes by hiding them from us.

Conscious beliefs—those beliefs that we are aware of—represent only a fraction of our personal belief system, like the tip of an iceberg. The stuff that sinks ships is hidden beneath the surface, in our unconscious. It is this subsurface mass of personal beliefs that gives rise to self-depriving behavior.

As these self-destructive beliefs try to escape from the confines of our inner self, our unconscious works harder and harder to keep them under wraps. But eventually, in one way or another, the beliefs leak through our resistance, usually in disguised form. They may express themselves as behavior—often unfulfilling or self-defeating behavior. Or they may emerge as depression, anxiety, or even physical symptoms.

Beliefs about our own undeservedness lurk at the core of all self-depriving behavior.

Giving Voice to the Demon

I couldn't just *ask* Sally what inner beliefs were making her feel undeserving because, on a conscious level, she really didn't know. So I suggested we use a technique that I call Giving Voice to the Demon.

I put an empty chair in front of Sally and asked her to move into it from her seat on the couch. She was a bit confused by this, but she did as I asked. I then told her to imagine herself still seated on the couch and to speak to herself as the voice of her own deprivation, as if her deprivation were a separate person. I asked her to reach deep into herself and try to find those things that her deprivation says to her at those moments when she feels most guilty about wanting something for herself.

For a moment, Sally thought about this. Then she started admonishing the empty couch.

SALLY

You shouldn't buy it. . . . You don't deserve it. . . . You didn't do anything to deserve it.

She started out slowly, uneasily, but as she got going, she picked up steam.

SALLY

How dare you even think you can have it. . . . You're so greedy. . . . There are other people you should be spending money on. . . . You are so selfish. . . . You shouldn't have it. . . . You *can't* have it. . . . You can't, you can't, you can't!

By this time she was fighting tears, clearly struggling with very strong emotions.

SUSAN

Stay with those feelings, Sally. Why can't you have it?

SALLY

Because I just can't. It makes me feel too guilty.

Somewhere along the line, Sally had been programmed to believe that she either wasn't good enough or that she hadn't earned the right to want anything. And if she did want anything, there must be something wrong with her. Beneath Sally's stoic exterior was a powerful guilt that she acted out by depriving herself. No wonder she felt depressed.

How could Sally do anything nice for herself if she believed that to do so would only confirm her worst fears about her own

stays away from
no needs = safe

greed and selfishness? How could she enjoy giving herself a gift if it came wrapped in feelings of guilt?

In the first few weeks that I worked with Sally, a picture emerged of a woman who at work was selfless and diligent beyond the call of duty and at home was devoted to her children, financially responsible, and highly motivated to getting her marriage back on track. She worked hard in both her career and her life to make things better for others, yet she couldn't look at a hat and say, "I've had a rough week. I've earned a treat."

As is true for so many self-depriving women, Sally spent the bulk of her life doing worthwhile things for other people, yet no matter how much positive feedback she got from giving to others, it had no impact on her own negative beliefs about herself.

The Roots of Self-Deprivation

To many people, the very word *deprivation* brings up images of homelessness, tattered clothes, bare feet, and starvation. But not every woman who lived a childhood of economic hardship grows up to deprive herself. Many of these women come from such emotionally rich families that their sense of deprivation is ameliorated by love.

There *is* a form of poverty, however, that is virtually guaranteed to damage our self-image—emotional poverty. Our developing personality needs emotional nourishment just as surely as a developing body needs food.

When Your Needs Aren't Important

Sally's early childhood was relatively happy and healthy. Her father was a fairly successful small businessman, and her mother was an active volunteer at the local art museum and took extension classes at the local university.

But a few years after Sally's younger sister was born, their house was broken into. Sally's father became preoccupied with fear that the city was too dangerous a place to raise children. So despite his wife's objections, he moved the family to a farm in Oregon.

Sally's mother hated rural Oregon. Her life had been exciting in the city. Now she felt isolated and bored. Her husband had given up his business when they moved, but he was working as an independent consultant, so he got to travel. Sally's mother felt trapped on the farm, and unconsciously, she blamed the girls as well as her husband. After all, it had been the girls' welfare that had motivated their move in the first place.

Sally's mother became increasingly moody and resentful, especially when the girls made any kind of demand on her. She saw her role in life as reduced to that of a cook and chauffeur for her children.

Then the accident happened. When Sally was seven, her sister Emily fell off a horse and was partially paralyzed. For the next four years she required almost constant attention and intensive physical therapy.

SALLY

My mother became totally wrapped up in Emily's recovery. She finally had something to throw herself into. And I wasn't part of it. So it was like, "I can't right now, Sally. Your sister needs me." Whenever I had to go somewhere, I had to ride my bike because my mom couldn't leave Emily alone in the house long enough to drive me. And my dad was always working, trying to catch up with the medical bills. Sometimes I felt as if they didn't even know I was there. Whenever I wanted something, they'd say, "Let me just finish with Emily first," and then I'd never hear about it again. It wasn't their fault—it was just the way things were. I had a few friends. But none of them lived nearby, and their mothers got tired of doing all the driving, so I didn't see them too much outside of school. It was lonely, let me tell you.

Sally's parents were not "bad"—they were simply overburdened and stressed beyond their emotional resources, and Sally got the short end of the stick.

Unfortunately, Sally was not old enough to understand why she was suddenly being ignored. With the best of intentions, her parents nursed her injured sister back to health, forgetting that Sally, who appeared so self-sufficient by comparison, needed nurturing, too.

Sally was getting very clear, if inadvertent, messages from her parents—that her sister's needs were more important than hers. That her mother's needs were more important than hers. And that her father's needs were more important than hers. In short, Sally's needs were unimportant.

As a result, she learned not to ask for things or to expect them because she would only be disappointed. Again and again, this lesson would rise to the surface to influence Sally's behavior in her adult life, both in her love relationships and in her relationship to money.

The Finger of Blame

As children, when our basic emotional needs for love, respect, attention, and a sense of security are not adequately met, it is only natural for us to assume that there is a reason for our feelings of deprivation.

SALLY

I used to sit on a rock over this creek near our house. . . . I'd sit there for hours trying to figure out why they didn't love me anymore. I mean, that's how I felt. I figured it had to be something I'd done, but I couldn't figure out what it was. Maybe I asked for too many things, or maybe I wasn't spending enough time reading to my sister, or maybe I wasn't doing enough around the house. . . . I just couldn't figure it out. Sometimes I'd wish my sister would just die so I'd have my parents back. And I'd feel horribly guilty about thinking that. Then I'd think maybe that's why they didn't love me, because they could read my thoughts.

When a child tries to make sense of emotional pain, she invariably points the finger of blame inward. When a child feels hurt, she tends to translate that feeling into guilt for what she imagines she's done and shame for who she imagines she is.

Guilt and shame so often go hand in hand that many people think of them as synonyms. But they are different feelings based on very different belief systems.

- *Guilt* comes from having thought, felt, or behaved in a way that you believe is wrong or bad.
- *Shame* comes from believing that you *are* bad, that at your core you are unlovable, inadequate, or inferior.

Guilt is about what you've *done;* shame is about who you *are*. Sally didn't just feel guilty for having done something she considered selfish and greedy; she felt ashamed of whatever it was in her character that made her act that way.

In her desperation to make sense of her confusion, Sally—like so many children—concluded that if she felt bad, and there was no apparent external reason, the explanation must lie within her. There must be something wrong with her.

Children equate parental neglect, anger, favoritism, rejection, or abuse with punishment. And they assume that there must be some reason for it. If they feel bad, they must *be* bad, especially if they're getting punished. In a child's mind, this explanation is the only one that makes sense.

When Wanting Shames You

Sally's mother's inadvertent neglect was bewildering enough to Sally to make her imagine all sorts of explanations for it. She must be selfish, so she felt ashamed of that. She resented her sister—quite normal in situations like hers—so she felt guilty for that.

SALLY

You know, I haven't thought about this in years, but I got a part in this school play once. I was really excited about it because we got to dress up in fancy costumes. They had these old evening gowns at school, and I picked out this gorgeous red-sequined one that actually almost fit me, except it had to be shortened. So I asked my mother—I'll never forget the look she gave me. She kind of rolled her eyes to the ceiling and gave out this sigh like I was putting the weight of the world on her shoulders. I'm sure she was just feeling especially overloaded that day, but it made me feel that I was totally self-centered and thoughtless. I wanted to just go crawl up under the house and hide.

Sally remembered a number of stories like this one. Her mother's aggravated reactions to perfectly reasonable requests on Sally's part set Sally up to be oversensitive to any little sign of disapproval that her parents might give her. Her mother's irritation reinforced Sally's general feelings of undeservedness, and in this context it had the effect of a major reproach. A less sensitive child might hardly have noticed, but once again Sally felt as if she had done something terribly wrong just by asking for something.

Once a child is sensitized to this mode of response, she may experience even compliments or kind gestures as negatively as she does disapproval.

Imagine, for instance, an attractive woman who is convinced that she is ugly. When a man compliments her on her appearance, she assumes that he's being insincere because she can't believe anyone could find her attractive. She becomes convinced that he is covering up for disparaging thoughts about her, and this makes her even more self-conscious about her own perceived unattractiveness. The more she thinks about how ugly he must think she is, the more ashamed she feels. She has turned his compliment into a source of pain.

In the same way, feelings of unworthiness or undeservedness can turn a gift or a favor or a treat for yourself into a painful experience. Better to go without than to put up with the embarrassment and self-denigration of self-imposed shame.

The Payoffs of Self-Deprivation

Selp-deprivation, like every other self-defeating behavior, has its silver lining. At the very least, the emotional pain that drives the self-deprivation is momentarily soothed by feelings of being ennobled through self-sacrifice. Though this is only a temporary gain or "payoff," it is unfortunately sufficient to keep a lot of women coming back for more.

I can remember a Christmas Eve many years ago, when I was married to my first husband, had two small children, and lived in a small tract house near Los Angeles International Airport. As usual, for Christmas Eve dinner we headed to my parents' magnificent mansion on three acres in one of the city's most expensive neighborhoods.

After dinner we gathered before the fireplace to open the presents from my parents.

My children opened their presents first—a generous assortment of clothes and toys. Then my sister opened hers—a lovely double strand of pearls with a diamond clasp. And finally, it was my turn. I ripped open the wrapping to discover a drab tan poplin raincoat.

My first reaction was disappointment and hurt. But then I felt ashamed for being ungrateful and for wanting more than I deserved. I spent the rest of the evening feeling miserable and trying to hide it.

The day after Christmas I returned the raincoat for a cash

refund of thirty-four dollars, and instead of using the money to buy something else for myself, I spent it on groceries.

In returning the raincoat I was getting back at my parents for hurting me. In spending the money on groceries, I was indirectly reproaching my husband for not being an adequate provider. And in giving up my Christmas present, I could prove to myself that I was somehow spiritually superior. Through my selflessness, I could experience the delicious feeling of righteousness. What a wonderful series of payoffs from such a simple act!

The fantasy of virtue through martyrdom is a powerful motivator for repeating self-depriving behavior.

The Bag Lady Syndrome

Many self-depriving women are preoccupied with insidious premonitions about their future. They become obsessed with hoarding money to fend off their fear of a dark and terrible fate: becoming a bag lady. This catastrophic fantasy is quite common, especially among women who went through, or whose parents or grandparents went through devastating financial times like the Depression or family bankruptcy.

The Bag Lady Syndrome, as it has come to be called, is ruthlessly democratic, popping up among women of every economic and social group.

My friend Helaine averages about sixty thousand dollars a year as a loan broker. In addition, her husband Phil makes about twice that as a partner in a CPA firm. Their two children are grown and on their own. Between their savings and their combined income, Helaine's financial situation is secure. Yet she is still plagued by the recurring terror that she will somehow lose everything.

HELAINE

Don't laugh, but every time I see one of those homeless women picking through a garbage can or pushing a shopping cart down the street or holding one of those signs asking to work for food, I think, "That could happen to me." What if Phil had some kind of bizarre accident that our insurance didn't cover? Or what if we both got sick and couldn't work? What if the economy crashed? Part of me knows it's irrational, but that doesn't make any difference. I still worry all the time, and the more I worry, the more I'm afraid to spend money. I save newspapers, I save old foil, I save rubber bands. . . . You can hardly walk into my garage anymore—it's like these tiny aisles between junk piled to the ceiling. But I just hate to throw something away if I know I might have to spend good money to replace it someday. Phil's always yelling at me to give it away or throw it away or something, but I can't bring myself to do it. So I'll go in there and rearrange everything so it looks neater. Then I'll lie and say I threw some of it out, just to get him off my back.

Instead of being able to enjoy the rewards of the success that she and Phil have achieved, Helaine lives in fear. Helaine knows that her fear is unreasonable, but she is still hard pressed to spend on herself. She is also a pack rat, as if this will help her ward off an inevitably painful fate. By hoarding her financial resources, she tries to assuage her fear and gain some sense of control over her future.

The Bag Lady Syndrome is deeply embedded in our collective unconscious. It reflects more than just the fear of financial ruin—it is the ultimate manifestation of all our fears about being alone, pitiable, disdained, and outcast. These fears have been with women for centuries. And while many of us *know* that we are fully capable of taking care of ourselves financially, in some dark, irrational recess of our mind, most of us still live with the simmering fear that we can't.

Hoarding and self-deprivation can seriously disrupt a relationship, but these behaviors *do* help some women to temporarily control their fears of destitution. This can be a potent payoff.

Confronting the Demon

The first step toward overcoming the seductive lure of payoffs is to uncover the all-important connections between them and the money demons that empower them. This is what Sally did.

When she told me the story about the costume for her high school play, I remarked that the feelings she described sounded exactly like the feelings she had described in buying the hat. She agreed. I told her it was time to face up to the fears that were driving her self-depriving behavior so that she could diminish their power.

Drawing the Demon

I gave Sally a homework assignment called Drawing the Demon. She reacted to the idea as perhaps half of my clients do: by feeling intimidated. The assignment involves drawing a picture, and many people are afraid to try it because they lack faith in their artistic ability. But as I explained to Sally, this exercise is not about artistic technique—it's about emotional expression. If her drawing turned out to look like a ball of steel wool, fine.

SUSAN

As long as this demon's hidden in some dark place inside of you, you can't deal with him. So by next week I want to see this turkey out in the open. I want to know what he looks like.

SALLY

Are you serious? You want me to literally draw you a picture?

SUSAN

You bet. Take some paper and a pencil, and put a face on this creature who's making you feel too ashamed to spend any money on yourself. It doesn't have to be any great masterpiece—it can even look like a kid's drawing. After all, you were a kid when he moved in. I don't care if he's funny, or scary, or grotesque, or disgusting, as long as you wind up with a clear visual image.

The following week, Sally brought in a drawing that looked like a cross between Snoopy and the creature from the black lagoon.

She told me that when she was drawing her demon, she had experienced a strange feeling of mastery over it. Not that she had exorcised the demon—she had considerable work to do before she could approach that goal—but by externalizing it, she was turning what had been a nameless, faceless force into something tangible that she could confront.

She told me that when she finished her drawing, she stepped back to consider it, and its cartoonish, childlike style had made her laugh. This, too, gave her strength to combat it because her laughter helped to lighten some of her money demon's emotional load.

Now that Sally had a visual representation of her demon, she could put it to use. I suggested that she commit the face of her demon to memory so that the next time she found herself feeling anxious over a purchase, she could invoke its image to remind her that her conflict was due, in large part, to some outdated beliefs and feelings that she would be foolish to allow to control her.

Therapeutic Shopping

Once Sally understood how to use this new visualization of her money demon, I told her that I wanted her to go into a store sometime that week and buy something for herself. Not a vacuum cleaner, not new dish towels—nothing practical—she was to buy something for herself that she wanted *just because she wanted it,* not because she needed it. It didn't have to be expensive, but it had to be something that caused her some discomfort when she contemplated buying it.

As she did this Therapeutic Shopping, she could invoke her demon image and silently repeat a little Self-Affirming Mantra to it—a mantra that I developed long ago to help soothe my own anxiety:

> At this moment, in this store, with this purchase, I have nothing to feel guilty about. I deserve to buy this for myself; I've earned it.

This exercise wasn't about turning Sally into a spendaholic. But armed with a new perspective, she would be more apt to make spending decisions based on whether she could afford a particular purchase rather than on whether she felt she deserved it.

Sally wound up going back and repurchasing the hat she had returned. Ward *did* grouse about it for a day or two, but he didn't get nearly as upset as she had feared he would. Though this experience did not magically eliminate all of Sally's internal conflicts overnight, it was a great symbolic victory for her.

We built on this victory by setting up a weekly Therapeutic Shopping trip during which she would buy herself a gift. Some weeks she did better than others—one week she bought herself a leopard-print silk scarf, but the next she managed only a lipstick. Still, Sally was making positive changes in her behavior in the face of great emotional obstacles, and she was feeling better and better about herself as a result.

Nothing is more disempowering to the money demons of deprivation than a shot of self-esteem.

Picking a Partner to Keep You Deprived

An alarming number of women set themselves up to relive, in their adult relationships, the very deprivation they suffered as children.

You'd think that if a woman felt deprived as a child or as a teenager, she would be driven to find a partner whose love would compensate, at least a little, for all those things she felt she missed. But instead, most women who suffer deep core feelings of undeservedness gravitate toward potential partners who seem destined to give them exactly what they think they're entitled to: very little.

This appeared to be exactly what Sally did by marrying Ward—a man she described as extremely penurious.

A marriage between a self-depriving woman and a penny-pinching man would seem to be a match made in heaven. If she couldn't bring herself to spend money and he felt compelled to hoard, there should be no basis for money fights, right?

Wrong. Money behavior is not an isolated psychological phenomenon. It mirrors all sorts of other behaviors, including expressions of emotion. A person who is withholding with money is likely to be withholding with feelings as well.

Though Sally described Ward as a decent, responsible man, he seemed unresponsive to her emotional needs. In picking a man who had trouble being giving, both financially and emotionally, Sally had unconsciously found a way to perpetuate the deprivation and neglect that had characterized so much of her childhood. It was becoming increasingly clear that Sally's choice of Ward as her partner was motivated as much by her need to validate her feelings of undeservedness as it was by love.

Setting Him Up to Say No

Soon after Sally began therapy, she brought Ward in with her for a session. After a few minutes together, it seemed evident to me that both Ward and Sally were genuinely committed to their relationship. But before they could turn that commitment into meaningful change, they needed to identify some of the behavior patterns that were holding them apart.

WARD

We fight a lot, and it's usually about money. I really hate it because *I've* always got to be the bad guy. *I'm* always the one who has to say no. *I'm* always the one who has to say, "Enough."

SUSAN

I don't understand. Sally tells me that she has a really hard time spending any money on herself, so why would you have to say no?

WARD

I don't know about when she's alone, but when she's with me . . . I mean, just last weekend she all of a sudden got the "I wants" for a new car. We don't need a new car, we can't afford a new car, but we ended up fighting about it anyway. It's always something that . . . we'd have to be the Rockefellers.

SUSAN

This doesn't sould like the Sally I know.

SALLY

Well, I was just sort of talking about it, you know? Kind of dreaming about it. I wasn't all that serious, but then he gave me "The Look," and it just ticked me off. The more he said no, the more I wanted that car.

Sally and Ward were caught up in an intriguing drama. His complaint, about always having to act the heavy, was telling. By inadvertently creating situations in which Sally knew that Ward would say no to her, she was virtually scripting scenes

in which he played the villain and she played the poor little
match girl.

The dynamic was fascinating. When she was out by herself,
she felt guilty just for wanting something. But when she was
with Ward, she could feel freer to yearn for things because she
knew that he would take responsibility for depriving her of
them.

An Emotional Dance

Sally's drama had two leading characters: the rejecting, withholding parent and the needy, frustrated child. When she was
alone in a store, or in the cafeteria, or anywhere else where
doing something for herself could be an issue, she had to play
both roles in order to act out her feelings of undeservedness.

But when Ward was *with* her, he could actually play the withholding parent, and *she* was free to play the part of the needy
child to the hilt.

And the more she wanted something she couldn't have, the
more deprived and resentful she could feel, once again repeating her childhood feelings of hurt, frustration, and undeservedness.

Sally had been caught in the same repetitive pattern since
childhood.

1. She would want.
2. She would feel guilty.
3. She would not get what she wanted.
4. She would feel resentful.
5. She would be hurt.

This was the only pattern she knew. And Ward's emotional
distance made him a perfect choice to help her continue to do
what she knew best. As a result, their relationship served to
reinforce both her self-deprivation *and* his tendency to
withdraw.

When Ward gave Sally "The Look," he was reactivating the same emotions that she had felt when her mother gave her looks of impatience or disapproval as a child. He was doing exactly what Sally unconsciously wanted him to do. Deep down, she was encouraging him; but consciously, she was growing to resent him more and more. This only increased her internal conflict, cranking up her anxiety level even more.

For his part, Ward felt ground down by the unrealistic material demands that Sally used to ensure that he would, in fact, continue to deny her. Aside from his predisposition to be withholding, he resented being set up to play the authoritarian parent. And the more he resented it, the more he withdrew.

As a couple, Sally and Ward were doing an emotional dance with money, using it to feed each other's resentments and ultimately to push each other away.

Choosing an Unavailable Man

Some women perpetuate their self-deprivation by gravitating toward men who are unavailable to be partners—men who live far away, are unavailable emotionally, or are already in a relationship with someone else.

My client April did this by becoming romantically involved with Steven, a pilot who flew for the same airline that she worked for as a flight attendant. By the time she came to see me, they had been together for five years, but there was a slight hitch: He was married.

APRIL

All my friends have this romantic notion about being a mistress—black negligees, champagne and caviar, dancing in the moonlight stuff. But the reality is, we spend most of our time at my place with me cooking for him. He never spends any money on me. I mean, he never offers to pitch

in on the food. And when we go out—which isn't much—
half the time he finds some excuse not to pay. He doesn't
carry cash, and he's afraid his wife will see the credit card
bills, or he forgets his wallet or something. This is all fine
with me—I don't need a lot of material things to be happy.
But then for my birthday this year, he did a complete 180.
Usually he gets me some little thing—a book or a CD—
but this year he took me to Nordstrom's and told me to
buy whatever I wanted. All of a sudden I felt my insides
knot up. I was really uncomfortable and I didn't know
why. Of course, I didn't say anything to him about it, but
I was a wreck inside. So I got really picky and pretended
that I couldn't find anything I liked. He finally insisted that
I try on this one black dress. I'll never forget the feeling
when I went into the dressing room—I started to hy-
perventilate, my heart was pounding, it was awful. Nothing like that had ever happened to me before.

As long as Steven was withholding with money and gifts,
April felt comfortable in the relationship. But when he changed
his pattern, her emotional response was so violent that she had
an anxiety attack. It seemed apparent that Steven's offer vio-
lated some unwritten law in April's unconscious, and she was
suffering the consequences.

But that black dress wasn't the only thing April wouldn't
allow herself to have. By remaining in her "relationship" with
Steven, she was effectively cutting herself off from the possibility of having a truly loving relationship with someone else. In
choosing a married man, April was practically guaranteeing
herself heartache.

Why would a young, attractive woman with a good job
choose to close off her options by entangling herself with a
man who was usually not a giving individual and who, from
all indications, had no intentions of leaving his wife?

APRIL

I know it's a dead end, but I don't want to leave him just to go back to one-night stands. What's the point? At least now I've got some tenderness, some consistency.

The option of a healthy relationshp with an available man didn't even occur to April. Nor did she consider the option of finding contentment outside of a relationship. Her negative self-image allowed for only two possibilities: an unfulfilling relationship or loneliness.

April's bleak outlook was the result of harsh experience.

When the Solution Compounds the Problem

Even before April walked into her junior high school prom, her stomach began to knot. She knew that all the other girls would be wearing new dresses while she wore the same old party dress she'd worn last year—and her mother had bought it secondhand at that.

When she stepped into the gym alone, she felt the eyes of her classmates turn toward her like so many heat guns. Most of the boys looked interested, while most of the girls looked resentful, even contemptuous. She envied them their social graces, their expensive clothes, and their easy lives. She even envied the arrogance that they directed so pointedly at her.

Her mother kept telling her that she should thank the Lord for allowing her to go to such a fine school in one of the wealthiest suburbs in town, but April didn't feel very thankful. Her classmates all lived in big houses with big families, while she lived with her mother in a tiny apartment above their minister's garage—her mother cleaned the church and the reverend's house in exchange for the quarters.

April's father had died six months earlier after spending several years on disability for a back injury from a construction job. Since his death, April and her mother had survived on welfare checks and on occasional gifts of food from the church. They had to share a bedroom and they had no kitchen, but there was a roof over their heads, and for that April's mother felt extremely lucky. April just felt poor.

As she crossed the dance floor, she felt as if she were walking through a thick cloud of scorn and ridicule. They had it all; she had nothing. But before the night was out, she was going to turn that around. The other girls could keep their money and their fancy dresses, because tonight, April was going to walk out of that dance with the one thing all the other girls wanted—Tommy Sheffield.

At the moment, Tommy was talking to Debra Richmond—blond, blue-eyed, rich, and confident. But April had something Debra didn't: nothing to lose.

At thirteen, the other girls were just beginning to make out with boys. But April had gone all the way with Harry Longstreet one fateful night. And the next day her social life had turned around. The other girls could keep their money and their fancy dresses—the boys all wanted to be with April now. And tonight the lucky winner was Tommy.

April walked up and boldly asked him to dance, interrupting Debra in the middle of a sentence. Debra's jaw dropped at April's audacity. For a moment Tommy seemed confused, torn between two worlds. But when she took his hand and pulled him toward the dance floor, he went willingly, sending a kind of "What can I do?" shrug back to Debra.

As they started to dance, April rubbed up against him suggestively. He let out a little moan. That was when she knew she'd won. In a few minutes they'd be behind the gym, and Tommy Sheffield would be hers. She knew that tomorrow he'd probably go crawling back to Debra, begging her to forgive him. Boys always seemed to do that. But at least for tonight, all the other girls would envy her.

Fifteen years later, April sat across from me in my office and started to cry at the memory.

Like so many girls during puberty and adolescence, April had become extremely self-conscious, overly sensitive to the kindness or cruelty of her peers. In her desperation for approval, she had chosen to sacrifice herself, body and soul, for a series of brief, precious moments of acceptance.

Acceptance at Any Price

During her teens, April's lack of money and status had made her feel inadequate next to her classmates. In order to defend against this, she had felt compelled to find alternative ways to compete with the other girls. Indiscriminate sex became her weapon of choice.

She used her body to try to match their fancy clothes, their swimming pools, their country club memberships, and their upper-class manners. Their money made her feel inferior, but she hoped social acceptance would help her overcome that. Unfortunately, her sexual behavior only increased her alienation from her classmates. By and large, the girls ostracized her as a "slut," while the boys used her for sexual gratification before going back to their girlfriends.

The very behavior she was using to defend against her feelings of deficiency ended up making her feel even more inferior and degraded.

With such negative feelings about herself, it was only natural for April to believe that her material poverty was no accident of fate, that she was getting exactly what she deserved.

Not surprisingly, her high school patterns continued through college, where she became involved in a string of unfulfilling, desultory, short-lived affairs.

When she graduated, she finally decided that she had had enough of the emptiness of one-night stands. She determined to find a lover with whom she could develop a "meaningful" relationship. Unfortunately, without dealing with the unfinished business that was driving her to choose inappropriate partners, her chances of making a consequential change in her patterns of behavior were slim to none. That was when she had found Steven.

Right Problem, Wrong Solution

While April's relationship with Steven, because of its *relative*
stability, may have been a welcome change from her previous
encounters with men, she was still being treated like a second-
class citizen.

APRIL

He comes over, I cook for him, we make love, and he goes
home. While he's here, I feel like he cares for me, like he
loves me even. But as soon as he walks out the door, I get
hit by the loneliness. I'm so jealous of his wife, I could die.
God, it's frustrating.

SUSAN

So Steven goes back to his wife just like the boys in school
went back to their girlfriends. And you wind up feeling
awful all over again.

The realization that she was continuing a pattern hit April
like a ton of bricks. She thought she had made a significant
change in her life by entering into her relationship with Steven—for the first time, she was being monogamous, the relationship was long-term, and she believed she was in love. But
in fact, she was still acting as she had when she was fifteen years
old, only now she was depriving herself emotionally by being
with one unavailable man instead of many.

April was on the right track in seeking more emotional intimacy in her love relationships, but she was on the wrong train.
And for the first time she was beginning to understand the im-
plications of this.

APRIL

I'm going to have to break up with him, aren't I?

SUSAN

It's pretty hard to turn your life around when you're neck-
deep in an unhealthy relationship.

April knew what she had to do, but that didn't make it easy for her to do it. It took several more weeks of work before it really sank in that by continuing to see Steven, she was reinforcing the very feelings she needed to change—the feelings of unworthiness that had led her to choose an unavailable man in the first place.

Creating New Relationship Patterns

While Steven was unavailable to April due to circumstances, Ward was physically present to Sally. But emotionally, Ward was just as unavailable as Steven, and this was becoming increasingly unacceptable to Sally.

The day Sally brought Ward into my office, it became clear to me that they were locked in an almost ritualistic pattern of conflict about money that was masking more significant problems in their marriage. Until they interrupted these patterns, they could not hope to salvage their relationship.

The Naked Truth Exercise

To help Sally and Ward understand the emotional underpinnings of the money fights that were pulling them apart and reinforcing her deprivation, I asked them to do what I call the Naked Truth exercise.

There was only one constraint in this exercise: They could not mention money. Even though money was central to most of their fights, I wanted them to dig deeper into their hearts.

SUSAN

I want you to look each other in the eye and complete four sentences . . . truthfully. Don't hide anything, don't hold back, don't worry about hurting each other's feelings, just let it out for once. The first sentence begins with: "I

want . . ." The second with "I *need . . .*" The third, "I
feel . . ." And the last, "I *wish . . .*" I want you both to
really dig down inside and try to tap into some real hurts,
some real longings, some real fears, some real hopes.

I gave them a minute to think this over, then asked Ward to
start. He seemed to have no trouble at first.

WARD

I *want* to stop fighting so much. I *need* for you to spend less
money on the kids—whoops, no money talk.

Once Ward realized he couldn't use the easy answer, the exercise became more difficult for him.

WARD

I *need* for you to . . . I don't know, I mean—I guess I *need*
for you to be . . . happier, so that we can lighten up a little
bit . . . just to get over whatever it is that's bothering you.
I *feel* confused—and tired. And what do I wish? . . . I *wish*
this exercise was over.

Ward looked at me mischievously, expecting me to ask for a
serious response to his wish. But I didn't need one. His joke
was another way of saying, "I wish I didn't have to talk about
my feelings," a perfectly legitimate and revealing answer. His
willingness to try to open up despite his discomfort with the
process was to his credit.

In articulating his "need," he made it obvious that he was
not as insensitive to Sally's unhappiness as she believed he was.
But his past behavior indicated that he didn't know what to do
about her unhappiness, so his unknowing solution was to ignore it. As a result, the chasm between them just kept getting
wider.

Sally had a lot less discomfort with the exercise than Ward
did, having worked hard on identifying and expressing her beliefs and feelings for several weeks now.

SALLY

I *want* you to care about how I'm feeling. I *need* you to . . .
act more loving with me. I *feel* lonely, even when we're
together. And I *wish* . . . I *wish* we could go back to the
way we were when we met.

Sally was surprised to see Ward's eyes well up with tears. She
took his hand comfortingly. I was pleased to see that these simple statements of truth were bringing them closer before we
had even had a chance to deal with the content of what they'd
both said.

Of course, this simple exercise was not enough to undo their
years of growing distance, but it was a start. Sally had previously been able to tell *me* about the emptiness she'd been feeling in the marriage, but this was the first time she'd been able
to tell Ward. Since Ward had been so consistently unreceptive in
the past, Sally had always thought "Why bother?" when she'd
considered revealing her feelings to him. She was wary of making herself vulnerable to being hurt, especially since it seemed
unlikely to pay off.

From Adversaries to Partners

Sally and Ward were living under one roof, but they were leading very separate emotional lives. Though they spent most evenings together in the same room, they rarely spoke. He would
watch television and grade papers or do the bills, while she read
library books or leafed through magazines. Sex between them
had become mechanical, infrequent, and unsatisfying for both
of them--another thing they "couldn't talk about."

In the verbal exercise they'd already done, Sally and Ward
talked honestly about their feelings for the first time in many
years. I encouraged them to continue doing so at home, and if
they had trouble, to try repeating the exercise to help them
get going.

But it was also time for them to implement some specific behavioral changes to immediately address the specific desires and shortcomings that each had described.

We still hadn't addressed their fights about money. So far in their relationship money had been a divisive issue. It was important for them to find a way to feel like financial partners instead of continuing to play out the habitual withholding-father/demanding-daughter relationship they had developed.

One thing they could do immediately to help stop this destructive role-playing was to change the way they managed their household expenses. At the time they came in, Ward handled all the bills. The only thing Sally knew about their finances was that he would accuse her during their fights of having no appreciation for how little they actually netted after taxes and expenses.

There was a simple solution to this information gap. I suggested that from now on, they sit down *together* to do the bills. Then they could become partners instead of adversaries. This hard information would undercut the tape of Ward's disapproving voice that Sally carried in her head to help her stay deprived when she considered even the most minimal purchase. For Ward's part, it would relieve him of the sense of isolation that the sole responsibility for finances had been making him feel.

Once Sally became more of a participant in family finances, she would feel like more of a grown-up in regard to money, and it would be more difficult for her to fall into the needy-child role.

Growing Close Again

Two weeks later, Sally and Ward went out together looking for some new bedroom furniture. She saw something she really loved that was beyond their budget. But instead of setting Ward up to say no, as she would have in the past, she told him how much she loved it but acknowledged that they couldn't afford it.

This may seem to be yet another example of Sally depriving herself, but this time she didn't do it out of a sense of guilt or out of unconscious feelings of unworthiness. Instead, she made a rational, adult choice based on the reality of their financial situation.

Ward's response was different, too. He empathized with Sally's disappointment, admitting that he liked the furniture as well. In the past he never would have agreed with her because he would have been afraid of weakening his position in the inevitable argument that would follow. They would have walked out of the store feeling angry and resentful.

But on this day, they walked out of the store feeling closer. Their new financial collaboration—along with Sally's continuing work in therapy on her personal money demons—turned their relationship around. At my urging, they began to budget their time as well as their money to give themselves a few hours a week to spend together without children, without bills, and without television or term papers.

For Sally, who had been so starved for attention, these few changes made an incredible difference in her sense of emotional fulfillment. She began to feel better about herself, which made it more enjoyable for Ward to be with her. And the more he enjoyed being with her, the more attention she got.

Ultimately, Sally's inability to buy herself a five-dollar lunch turned out to be the key to unraveling the mystery of her self-deprivation. And this revelation turned the downward spiral of alienation in her relationship into a self-perpetuating cycle of renewal.

Self-Help Strategies

Giving Voice to the Demon

This exercise will work for any money demon, not just demons that cause self-deprivation. When you hear yourself saying the words of your demon, catalog those words in your mind. The next time you catch yourself feeling guilty or anxious, remind yourself of the demon's words, and ask yourself whether you are responding to those false beliefs.

Drawing the Demon

The money demon you draw can represent your feelings of guilt, of shame, of undeservedness, of anxiety, or any other painful feeling that is inhibiting your ability to give to yourself or to receive from others. Like the previous exercise, there is no reason to restrict this exercise to demons that cause self-depriving behavior.

Therapeutic Shopping

The key to this exercise is to learn to tolerate the anxiety of shopping for yourself, not to spend a lot of money. Trust me—the more you do it, the easier it gets. Don't just do this once. Try to pick a regular time, perhaps once a week, and set it aside just for you.

The Self-Affirming Mantra

You can use my mantra, just as Sally did. Or you can make one up that is more specific to you. In addition to saying it to yourself, you can write it on Post-its and stick it where you'll see it around your home or even on your checkbook.

The Naked Truth

Our culture does not encourage men to be open with their feelings, so many men do not know how to access, much less express, them. Be patient with your partner. The fact that he's willing to try this exercise may be a big step for him, and your understanding may help motivate him to take the next step.

3

Sabotaging Your Success

It was almost a relief to get fired. At least I could stop pretending I thought I could do it. Of course, when I got home, I had to tell Joe. That part was awful.

—*F.D., age 32*

After ten years of bit parts and auditions, I finally got a job on a soap. I couldn't believe my luck. But then I started to gain weight. I knew it was suicide, but I couldn't help it. I'd sit there eating and thinking, "What are you doing?" but I'd still keep eating. So I gained thirty pounds in six months, and the next season they decided to drop my character.

—*L.R., age 40*

The day I won my first case I went to my folks' house for dinner. I was bursting with the news, but I couldn't bring myself to tell them. My mother'd been a secretary for twenty-five years—I didn't want to rub it in.

—*S.M., age 41*

Some women are driven by money demons to turn success into failure. By undermining themselves in the workplace, they sabotage their employment, their advancement, and their finances in a particularly bewildering way.

The Danger of Achievement

Jeanie sat near the end of the conference table and stared at the polished blond grain of the bird's-eye maple that stretched to the far end of the conference room. She'd worked hard to get to this table, but now that she was here, she couldn't understand why she felt so unhappy. She heard one of the other vice-presidents rambling on about consolidating operations, but she had trouble concentrating on his words—she was too preoccupied with trying to appear alert.

"Relax," she said to herself. "Sit still. Pay attention. Okay, try to look like you're paying attention. God, I hope Mitchell doesn't ask my opinion."

She tried to focus on the little swirls in the wood, but no matter how hard she strained, she couldn't stop seeing double. She yearned for a breath mint, but she'd neglected to bring any into the meeting with her, so she made an effort to exhale in shallow breaths to keep the smell of her three lunchtime margaritas from traveling beyond her place at the table.

"What if he wants me to report? I'm in no condition to talk straight, much less think straight. Why the hell did I drink anything? I wish I'd never started again."

Suddenly everyone's gaze was upon her. Mitchell's eyebrows were raised expectantly. The realization hit her like a brick: He'd asked her a question that she hadn't heard.

"I'm sorry, Mitchell. My mind wandered off there for a second."

His eyes narrowed. Had she slurred her words? Could Mitchell tell she was drunk? Could they all tell?

"Are you feeling all right, Jeanie?"

They all stared at her expectantly. She wanted to say something, but her mind was a blank. Then, as if an emotional floodgate had opened, panic and shame surged through her. She grabbed her purse and her note pad, mumbled something about the flu, and rushed out of the room.

Twenty minutes later, Mitchell came into her office.

"Feeling better?"

"Much. Thank you."

He sat down and stared at her silently for an uncomfortably long moment. Finally, she couldn't take it anymore.

"Look, Mitchell, I'm sorry about the meeting. I just . . . I haven't been feeling well for a couple days, and I think it's just catching up to me, that's all."

"I think it's the medicine you're taking that's catching up to you." *He spoke softly, gently, but his words struck fear in her heart. He knew.*

She began to cry. "I'm sorry. I just had this one margarita for lunch, and they must have put like a triple shot in it without telling me, and—"

He interrupted her. "I'm not interested in excuses, Jeanie."

"Are you going to fire me?"

"I'm going to give you a choice. Either you can resign, or you can check into a rehab program and get sober. The insurance plan has one all set up. All you have to do is call."

The next day, Jeanie checked herself into a residential substance abuse hospital, where I was running therapy groups several times a week. Over the next thirty days she attended Alcoholics Anonymous meetings every night and came to my group twice a week.

When she first started seeing me, I assumed that Jeanie's problems were due to chronic alcoholism. But as I got to know her, it became increasingly clear that there was an unusual pattern to her drinking that implied a different kind of demon. Jeanie didn't drink when she was depressed, or lonely, or bored, as so many alcoholics do. When things were going wrong, she made an effort to stay sober and work harder. It was only when things were going right that she celebrated by drinking. Whenever she got promoted or achieved something at work, she would start getting drunk.

The episode that brought her to my group was not the first

to affect her career. It was just the first time an employer had given her a second chance. Several years earlier, she had lost two jobs in a row because of alcohol-related incidents and had had to climb back up the ladder from the bottom as a result. Each one of these incidents had occurred soon after some kind of professional recognition. Ironically, it was success that triggered her drinking.

When Success Feels Bad

Jeanie had no idea why she kept torpedoing herself when things were going well for her at work. So I asked her to try to describe the feelings she had during those times—for example, when she got her last promotion.

JEANIE

You'd think I'd just lost my job instead of getting promoted. My heart was pounding, my stomach was in knots, I was really nervous. I knew I could do the work—I mean, I'd already been doing it for a year without the recognition—so I had nothing to be scared of. I don't know . . . the big title, the big office, the money—I mean, it was really exciting, but at the same time I felt awful, don't ask me why. And then there was Jess. I remember getting home and not even wanting to tell him because he'd been so down about his own stuff—with real estate being so slow. And I was right—it just depressed him. I don't know why I even told him about it. I ought to just keep these things to myself.

As Jeanie talked, I felt a knot in *my* stomach. I recalled an incident from my own life—an incident I've written about before. It was the day I made my deal for my very first book contract. I came home filled with excitement, hoping to celebrate my good news. But the moment I walked into the house, I could feel the cloud of my husband's bad day. I was filled

with compassion for him and felt the need to conceal my good
fortune to keep him from feeling worse. So I poured a small
glass of wine and quietly took it into the bedroom to share a
lonely toast with myself in the mirror.

As I told this story to Jeanie, she nodded empathetically.

JEANIE

I feel exactly the same way. We've been married four years
now, and I still feel guilty for being more successful than
he is.

It was this guilt, to a great extent, that was making it so
hard for her to enjoy her own achievements, and Jess's behavior
didn't help.

Knowing He's Wrong, Fearing He's Right

During Jeanie's second week in the hospital, Jess came to visit
her one night, and they got into an enormous fight.

JEANIE

I asked him how his sales were going, and he said pretty
well, and I told him I'd been thinking about how it might
help his business if he did a mailing. And he got all defensive and started yelling at me about he was doing just fine
without me telling him how to run his own business and I
should get off my high horse. . . . Then he says—if you'll
excuse my French—"You think your shit doesn't smell—
remember which one of us is in the mental hospital." And
I felt like he was really pulling away and that maybe he'd
leave—and I panicked. Then I thought, maybe he's right—
maybe I *do* have a swelled head, maybe I *have* become too
much of a big shot. But then I hated myself for thinking
that because, first of all, he had no right to talk to me that
way, and besides, I knew he was wrong. I don't lord it
over him, that's just not my way.

Like so many women, Jeanie was conflicted about her role, her image—and her lovability.

On the one hand, she felt understandably insulted and angered by Jess's abusive comments. In addition, the healthy part of her was convinced that he was dead wrong.

On the other hand, another part of her—the insecure, fearful, anxious part—was afraid he might be right. Deep down, her beliefs were at war with one another.

Part of Jeanie believed Jess, not because he was persuasive but because she was susceptible to his anger—like most women, she had a programmed tendency to appease men. All her life, she had been getting the cultural message—perhaps not out loud, but subtly and repeatedly—that this was what women were supposed to do.

When His Self-Worth Is Threatened

Through the years I have seen many women, like Jeanie, undermine their own career advancement for fear of upsetting a lover who is less financially or professionally successful than she is. For some couples, this discrepancy is not a problem. Some men can share in their partner's success without feeling uncomfortable or overshadowed.

But the great majority of men have been socialized to believe that their adequacy, their worth, and to a great extent their masculinity are directly tied to their earning ability and their job status. Because of this, it is hardly surprising that so many men feel humiliated, resentful, and envious when their partner surpasses them in earning power.

Most men have trouble expressing these shame-filled feelings openly. Instead, they may try to compensate for their feelings by becoming angry and belligerent—as Jess did—or depending on personality style or temperament, they may withdraw into moodiness or depression.

Protecting His Feelings

No matter how these men express their pain, they deliver a message to their partner—sometimes directly through words, sometimes indirectly through behavior, sometimes consciously, sometimes not. And no matter how the message is delivered, its content is the same: *Her* success is the cause of *his* unhappiness.

JEANIE

My heart goes out to him. I know how hard it is for a guy to feel emasculated. It happened to my father when his business went under. I mean, he was strong and proud, and overnight he became a beaten man. And then he had to go crawling to this guy, who used to be his big competitor, for a job. It was totally humiliating. I remember watching him cry . . . my mother hugging him. . . . And she just kept saying, "Don't do this, Jack. You're not a failure. You're not a failure." I must have been about ten at the time. . . . I'd never seen him cry before. It really scared me. . . . So I really sympathize with Jess's pain. I just wish there was more I could do to make him feel better.

Without realizing it, Jeanie was doing a *great deal* to make Jess feel better. Because of her feelings of guilt, she was downplaying and even reversing a great source of pain from his life—her success.

After all, Jeanie had seen how devastated her father had been by a career blow, and she had seen how noble and nurturing her mother had been by supporting him through it. She wanted to be as noble and nurturing as her childhood vision of her role model had been. In her mind, if her prosperity was exacerbating Jess's depression, then she was responsible for doing something about it.

Jeanie would have been doing what any loving partner might be expected to do if she had comforted Jess as her mother had done her father. But Jeanie didn't *just* comfort Jess—she went far beyond that. She was driven more by the childhood memory of her father's pain than she was by the memory of her mother's specific behavior. The experience of seeing her father cry was still a powerful motivator for Jeanie, and when she transferred those same feelings of empathy to Jess, she could not bear her own feelings of responsibility for his pain.

No wonder she felt guilty about being promoted. She knew that it would increase Jess's feelings of inadequacy and humiliation, and she knew that this would escalate the tensions in their relationship. To avoid all this, she effectively deprived herself of money, prestige, satisfaction, and self-esteem—all in the name of love.

This was an eye-opening insight for Jeanie—for the first time, her self-sabotaging behavior began to make some sense.

The Martyrdom Exercise

Even though Jeanie had made the intellectual connection between her guilt over being more successful than Jess, and her self-sacrificing pattern of sabotaging herself to protect his feelings, she still needed to confront the money demons that were behind it all.

She had taken a big step forward by checking herself into the hospital and going to AA. These steps were essential to help her stop drinking. But even if she gained complete control over her alcoholism, her money demons were still agitating on an *emotional* level. If left unchecked, these demons would merely reemerge in the guise of some other self-destructive behavior.

One of the simplest things she could do to deal with her demons was to engage the healthy part of herself as an ally. I suggested that she might achieve this with the help of what I call the Martyrdom exercise.

Now that Jeanie was aware of the connections between her

professional self-sabotage and her relationship, I wanted her to use her imagination to push her behavior to the limits of absurdity. I asked her to think of the wildest, most ridiculous, most excessive promises she could make to Jess in order to be a *totally* adoring, unselfish, unabashed martyr.

Jeanie took a few moments to think, then came up with this set of martyr's vows:

> JEANIE
>
> I love you so much that I will wreck every opportunity that comes my way so that you can . . . feel superior. I will get drunk right in my office in front of my boss so that there's no chance that I'll ever be able to get a better job than you. I will refuse to allow anything good to happen to me—and I will always put your needs and your feelings first, before even thinking about my own. I'll be a slave to your ego so you won't ever have to feel less than totally perfect. . . . I will fake orgasms to make you feel like a stud.

At this point, Jeanie started to laugh.

> JEANIE
>
> This is so ridiculous.

> SUSAN
>
> Good. I'm glad you think so. Now I want you to go home and say that all to Jess.

> JEANIE
>
> Are you crazy!? I could never say those things to him.

> SUSAN
>
> Isn't that what you've been saying to him all along through your behavior?

This caught Jeanie off guard. She had thought her exaggerations were far from the truth, but in fact, when she was forced to consider really saying them to Jess, she realized how unsettlingly close to the truth they were. She might have been embellishing, but when she stepped back to consider, she was shocked to see how little exaggeration she needed to strip away before she recognized her own behavior.

When she realized how uncomfortable she would be taking her martyr fantasy out of the therapy session and into her relationship, she recoiled. That was what the exercise was all about. It gave the healthy part of her an opportunity to come to grips with the true nature of her past behavior.

Changing the Rules

When Jeanie went home from the hospital, she sat down with Jess and had a long discussion about what she had learned about herself in the hospital and what she was planning to do to change.

JEANIE
He wasn't too keen about the idea that I was going to stop taking responsibility for how he feels, and that he was going to have to do that himself. His first reaction was to deny that any of this was true. He had no idea what I was talking about when I said that I'd been trying to make him feel better by screwing up at work. I told him that I didn't care whether he understood or not, as long as he was willing to work with me on our relationship. For one thing, he had to stop insulting me. If he was feeling lousy about something, he had to talk about it instead of lashing out at me. That was a big one. For my part, I promised to stop telling him how to do his job and to keep going to AA.

I told Jeanie to anticipate some rough going. When you change the rules in a relationship, your partner will inevitably feel out of balance and will often react to this by trying to return things to their old, familiar patterns of interaction.

It is not uncommon for people to try to sabotage their partner's recovery progress (even if this means buying a bottle of wine for a recovering alcoholic). I warned Jeanie that in her relationship, Jess might do this unconsciously by becoming especially moody in an attempt to manipulate her back into her role as his emotional caretaker. Or he might become verbally abusive again as an indirect way of expressing his discomfort with her success.

But she was much better prepared than she had been before her hospitalization to deal with these potential obstacles. Now that her healthy self had become activated, it would be much more difficult for her money demons to drive her to "martyr" herself in the future.

The Need for Permission

A husband and lover is not the only person for whom a woman may unconsciously sabotage herself. A woman who is in a relationship with a man who is successful in his own right or not the least bit uncomfortable with her success, or even a woman who is not in a relationship at all, may still sabotage herself financially or professionally to protect the ego of a parent or sibling.

We would all like to think that every parent wants his or her child to do well. But as we all know, this is not always the case. On an unconscious level, some parents feel frustrated, thwarted, angry, and disappointed in the failure of their own dreams and goals. As a result, they unconsciously withhold permission for their children to surpass them financially, artistically, educationally, or professionally.

Frustrated parents often communicate, either through words or through behavior, that you do not have permission to do better than they—to do so would be disloyal, it would be a betrayal, it would be a public humiliation to shine the light of your own success on their past failures, their inadequacies, or their loss of control over you.

As a result, many parents, whom one would expect to be joyful and approving of their children's success, instead respond in bewildering negative ways—with depression, unjust or unkind criticism, or even ridicule.

It's as if they were saying, "How dare you rub my nose in my own failure."

Pursuing Mother's Dream

Melanie, a friend of my daughter's, was an accomplished modern dancer. She was a student at one of New York's most prestigious dance academies (as her mother had been before her), and she showed considerable talent and artistic promise in class. But every time she auditioned for a paying job—a Broadway show, a television commercial, or even one of her own company's professional performances—she blew it. She would either be late, or she would lose the address, or she would forget her music, or she would perform, as she put it, "like an arthritic camel."

Melanie's mother had always wanted to be a professional dancer herself. She had trained hard since she was a child to pursue her dream. But when she became pregnant with Melanie, she had been forced to give up her career to raise her child. As a result, in an unhealthy attempt to live out her own dreams through Melanie, she had pushed her daughter to become a dancer.

At first, Melanie enjoyed the attention she got from her mother for dancing. But as Melanie began to show promise, she began to notice a change in her mother's supportiveness. Whenever Melanie had a good recital or received accolades, her mother seemed to get moody.

MELANIE

She never said anything that wasn't positive and supportive, but the way she said it and her whole demeanor . . . I always had this strong feeling like she was burning with envy, like she longed to be doing what I was doing, like I was hurting her somehow by doing well. And the better I got, the stronger I felt that. It got to the point where I wished she wouldn't come see me dance because it made me feel so guilty.

I had no way of knowing whether Melanie's childhood perceptions were accurate, but in terms of her emotional healing, it didn't really matter. What was most important to Melanie was her *experience* of her mother's sadness and envy, and Melanie's beliefs about where those feelings came from. Whether or not Melanie's mother was actually having trouble dealing with her daughter's success, Melanie's belief that her mother was having trouble was enough to cause her enormous guilt.

When Melanie grew up, these guilts undermined her confidence and her drive, so that anytime an opportunity arose for her to progress from student to professional, she found some way to insure that she didn't make it. Unconsciously, Melanie believed that to perform for money would be to belittle her mother, because money was such a blatant symbol of success. And if she belittled her mother, she might lose her mother's love.

The Good Girl Syndrome

There are other ways to sabotage your job or career besides screwing up. It's quite possible to perform well at work and still undermine your own best interests.

This is how Sandy sabotaged herself in her job as a midlevel product development manager for a large computer software company. Sandy had been a key player in the development of one of their best-selling software packages and had initiated two others that were innovative and promising. She first came in to see one of my staff members for clinical hypnosis to deal with a weight problem. When she learned that I was working on this book, she volunteered her story.

SANDY

My husband Mike's always telling me how I undervalue myself and how I should be getting promoted and how I should go in and demand a raise and how all the other managers at my level are making much more than I am, even though I'm one of the most productive. And he's right. I know I deserve more. I know I've earned more. But I just can't bring myself to ask for it.

SUSAN

What do you think would happen to you if you went in to your boss and asked for a raise?

SANDY

I'd probably get it. My friend Margie did, and she hasn't even been there as long as I have.

SUSAN

So what's the worst thing that could happen?

SANDY

I don't know. I'm just afraid of rocking the boat.

SUSAN

What could happen to you?

SANDY

It's not a logical thing, it's a physical thing. I feel like I'd throw up or something.

Sandy was clearly terrified of doing anything that might upset her boss. Yet from her friend Margie's success and from her own expectation that she would get her raise if she asked for it, it seemed clear that her boss was not a tyrant. Sandy was a victim of her own timidity and fear. She was struggling with the Good Girl Syndrome.

The Good Girl Syndrome combines a powerful need to be liked with a deep fear of incurring other people's displeasure or anger. In one way or another, it afflicts almost all of us. When it's mild, it's more of a personality style than a problem. And in fact, there's much to be said for being cooperative and easy to get along with.

But when taken to extremes, unconditional people-pleasing can undermine your ability to stand up for yourself, and when it constrains you, it can immobilize you. The Good Girl Syndrome can set you up to be exploited, cheated, and even abused.

In relationships, this syndrome may not be all that obvious— women may appear cheerful, quick to please, and selfless. But in the workplace, the need to be seen as a "good girl" keeps you from negotiating effectively for yourself and causes you to undervalue the worth of your services and to accept less compensation and slower advancement than you deserve.

This can compound your own lack of initiative in holding you back in your career, because when you undervalue yourself, others undervalue you as well.

The Fear of Authority

There's a reason why this syndrome is called Good Girl and not Good Woman—it is typically developed in childhood.

SANDY

My father was a very strict disciplinarian. I mean, *really* strict. If we got him mad, he'd take off his belt and we wouldn't be able to sit for a week. Believe me, you didn't want to get Daddy mad. So we'd never complain, we'd never talk back, we'd never make noise when he was around, we'd never do anything to get his attention.

The source of Sandy's fear of rocking the boat was pretty obvious. Unfortunately, she was unable to separate out the past from the present. She projected many of her fears of her father onto her boss, because her boss, like her father, was a strong authority figure in her life. She had learned as a child that authority figures are unpredictable and volatile and that the key to avoid being hurt is to avoid calling attention to herself. As an adult this fear refused to let go.

She was afraid to ask for a raise. She was reluctant to take credit for the contributions she made to the products she developed. She would communicate with her supervisors primarily through e-mail to minimize the threat of confrontation, and she rarely spoke up at meetings for the same reason.

A Convenient Arena

Families and workplaces are often strikingly similar—they are both complex webs of authority, rivalries, and alliances.

Because of this, the workplace often becomes a convenient arena for acting out or trying to resolve many of our family conflicts. We cast the people we work with as various members of our family. We'll often replay sibling rivalries with our coworkers, acting out unresolved issues of favoritism and competition. We'll turn a mentor into mother, a boss into father (or vice versa).

This is especially true for women whose childhoods were marred by parental alcoholism or abuse, and who grew up fearing authority figures. The Good Girl Syndrome is a defense against that fear. It can be extremely effective in creating the illusion of safety.

Fear of Failure

Women with the Good Girl Syndrome often feel quite secure in their own skills and abilities. But other women are not so fortunate.

Many women who lack confidence in themselves are so afraid of failure that they will sabotage their own opportunities to move up to a new job or a new level of responsibility in order to avoid the risk of falling flat on their face.

Needing to Be Perfect

Charmaine crossed out the words old age *with a blue pencil and wrote in the word* aging. *Then she sat back and stared at the page. She took another sip of coffee and considered her work, unable to decide whether it was any good.*

Another reporter strode by—"Hiya, Char. Howya doin'?"—and was out of earshot.

"I wish I knew," she responded under her breath. She read her lead sentence out loud: "The marriage between aging and infirmity may finally be on the rocks."

It wasn't easy to bring a breezy style to an article about a potential breakthrough in thyroid chemistry. She thought she'd done a pretty good job with the lead, but she felt uneasy about the rest of the story— it bothered her that she couldn't put her finger on what it needed. It just wasn't right yet.

Her reverie was interrupted by a sense that someone was standing behind her. She turned to see Ed, her managing editor. He was reading her story over her shoulder. She flipped the top page over so he couldn't see.

"Gimme." He put his hand out for the story.

"I'm still working on it."

He took the pages off her desk. "It reads fine. I need you to fill in for Dave."

She suddenly felt her heartbeat in her chest. "On the desk?"

"No, we need a fourth for bridge—of course on the desk!"

She didn't feel qualified to work on the city desk. She was unsure enough of her writing skills without having to edit other people's stories. She'd make the wrong changes, the reporters would start complaining, and she'd be exposed as the incompetent that she felt she was.

Her palms were beginning to sweat. She reached out and snatched the pages back from Ed. "I'm not through with the story."

Her heartbeat was now pounding in her temples. She could see Ed getting angry—he didn't like being challenged. But she couldn't think of anything else to do. The very thought of working the desk flooded her with panic.

So she hardened her resistance. "As long as my byline's on it, I'm the one who says it's finished."

"Maybe you didn't hear me, Charmaine. I read it. It's fine. I need you on the desk. Period." It was clear that his patience had run out. He extended his hand for the story.

Her anxiety was now so great that she was frozen, unable to even move her arm to give him the pages.

"Don't make me ask you again."

Something in her snapped. "Why are you being such a fucking Nazi? Just leave me alone!" She felt like an idiot, but she'd be damned before she'd admit it.

"You've got ten minutes to pack your things and get out. You're fired." And he walked away. Just like that.

She was stunned—not only by his behavior, but by her own.

When Richard arrived home that evening, he found Charmaine making dinner.

"I thought it was my turn to cook. You get off early?" He grabbed a Diet Coke from the fridge.

"I got fired."

The way she said it, so matter-of-factly, caught him off-guard. He wanted to think she was kidding, but this would be the third job she'd lost in four years, so he had a strong suspicion that it was true. "You didn't."

"I'm sorry."

"The same thing?"

"I couldn't help it, Richard. My brain just short-circuited. I couldn't stop myself."

"How could they just fire you? I thought you were doing so well."

"Well . . . it might have something to do with the fact that I, uh — I called Ed a — fucking Nazi."

Richard exploded. "We can't afford this again, Char! Don't you get it?! I can't support us both! I just can't! Not to mention the health insurance!"

"I didn't do it on purpose!"

"Bullshit, Char! That's bullshit! Nobody did this but you! You always do this! What the hell is the matter with you!?" He rushed out of the room.

Fear ran through her like a wildfire. "Where are you going?!" She heard the front door slam.

About midnight, Charmaine finally gave up waiting for Richard and went to bed. She was still awake two hours later when he finally came home. But he never came upstairs. The next morning she found him asleep on the living-room couch.

Charmaine and Richard had a long talk when he woke up. She acknowledged that she had been out of line when she blew up at her boss, but she insisted that the man was an unreasonable tyrant and chauvinist who had driven her over the edge with his impossible demands. Richard refused to accept her excuses — he'd heard them before. He pointed out that this was not the first time this had happened to her, and he insisted that she own up to the fact that she was responsible for what she had done. Charmaine continued to deny that she was to blame for her self-destructive outburst.

Finally, Richard told her that he was no longer willing to tolerate the anxiety and pressure of Charmaine's serial unemployment. He didn't want to end their marriage, but he was prepared to if she was not willing to see a therapist to deal with her self-sabotaging tendencies. This ultimatum really infuriated Charmaine — she told him she had no intention of seeking help for a nonexistent problem.

Richard packed a bag and left that same day. Two days later, Charmaine called him and told him that if he'd come back

home, she'd give therapy a try. She reluctantly joined one of
my groups the following week.

From Anxiety to Panic

Most people are afraid of failure to a certain extent. A touch
of apprehension when we're faced with doing something both
challenging and unfamiliar is not necessarily a negative emotion. A little anxiety about new challenges can be exhilarating,
it can motivate us, it can get our motor going to prepare ourselves for at least a reasonable chance for success. But money
demons can cause us to overreact to that healthy anxiety, and
that was what happened to Charmaine.

What should have been a little anxiety for her turned into
something more like full-blown panic. Instead of motivating
her to grab her opportunity, the panic motivated her to avoid
the professional challenge at all costs, driving her to behave in
ways that were guaranteed to end in disaster.

One day Jeanie—who after finishing her rehab program had
joined the same group Charmaine was in—asked Charmaine if
she thought she was self-destructing to protect her husband's
ego, as Jeanie had done for Jess.

CHARMAINE

Not at all. In fact, when I do well, he's really proud of me.
When we go out, he's always telling our friends about this
article I did or this scoop I got. Every time I get a piece in
the paper, he faxes it to my parents. He's very encouraging. It's *my* ego that needs protecting. The thought of being humiliated in front of everyone I work with—I
couldn't take it, I'd just die.

Charmaine seemingly had no need to protect her partner's
feelings as Jeanie did. Instead, Charmaine's self-sabotage was
driven by her fear of her own inadequacy. Like so many
women, she would oscillate between wanting career success and
being afraid of pursuing that success.

Charmaine was an extremely skillful writer. This talent often brought her opportunities to advance. But the prospect of advancement was always tempered by her fear of trying anything that might subject her to yet another round of frustration and humiliation. Despite the fact that her colleagues and editors seemed to have high regard for her skills, her fear of failure easily overshadowed reality in shaping her behavior.

Impossible Standards

When someone in a ski mask holds a gun to your head, panic is understandable. But when someone offers you an opportunity to advance and you panic, you are clearly not reacting to a real threat. The tendency to panic in the face of a job-related challenge doesn't just fall from the sky; it usually comes from a legacy of repeated criticism that makes the child feel inadequate.

I asked Charmaine whether either of her parents was particularly hard to please.

CHARMAINE

I guess my dad. I mean, he loved me a lot, I know that, but he was such a perfectionist . . . always pushing me to do better, to try harder. No matter what I did, he always had some way I could have done it better, something I didn't do right, or I overlooked, or I was careless about. He was constantly correcting me every time I picked up a fork with the wrong hand, or used *her* instead of *she,* or didn't tuck my sheets in tight enough. He would lecture me about everything.

SUSAN

How did you feel when he'd criticize you?

CHARMAINE

Well, obviously, it didn't feel good. . . . It's the pits to be a failure, believe me. I mean, not that I was a failure, but I was far from perfect. He was just trying to make me better, to make me have a better life.

Charmaine was set up for failure by the virtually impossible standards of her perfectionist father. And like a disease that is passed on from generation to generation, Charmaine inherited her father's perfectionism.

There's nothing wrong with aspiring to meet high standards, but when those standards soar to such heights that they are unrealistic, they become destructive. The need to be perfect often gives birth to a paralyzing fear of failure.

Even after Charmaine moved away from her father, nothing she did was ever good enough. In fact, nothing she did *could* ever be good enough, because perfection is unattainable.

But like most children of relentlessly critical parents, Charmaine came to see herself as the failure she saw reflected in her father's criticism. She couldn't imagine why else he would criticize her unless she deserved it. She couldn't imagine that he might have unhealthy reasons of his own for being so disparaging.

Leftover Anger

In order to feel better about themselves, perfectionist parents put extraordinary pressure on their children to reflect glory on them. Perfectionistic parents rationalize their constant criticism as encouragement to excel, but their children almost always experience this as their parents' disappointment and rejection.

Unable to do the impossible, these children feel frustrated and resentful of their parents for making them jump through hoops.

These were feelings that Charmaine brought with her into adulthood, feelings she acted out in her workplace.

We all hate being criticized, and when we are picked at and nagged continually, as Charmaine was, it is only natural that we build up an enormous well of resentment. This resentment cannot be held in forever, however, and with perfectionists, frustration is the key to releasing it.

When her editor exerted pressure on her, Charmaine reexperienced the frustration that had been so familiar to her in childhood. By stubbornly refusing to capitulate to her editor, Charmaine was able to assuage that frustration, if only momentarily, by not giving in to a man she saw as an unreasonable tyrant. At that moment, her editor became a stand-in for her critical father.

Charmaine had projected the same image on previous bosses, with virtually identical results—she had been fired before. In rebelling against authority—no matter how self-destructive this may have been—she was seizing the opportunity to overcome her childhood powerlessness. The workplace had become a battleground for her, a place to fight authority figures in the hopes of defeating her long-standing fears and resentments from childhood.

Unmasking the Internal Critic

In order to help Charmaine see how her childhood had forged patterns of fear and resentment in her, and how those patterns set the stage for her adult self-destructive behavior, I proposed an exercise I call Unmasking the Internal Critic.

I asked her to spend some time before our next session recalling some events in her childhood and young adulthood during which her father had made her feel like a failure. I wanted her to frame these memories by answering three questions for each event:

1. What did I do?
2. How did he react?
3. How did I feel?

The following week, she came back with nineteen events. The following four examples are typical:

What did I do? I flunked a science test at school, and the teacher sent a note home saying I wasn't working up to my potential.

How did he react? He didn't talk to me for two days, as if I'd totally disgraced him.

How did I feel? Totally disgraced, ashamed, like a worm, like a total failure.

What did I do? I wrote a poem for my father for Father's Day.

How did he react? He thought it was stupid because I tried to rhyme *love* with *hug* and he said any idiot would know they don't rhyme.

How did I feel? Discouraged, embarrassed, awful.

What did I do? My mother wasn't feeling well so I worked really hard to make dinner for the first time. I was only nine.

How did he react? He ate it all, but the whole time he kept complaining about how bland it was, how tough it was, how overcooked it was.

How did I feel? Angry, disappointed, and hurt.

What did I do? I was offered a job as a summer camp counselor.

How did he react? He told me it was up to me, but he didn't think I could handle being responsible for a bunch of little kids when I couldn't even keep my own room clean.

How did I feel? Stupid and helpless.

Needless to say, Charmaine didn't take the summer camp job. As an adult, though she certainly enjoyed many career successes, whenever she reached a new plateau in her career, her father's messages would come back to undermine her.

Making the Connections

As a result of the Unmasking exercise, Charmaine committed her personal history to paper. With her father's patterns of unwarranted criticism before her in black and white, she was forced to confront the fact that he had continually undermined her childhood confidence.

CHARMAINE

Not that I didn't know it before, but I'd always thought about specific incidents—I'd never really put them all together like this. I mean these nineteen are just a few—I could have just kept going. And the funny thing is, now that I'm in California, I've, like . . . taken over for him. When I think about the things he used to say . . . I mean, these days I say the same sorts of things to myself all the time.

Charmaine's father may not have been overtly abusive, but he certainly didn't provide her with the encouragement and praise that are so necessary for a little girl to develop a sense of self-worth. Armed with this self-knowledge, Charmaine could begin to nurture that damaged self-worth herself.

Once we unmasked her internal critic, we had an adversary with whom we could deal in the open and could ultimately conquer.

Self-Help Strategies

The Martyrdom Exercise

If you suspect that you are sabotaging yourself to protect your partner's (or a family member's) feelings, this exercise will help you get in touch with the discomfort your behavior should be giving you. Once you are ready to articulate the most ridiculous, pathetic, self-sacrificing things you can imagine doing for your lover, tape-record yourself saying them. Then play back the tape to get the full impact of the absurdity of martyrdom. The next time you feel anxious or guilty over success, replay that tape in your imagination and let the absurdity bring you back to reality.

Unmasking the Internal Critic

In the background of almost all self-saboteurs lurks a great critic. This person is usually a parent, though grandparents, siblings, friends, neighbors, or teachers may be responsible as well. When that critic's voice becomes indistinguishable from your own, it is next to impossible for you to have a realistic self-image. To get rid of the counterproductive self-criticism that is hobbling your ability to achieve, you must first unmask the identity of the true critic within you and identify the crippling messages that he or she left behind. This exercise— exactly as Charmaine did it—is a good first step.

4

Living in Debt

I would get really lonely for people, and I would go shopping. It was like I felt safe in a mall. It was a way to reward myself. I'd get myself something pretty, and I'd be on a roll. I've always been extravagant with myself—go out to buy powder base and end up spending seven hundred dollars. There was hell to pay when the bills came in.

—R.G., age 30

We were going from one crisis to the next, the landlord was breathing down our necks . . . bill collectors . . . we had to park the car a block away so they couldn't repossess it. . . . I don't know how we got by. His paycheck was always spent before we even got it, but that didn't stop me from spending more. By the end of the month, we would end up worse off than we started.

—P.B., age 34

I never should have grabbed the check. . . . I mean there were ten of us, and I certainly couldn't afford it. But I thought it would be such a grand gesture.

—K.K., age 35

We've all spent money on things we don't need. We've run up our credit cards and juggled our debts. Most of us have bounced a check at least once. But for all too many women, financial slipups have become more than occasional lapses— they've become a lifestyle.

Some women find themselves deeply in debt, yet they continue to spend impulsively, and they can't seem to stop, no matter how hard they try. Reckless spending has a lure all its own for these women, a drama and euphoria that seems irresistible.

The Siren Song of Reckless Spending

"Come on," Gina pleaded. "We'll just try a few things on."

Carol still held back. "I'm on a budget. I can't afford anything." She was already feeling guilty about ditching her job to play hookey with Gina; the last thing she needed was to compound the crime by spending money she didn't have. But she needed cheering up because she and her husband Chris, a loan officer, had had yet another fight about a bill she'd neglected to pay.

"We're not buying," insisted Gina. "We're just playing dress-up. Come on, it'll be fun." Gina grabbed Carol's wrist and dragged her into the jewelry store.

The topaz ring was the first thing Carol saw when she walked through the door. It looked like a big diamond, except that it had a pale aqua hue—almost exactly the color of her infant daughter's eyes. The color of love, she thought.

"Could I try that on?" she asked the salesman, then whispered to Gina, "Just for future reference."

As she slipped the ring on her finger, she could sense herself feeling different—better. She just knew that with this ring on her finger, people would see her in a different light. She would seem more beautiful, more important.

"It's only a hundred and eighty dollars," said the salesman.

Carol looked at the ring appraisingly, as if the price seemed reasonable to her. But she was thinking about the enormous debt she'd brought with her into her marriage—the debt that still hung over her like a wrecking ball.

She examined the ring on her finger from another angle. It did make her feel awfully good—a definite improvement over the drudgery of processing payroll, which is what she was supposed *to be doing right now. For the first time in weeks, she didn't feel burdened by that sinking restlessness that seemed to set in whenever her life became frustratingly routine.*

With great effort, she mustered her resistance and slipped the ring off her finger. "I like it," she said as she handed it back to the clerk, "but it's not quite what I'm looking for."

She looked around for Gina, hoping to get out before she changed her mind, but Gina was across the store, trying on an emerald pendant.

"You know what would look great on you?" said the salesman. "The matching bracelet."

"I don't think so . . . ," Carol said reluctantly as she turned to the salesman to make a graceful exit. He was already holding the bracelet, and before she could stop him, he had draped it across her wrist for her to see.

It was gold, with three aqua topazes set apart by little diamonds. Its beauty dazzled her. It was the kind of bracelet that she imagined on Elizabeth Taylor's wrist, not on her own. It was the kind of jewelry she had always dreamed about, the kind that as a child she had always imagined was designed exclusively for royalty.

She fastened the clasp—just to see how it looked. Gina walked up and gasped. "Oh my God, Carol. That is the most beautiful thing I have ever seen."

"Here," said the salesman. "Try them on together." He slipped the ring on her finger.

Carol looked at her hand as if it belonged to someone else. Then she held her hand in front of her face and looked in the mirror. She looked like a model in a magazine. She felt like a queen.

"The bracelet sells for seven hundred," said the salesman, "but I can give you both pieces for eight."

"Can I put it on layaway?" Carol heard the words come out of her mouth, but she couldn't believe she'd said them.

"Of course," said the salesman.

"Are you crazy?" Gina asked this with as much admiration as astonishment.

"Yes," Carol replied. As the salesman moved away to ring up the sale, she held her hand up for Gina to admire. *"I'm already nineteen grand in the hole. What's another eight hundred?"*

Carol turned back to the mirror and felt a rush of excitement as she stared at her new image. She felt completely transformed.

Carol lost the war between her best intentions to control her spending habits and her desire to lift herself out of her doldrums. The jewelry promised euphoria, romance, and glamour—a promise too seductive for her to pass up.

A Lifestyle of Debt

When Carol married Chris, she was already thirteen thousand dollars in debt from school loans, overextended credit cards, and a car loan. Chris knew about these debts, but he assumed they were the result of bad financial planning—something he could help her with.

Chris immediately took responsibility for putting their finances in order. He refinanced her debt to pay off her credit cards. Then he took her out to a romantic dinner to celebrate her new freedom. She agreed to cut up her credit cards—Chris called it "plastic surgery."

He had thought the matter would end there. He didn't realize how out-of-control Carol's debting behavior actually was. In fact, Carol's debting was compulsive.

Debting as a Compulsion

Substance abuse is a compulsion. Repetitive overeating is a compulsion. So are sexual addiction and uncontrolled gambling. These are all relatively obvious compulsions that have received a lot of attention from the media in recent years—most people are aware of them.

But far fewer people realize that reckless spending and irresponsible debting can be compulsions, too, just as powerful and controlling as any other.

In fact, chronically uncontrolled debtors and spenders are sometimes called *debtaholics* because the similarities between their financial compulsions and those of alcoholics are so great. But the suffix *aholic* strikes some people as being overused, or even derogatory. So when I refer to women caught up in compulsive debting, I prefer to use the term *money-reckless*.

The Cycle of Compulsive Debting

Money-recklessness leads to recurring financial troubles that invariably spiral out of control. These troubles can create an upheaval in a woman's life, not only financially but emotionally. And compulsive debtors try to relieve emotional stress by spending money. It is a vicious cycle.

Carol's story is a perfect example of how this cycle works.

Soon after Chris cut up Carol's credit cards, she became pregnant. They hadn't planned a baby so soon, and it meant even more pressure on their budget, but they were thrilled when Marla was born. Throughout her pregnancy, Carol resisted running up any new debt. But after she returned to work, she began to feel restless again. Between her job and the baby, she felt like she never stopped working. And she was more and more resentful of the financial limits that Chris had imposed on her.

She also felt deprived of the enormous highs—the druglike rush she would experience when she impulsively bought herself extravagant gifts. The more she longed for those feelings, the more difficult it was for her to resist her cravings.

So without Chris's knowledge, she applied for some new

credit cards. Their arrival marked the beginning of a new spending spree.

CAROL

I'd buy something for Marla, and then an expensive dress or sweater for myself. All the way home I'd be bouncing back and forth between the excitement and the guilt. I'd buy these beautiful things, but then I'd have to hide them in the back of the closet so Chris wouldn't see them. On the one hand I felt good about getting back at Chris for controlling me, but at the same time, I felt this incredible shame, as if I were some kind of criminal skulking around behind his back.

Five months later, Chris found one of Carol's credit card bills and discovered that she had racked up an additional six thousand dollars in new debt.

Chris was furious. He accused Carol of betraying his trust, of caring more about new clothes than she did about their family. He even consulted a divorce attorney.

Carol panicked. The thought of losing Chris just a year after their daughter was born made her miserable. Her resentment turned to shame and guilt.

CAROL

He'd sit there playing with Marla, and all I could think of was how I was tearing the family apart before it even had a chance to get going. And that just killed me.

She pleaded with Chris to give her another chance. She swore that if he would help her work out a rational solution to the problem, she would stick to it.

Chris finally sat Carol down and worked out a compromise that she could feel comfortable with—a small weekly allowance that she could spend as she pleased. Carol swore up and down that she would stay within it.

But it was only a month later that she blew away her budget and bought the topaz jewelry.

The Four Stages of the Cycle

Like almost all other types of compulsive behavior, the cycle of compulsive debting follows a predictable course. There are four basic stages:

1. The Triggering Feelings. Compulsive debting is always triggered by feelings that may or may not be conscious. Your triggering feelings may be the result of a specific event, such as an especially bitter fight with your partner, or the loss of a promotion or a job to someone else. Or your trigger may be an accumulation of small hurts or frustrations that become too powerful to contain. Though any feeling can trigger a compulsion, painful feelings like neediness, rage, emptiness, depression, or loneliness are the most likely.

2. Reckless Spending. Reckless spending is a means of both deadening and distracting yourself from your uncomfortable triggering feelings. It shifts your focus away from your feelings to something outside yourself, something you can splurge on, usually something you can't afford. The excitement of spending and acquiring causes your mood to shoot upward like a rocket, if only temporarily. This is more than a psychological reaction; it is the result of a mood-altering chemical release (adrenaline and/or endorphins) in the brain that physiologically mimics a momentary drug-induced high. You get lost in the pleasure of the moment, giddy from the euphoria and the heady boost to your self-image. The knowledge that you're doing something forbidden only adds to the rush.

3. Self-Reproach. Now that your mood is sky high, you're set up for an inevitable fall. Reality sets in. There is an onslaught of guilt, shame, anxiety and bewilderment. You berate yourself for having behaved in such an irrational, uncontrolled manner despite your better judgment. Because of this, it is quite common for compulsive debtors to become preoccupied with the conviction that they are morally deficient, that they are just plain "no good."

4. Good Intentions, Futile Efforts. The final stage entails making promises to yourself or to your partner about reforming your impulsive spending habits. You may be truly committed to keeping these promises and to making these changes, but taking control of your behavior is not as easy to do as it is to consider. The power of compulsion can undermine even the strongest of commitments.

As Carol experienced these four stages:

1. Her triggering feelings sprang from resentment over Chris's control, from cravings for the highs of spending, from anxiety over her tenuous marriage, and from boredom at work.
2. She spent recklessly.
3. She felt miserably guilty and ashamed.
4. And finally, she made voluntary, hopeful changes in her spending habits—guided by Chris.

But taking control of her finances was not enough. Her emotional life was still being dominated by her triggering feelings. Eventually these led her to jump back into the cycle all over again.

Driven to Deceive

Despite the emotional upheaval that compulsive debting creates, many money-reckless women still live in a dream world—a world in which bills never come due and the consequences of irresponsible spending magically work themselves out.

But when reality encroaches on this dream world, most debtors feel as if they were being pushed over a precipice, and emotional survival takes precedence over everything else, including honesty.

In desperation, compulsive debtors often resort to lies and secrecy to try to escape the consequences of their own behavior.

Self-deception is also a handy tool for building a wall of denial. It is as if by putting bills in a drawer, a debtor can make them cease to exist. As if by lying to her partner about having paid the rent, she is actually paying the rent. As if by promising never to lie again, the slate of past lies will be wiped clean.

Driven by deep feelings of shame over how low she's sunk, guilt over what she's done, and fears that her partner will become enraged or will even leave her, the compulsive debtor hides bills and purchases as an alcoholic hides bottles. Compulsion breeds deception.

CAROL

I hated myself when I lied to him, but I was positive he'd leave me if he found out. I didn't think I could live through that, so these lies just came out of my mouth. I guess I knew that sooner or later he was bound to find out, but I just tried to keep putting it off.

There was a classic paradox at work here. Lying, the very thing that Carol did to keep her relationship from self-destructing, was exactly the behavior that was likely to tear it apart.

You can't keep financial chaos hidden forever; there are too many telltale clues to trip you up—bills, creditors, bounced checks, credit card rejections, new purchases. Sooner or later, the woman who lies to her partner will be caught. And her partner's feelings of outrage and betrayal will almost always be more destructive to the relationship than his reaction would have been had she voluntarily admitted to her compulsive spending in the first place.

Sir Walter Scott said it best: "O what a tangled web we weave, When first we practice to deceive!"

Are You a Compulsive Debtor?

If you are in the throes of financial chaos, it's easy to lose perspective on whether you got there through money-recklessness or through ill-advised spending, poor planning, or just plain bad luck.

Not every woman who gets into financial trouble is compulsively irresponsible or careless. Anyone can hit a financial pothole every once in a while.

To help you clarify whether your debting or spending is compulsive, I've devised the following checklist. Consider your answers carefully before you respond—most people to whom these behaviors apply have an understandable tendency to deny them.

Do you repeatedly . . .

- go on spending binges when you feel depressed, lonely, or angry?
- ignore, hide, or throw away bills?
- write checks that you know will bounce?
- borrow money you can't possibly pay back?
- blame others for your own financial problems?
- lie to your partner about having paid bills that you haven't paid?
- try to impress people by picking up dinner checks, lending them money, or buying expensive gifts, even though you can't afford to?
- get anxious in check-out lines or with salespeople, knowing there is a good chance that your check or credit card will be rejected?

- seem incapable of holding on to any money you may make?
- accuse your partner of selfishness, greed, or short-sightedness whenever he complains about your spending habits or mounting debts?
- spend money on recreational activities or luxuries when you don't have money for necessities?
- expect someone else to rescue you financially?

The key to this checklist is the word *repeatedly*. If you answered yes to even one of these questions, and your behavior around money is *consistently* self-defeating, you may very well be a compulsive debtor. Two or three positive answers make it almost certain. Beyond that, there's no doubt.

I know it's frightening to realize that your financial problems may lie in your emotional world as well as in your checking account. It's always easier to make excuses, or to blame the fates or the economy. But until you acknowledge that inner demons underlie your financial troubles, you can't hope to begin the work of overcoming those demons and of gaining some lasting control over your behavior around money.

A Two-Pronged Attack

Carol's guilt over buying the topaz jewelry eventually led her to return it and to confess the incident to Chris. To her amazement, Chris didn't blow up at her. Instead, he suggested that she seek professional help because his financial solutions were clearly not working.

CAROL

I lost an eighty-dollar deposit on that jewelry, but I think it was the best investment I ever made because it got me into therapy.

When Carol first came into my treatment center for an assessment, I insisted that she attend meetings of Debtors Anonymous in conjunction with her work with me.

She was surprised at this, as if I were sending her to a competitor. Why did she need DA if she was going to be in therapy? I told her I firmly believe that the cycles of any compulsion must be attacked on two flanks at once—a behavioral one and an emotional one. Each approach bolsters the other, creating a powerful synergy.

Carol was still resistant. She knew that Debtors Anonymous—which is based on the famous twelve-step structure pioneered by Alcoholics Anonymous in 1934—had a strong religious overtone, and she found that discomfiting.

CAROL

It's not that I'm not religious; I go to church pretty regularly. But I just have a problem with the idea of turning over my will to God. I mean, aren't I supposed to be taking responsibility for *myself* at some point?

I've heard this same concern from many women. They are afraid that step number three, in which they are asked to turn their will and their lives over to the care of God, disempowers them from taking responsibility for their own actions.

But, as I explained to Carol, most twelve-step programs have adopted the use of general terms such as "a higher power" instead of "God," or have expanded their definition of God with the phrase "as we understand him." As a result, even people without strong religious beliefs can benefit from twelve-step programs by interpreting the "higher power" not as God in the traditional sense, but as a healthier part of themselves that needs to be actualized.

Twelve-step programs like DA have proven far more effective than individual or group therapy for controlling compulsions. These programs offer vital support, understanding, a sense of extended family, and a proven, structured method for dealing with behavior that would otherwise be out of control.

Many people are critical of certain aspects of twelve-step programs. And I can't say that I wholeheartedly subscribe to every one of the steps or to every single recovery technique in use. But there is no arguing with the overall results.

DA *does* have its limits, however, and that's where the second prong of the attack comes in. Twelve-step programs are not designed to address deep-seated emotional wounds or unconscious motivations as comprehensively as psychotherapy is. Twelve-step programs are also not set up to provide a "laboratory" for practicing new behaviors, as an individual or group therapy session can through rehearsal or psychodrama. This is why I believe so strongly in combining twelve-step programs with therapy or with some of the therapeutic techniques I'll be showing you here.

Jamming the Trigger

One of the most straightforward ways of interrupting the cycle of compulsive debting is to identify your triggering feelings, then use them as alarm bells, rather than allow them to push you into the reckless spending stage of the cycle. I call this technique Jamming the Trigger.

Whenever Carol's emotional triggers gave her the impulse to grab her purse and head for the mall, for example, I told her to sit down, take a deep breath, and think about what this impulse was telling her: that unhealthy influences were trying to control her. She'd be surprised how this little jog to her consciousness could empower her to resist those influences.

By recognizing that she was fighting a triggered impulse, she would reinforce the fact that following the urge she felt was a choice, not a foregone conclusion. Armed with this recognition, she could choose not to go, especially if she were fore-

armed with other kinds of behaviors that might defuse her triggering feelings.

I asked Carol to tell me what some alternative behaviors
might be for her. She suggested going to the gym or playing
some tennis.

These were both good ideas. Physical activity is always a
good way to blow off emotional steam. But any number of less
active pursuits can work just as well.

Going to a movie or a museum, reading a book, drawing a
picture, meditating—these are all terrific ways to divert your
attention from your compulsion long enough to take some of
the urgency out of your impulses. The longer you avoid acting
out your urges, the less powerful they become.

You can also talk to a close friend, which will allow you to
vent some of your feelings—another effective way of disempowering rage or frustration. When we talk something out, it
often eliminates the need to act it out. (Eventually, this would
become an especially valuable part of Carol's work when she
hooked up with a sponsor in DA.)

I told Carol that these diversionary strategies were tangible
and immediate things that she could try right away. They
would give her some sense of mastery over her compulsion.
Even if they weren't successful every single time, when combined with some digging into the deeper roots of her compulsion her success rate was bound to improve with them.

Money Messages

As children we are all steeped in messages about money, messages we get from our parents, whether intentionally or not.
Some parents do this outright by talking about money. It may
be as general a message as "Money is the root of all evil." Or
it may be more insidiously personal: "I don't trust you with
money," or "What makes you think you deserve any money?"

Other parents are not so overt, but the way they *use* money sends a powerful message. They may dangle money like a carrot on a stick to exercise control; they may withhold money to be punitive; they may use money to express favoritism within the family or to disempower a spouse. Or they may be so secretive about their finances that money seems somehow sinful, as if it were something to be ashamed of.

There are a thousand variations on the theme, but when our parents use money to control, to punish, or to deprive us, we learn to look to money for various kinds of emotional fulfillment that it can't possibly supply.

The Money Autobiography

Since money demons are created early on in our lives, compulsive debtors need to look at some of the messages about money they received as children to clarify the attitudes that drive them to act out in compulsive ways around money as adults. Only by doing this can they embark on the task of dismantling those attitudes.

It took some time in therapy before Carol was ready to do this. First she needed to work on settling down her marital and financial crises. But after a few months, her work in DA was giving her a handle on her spending, and Chris was beginning to regain some of his lost trust in her. As her home life calmed down, Carol and I could begin to work on some of her deeper, more unconscious issues.

To help Carol get started on this introspective journey, I gave her the same homework assignment I give to all my clients who act out through money. I call it a Money Autobiography.

As the name implies, the Money Autobiography is a personal history about childhood attitudes, beliefs, and behaviors around money, mostly derived from family interactions. I gave Carol this list of questions to answer.

- Who controlled the money in your family? Did he or she use that power to control others?
- Who gave you money? What did you have to do to get it? Were there any strings attached?
- Did you work when you were a child? Did you have to work? Were you allowed to keep your earnings?
- Did your parents always seem to give more money to your siblings than they did to you? Or vice versa?
- Did your parents spend money recklessly? Or did they hoard money?
- Did your parents trust you with money? Or did they mistrust you?
- Did your parents fight about money? What do you remember them saying?
- Were your parents ever in serious financial trouble?
- Did you ever have to lie about a parent's whereabouts to creditors, bill collectors, or welfare workers as a child?
- Did you ever steal money as a child? Were you caught? What happened?
- Did anyone ever accuse you of stealing as a child when you were innocent?

I told Carol not to worry about answering every question, but to concentrate on those that seemed to strike a chord for her, that seemed to prompt the strongest memories.

A Child's-Eye View

The day Carol brought in her Money Autobiography, she felt very self-conscious about the fact that it was only one page long. She apologized for answering only a few of the questions, but she had been able to identify with only a few. As it turned out, she had nothing to be concerned about. Her few replies provided a gold mine of important revelations.

I asked her to read me what she wrote:

CAROL

In my family, we never had enough money. My dad would take whatever we had and go out and spend it drinking. I remember once he lost all our money gambling. And once he just lost it. There was always a lack of money. I never got an allowance, so I had to work for everything I wanted. We didn't have new clothes, or ever go on vacations, or even have enough money to fix things in the house that broke. But even though he was totally irresponsible, we all really loved my dad. He got all the attention, he was the focus. We always did whatever he wanted to do; if he wanted to eat at a certain place, that's where we went. And if my mom complained that we were too deep in the hole, he'd sweet-talk her into it anyway. He was like that, just full of life. Everybody ended up doing whatever he wanted. And my mom ended up giving up a lot because of it. She had to take this horrible job to keep us afloat, and she hated every minute of it. She became like a drudge for him.

I pointed out to Carol that her Money Autobiography revealed some striking connections between her financially irresponsible adult behavior and two powerful messages she internalized as a child:

The message from her mother's behavior: Being financially responsible means being dreary, sacrificial, and joyless.

The message from her father's behavior: Being financially irresponsible means being the center of attention, getting your way, and enjoying life.

In light of her two primary role models, Carol's cycle of compulsive debting looked a lot less bewildering. To her child's-eye view, her mother seemed miserable, while her father seemed blissfully carefree and self-indulgent. It doesn't take much imagination to see why Carol, as an adult, unconsciously chose to identify with her father.

Though she had lived out that identification by going shopping instead of going to a bar or to the track as her father had, the results were the same—chronic debt.

The Rewriting Exercise

Carol's Money Autobiography revealed that she had some mixed feelings about her father. On the one hand, she understood the damage he had done and she knew the pain and suffering he had caused his family. On the other hand, she romanticized him.

The child part of her still yearned for attention and aspired to be like him in order to get it. Her desire to identify with what she saw as his glamour and excitement was keeping her stuck in her pattern of freewheeling spending.

One way for her to loosen the grip of that desire was to look at her father from a different perspective, a truer perspective. This would help her to defeat the distortions that were feeding her compulsive spending.

To help Carol find this perspective, I asked her to do an exercise I call Rewriting. I told her to imagine that her infant daughter Marla was now grown and wanted to marry a man exactly like her father. In essence, I was asking her to "rewrite" her father's role as if she were rewriting a character in a play. Her father would become her prospective son-in-law.

Rewriting the family roles in this way would force her to look at her father's behavior differently. Instead of idealizing and making excuses for him, she would be moved by her maternal instincts to protect her daughter. This would give her a far less romantic view of the kind of man her father really was and of how his behavior had affected her family.

I asked Carol to role-play what she would tell her grown-up daughter under these circumstances. I played the part of Marla.

CAROL

Are you out of your mind? Are you completely nuts?
Who's going to support you? Him? He blows all his

money on booze—if he ever makes any. And he gambles,
can't hold a job, can't hold on to money. . . . He just wants
to play all the time, like an overgrown kid. Is that what
you want for your life? Working overtime to support a pe-
rennial teenager *and* to take care of the house *and* to take
care of the kids while he's running around the whole time
blowing every dime you make? He's going to make your
life a living hell. You'll never have money to go anywhere
or do anything, your kids won't have clothes—

SUSAN *(as Marla)*

He's just had a string of bad luck, that's all.

CAROL

Bad luck is when you get robbed, not when you go out
and drink up the rent, not when you blow the rent at the
track.

SUSAN *(as Marla)*

He'd never deliberately do anything to hurt me.

CAROL

He may not *mean* to hurt you, but he's not going to be
thinking about you, either. He only thinks about himself. If
someone's going to suffer, believe me, it's not going to
be him.

SUSAN *(as Marla)*

That's not true. He's sweet and he's funny and he's full
of life.

CAROL

Sure he is. Just like a big baby. But a big baby's never going to be anything but a weight on you. And there's nothing you can do to change that.

I could tell that Carol was becoming uneasy about the exercise. It's tough to demystify someone you've always adored,

especially someone who you're genetically predisposed to look up to and to love. I asked Carol how it felt for her to say such negative things about her father.

CAROL

To tell you the truth, it feels pretty shitty. I mean, I've told you about all those things he did to us, but I never really put it all together like this before. He sounds like such a jerk, it makes *me* feel like burying my head in a pillow and just crying.

Despite her sadness, Carol was making tremendous progress by acknowledging how her father had failed both her and her mother. Even though Carol had known this before on an intellectual level, it was not until she had done the exercise that she allowed herself to *feel* the pain of his recklessness. She had been stuffing her resentment and disappointment all her life because those feelings seemed disloyal to her. She had never before given herself permission to experience the full impact of what he had done to her.

Once she was honest with her feelings, Carol was able to see her father's behavior and understand his character more objectively, as an outsider might. This gave her the new perspective she needed to begin the process of disentangling herself from the attitudes toward money that she had inherited from him.

The Payoffs for Money-Reckless Behavior

Carol's unconscious identification with her father was only one factor in a knotty equation. It was easy to see why she would want to identify with him, but why would she continue to do so after her self-defeating behavior backfired in her face—over and over again?

The answer lay in one of the most tragic ironies of human behavior: Even the most self-destructive behavior can offer temporary gains. These are the "payoffs" that make lasting behavioral change so difficult.

It may seem bizarre to talk about gains from behavior that can destroy you financially, throw your life into turmoil, and overwhelm you with feelings of anxiety, shame, guilt, anger, and depression. But these gains are very real and very compelling to the unconscious.

Getting Attention

On a conscious level, Carol had no idea why she was driven to spend the way she did. In fact, she didn't even realize that she *was* driven.

But unconsciously, Carol was accomplishing an important goal. By plunging her life into financial chaos, she was forcing Chris to notice her, to spend time with her. She was doing exactly what her father had done to get attention—acting like an irresponsible child.

CAROL

When I was a kid, nobody paid any attention to me as long as I was doing okay. My father was out carousing and my mother was out working, and when they were home they were fighting. I might as well have been dead for all they cared. But if I got into trouble, everything changed.

SUSAN

What happened when you screwed up?

CAROL

I got attention.

SUSAN

So what do you do now to get attention?

The realization hit Carol hard.

CAROL

I screw up.

Attention was an important payoff for Carol. She felt left out and starved for attention as a child, and now, as an adult, she still felt the need to fill that void.

Though her compulsive spending infuriated Chris, it *did* get him to focus on her at a time when she thought he was withdrawing from her. This was a successful payoff, at least on an unconscious level — negative attention was better than no attention at all.

For Carol, it felt better to be chastised than to be ignored. When Chris sat her down and worked out a budget with her, he was proving to her that she existed and that he cared about her. For a little while, she could escape the feelings of invisibility that still haunted her from her past.

Avoiding Drudgery

Of course, Carol's unhappiness was not entirely rooted in the past. Her work made her feel like a dreary wage-slave — just as her mother had always complained of feeling. The idea that she was turning into her unhappy, ultraresponsible mother was appalling to Carol. So she rebelled against it, as if to say, "I'll be damned if I'll grow up."

By creating chaos through compulsive spending, Carol could stay the rebellious child and avoid the adult responsibilities she so dreaded — another big payoff.

CAROL

It's like, if I'm responsible with my money, then I have to be the drudge. I have to be serious. I have to give up myself to make money — give up the things I really want to do. I mean, look at my job. It's the most boring, depressing, horrible waste of time — it's just bean-counting. I have to be a grown-up, and grown-ups never have any fun.

As with many money-reckless women, Carol's need to escape adult responsibility became an almost full-time preoccupation. She was on a crusade to avoid her mother's joylessness.

As far as Carol was concerned, budgeting, saving, paying bills, and delaying gratification were symbols of oppression. By spending compulsively, she could throw off the chains—at least until Chris found out.

Rescue Fantasies

When Carol and Chris first married, he took over the management of her debts, cut up her credit cards, and dealt with her creditors. When she ran up a new debt, he again sat her down and made her promise to adhere to a strict budget.

Like a financial knight in shining armor, Chris would always ride to her rescue—another payoff.

CAROL

When I screw up really bad, Chris's always there for me. I feel like there's finally somebody standing on deck to throw out that life jacket when I start drowning. I never felt that before I met Chris.

By creating one financial disaster after another, Carol was setting Chris up to be her rescuer. In this way, Carol was getting Chris to provide the kinds of structure and protection that she never got from her father. Though she romanticized and emulated her father's carefree money-reckless behavior, it never provided her with the sense of security and stability for which she yearned. Now, as an adult, she was finally getting that safety net from Chris, despite the money fights that inevitably came along with it.

Almost all compulsive debtors cling to rescue fantasies. They become convinced that if they can just hold on long enough, a lover, or a friend, or a family member will come along to bail them out. Or they'll win the lottery. Or they'll be given a substantial raise. Or some long-lost relative will die and leave them a fortune.

Rescue fantasies are a big payoff for money-reckless women,

providing them with an alternative to taking personal responsibility for their debts, no matter how farfetched that alternative might be.

Image Fantasies

There was another fantasy that Carol's compulsive spending was feeding: the irresistible fantasy that others would find her more beautiful and more prosperous, would admire her more, because of a flattering piece of jewelry, an item of clothing, or her lavish spending.

Compulsive debtors often try to pump up their self-image through futile attempts to pursue the approval of others.

CAROL

I always felt like I wasn't as good as the other kids because they always had nice things and I never did. I remember this one year—it was after the Christmas holiday—some boy on the playground announced that I was a charity case because I was the only kid who came to school in old clothes. I felt like shriveling up and crawling into a hole. The other kids' parents were always doing stuff for them . . . taking them places. . . . Mine never did that. So now I do it for myself.

Feeling ashamed and inadequate for most of her childhood, Carol grew up convinced that her happiness was dependent on the favorable opinions of others. Now that she was an adult, this belief translated into a need to try to buy desirability. In essence, she was hoping that beautiful clothes and jewelry would make others see her in a better light than she saw *herself*.

When she tried on the topaz jewelry, she faced the mirror and "looked like a model in a magazine." That was how she believed she appeared to others. And that belief boosted her self-image, if only for a moment.

"Big spenders," in their desperate attempts for approval,

take expensive vacations they can't afford, buy extravagant gifts they can't afford, grab for checks in restaurants that they can't afford, buy or lease cars or homes they can't afford, buy furniture, adult toys, even artwork they can't afford.

These generally grandiose compulsive debtors may buy things they don't even like. When they're spending money to impress others, it doesn't matter what they spend the money on, as long as they're spending freely. The payoff lies not in the object itself but in the impression it makes.

Rx for Loneliness

Marie's money-reckless behavior was similar to Carol's, but her payoffs were considerably different.

Marie got into her car and let her head fall back against the seat. She needed a massage—or something. It had been a long, stressful day. But a productive one. She'd met with three different boutique owners and had managed to persuade them all to pay higher wholesale prices for the one-of-a-kind appliquéd jackets she designed and manufactured. Maybe now she could afford to cut back on her ridiculously long hours.

She felt like celebrating, letting loose. She thought about going home and talking her husband Joseph into taking her out for a night on the town, but the thought was more of a private joke than a serious consideration. The last time they'd gone out was almost two months ago, and it had been a disaster. She'd picked the restaurant, and he hadn't liked his food, so he'd spent the entire meal ranting about her incompetent choices and bad taste. "That's what I get for marrying a CPA," she thought. Then she reconsidered; "No—that's what I get for marrying Joseph."

Going home was out of the question. She really didn't feel like being criticized for her housework or her opinions, and that's all she ever seemed to be getting from Joseph anymore.

She could feel her loneliness closing in on her. In the old days she would have called a friend and gone out for a Virgin Mary—she didn't like alcohol. But now she couldn't think of anyone to call. She'd become so far removed from all of her old friends over the last year or so. For one thing, she'd been working ten-hour days, seven days a week, which made it impossible for her to find time for her friends. And for another, Joseph didn't like any of them. So she'd wound up simply drifting apart from everyone.

As she started the car, she really yearned for the warmth of human companionship. She needed someone to congratulate her, to share her feeling of accomplishment. After all, she'd made an extra twenty-eight dollars a jacket just by renegotiating.

She deserved a treat. Especially after having just paid off her six-thousand-dollar loan from Joseph's brother. For ten months, she and Joseph had been fighting about that loan. Now, after seemingly endless hours of overtime, it was finally behind her.

She didn't think about the fact that if she hadn't run up her credit cards in the first place, she wouldn't have had to take out a bank loan to refinance her debt. And she didn't think about the fact that if she hadn't fallen behind on that bank loan, she wouldn't have had to borrow from her brother-in-law. And she definitely didn't think about how Joseph would react if he were to discover that she'd allowed her credit card debt to pile up again.

Instead, she thought about the mall and how cozy she would feel there in the warmth of her favorite stores. She thought of the effusive greetings she'd get from the salespeople she knew, and the joy she'd get from trying things on—how they'd compliment her on the things that looked good or joke with her about the outfits that didn't quite work.

The prospect of going to the mall brought back memories of shopping in department stores with her mother. There had been a particular saleswoman with a French accent who always used to give her mother a kiss on both cheeks when they walked in and then give Marie a chocolate when they left. Marie had always felt so welcome when they visited her.

Marie's mother used to take her shopping a lot—whenever Marie's father would get on his daughter's case about how thoughtless she was or how irresponsible she was or how stupid she was. Marie would

*invariably wind up running out in tears as her father called after her,
"Don't turn your back on me!"*

*Marie's mother never intervened during these all-too-frequent epi-
sodes, but later that day or the next morning, she would knock on
Marie's door, tell her her father was sorry, and ask her if she was up
for an "apology trip." Then they'd go to Macy's or Bloomingdale's.
Marie's father never once apologized himself, but somehow shopping
with her mother always seemed to make up for that.*

*Marie pulled out of her parking spot and headed for the mall. She
wasn't going to spend a lot of money. Just taking an hour to relax in
the shops would be treat enough. She could just pick up a pair of those
eighteen-dollar patterned stockings she'd been wanting.*

*Four hours later, she left the mall with $3,700 worth of clothes.
After all—as that delightful salesgirl had pointed out—what good are
eighteen-dollar stockings without an outfit to match?*

For Marie this was no simple trip to the mall. Shopping for
her was a complex tangle of associations, reenactments, and
unconscious payoffs.

She and Joseph were barely earning enough to meet their basic expenses, especially since they had enrolled both of their
sons in private school. Thirty-seven hundred dollars was a lot
of money to them.

Nor was Marie's spending spree an isolated incident. She had
thrown their marriage into turmoil several times in the past by
running up her credit cards past the limit. And every time, Joseph's patience grew thinner. She knew there would be hell to
pay when he found out this time, but she did it anyway.

Every time she and Joseph managed to climb out of debt, she
found herself impulsively sinking them back in. This not only
hurt their relationship, it was having a serious impact on the
future of her children. She and Joseph were trying to save for
their boys' college educations, but Marie's compulsive behavior
was making that impossible. Why did she keep doing it?

One of Marie's payoffs was clear: She was able to quell some

of her loneliness through the companionship of doting salespeople and through an activity that had provided comfort for
her as a child.

When Marie was little, the pain of her father's verbal abuse
was eased by the pleasure of her mother's apology trips. Instead
of protecting Marie from her father's tirades, Marie's mother
tried to undo the hurt with material things. And the shopping
sprees paid off for Marie, making her feel special and adored.
This sent Marie a powerful message that stayed with her into
adulthood—that spending money on pretty things was a way
of coping with unhappiness.

And indeed, Marie was now taking that message to heart.

MARIE

I feel like I'm in a morgue when I'm at home, it feels so
dead there. We never laugh, we never touch, we never have
sex anymore. . . . Maybe he's having an affair, or maybe
it's because I'm always working, or maybe it's that he just
doesn't love me anymore. I don't know. We never talk
about it. But when I go to the mall, it's like a party.
There's always people there. And I feel somehow that nobody will hurt me there. I don't know whether it's because—I thought once that it's like the womb, a mall. It's
all enclosed and well ordered and well lit, and the tempera-
ture is regulated, and it never rains. People are nice to
you. . . . It's like you're not alone.

Clearly something was wrong if Marie was finding the mall
more fulfilling than the companionship of her husband.

The feelings of loneliness that result from a troubled relationship leave us desperate for *more*. Sometimes we're not sure what
we want "more" of, but our sense of emptiness and lack of
fulfillment are tangible. At other times the deficit is painfully
clear—we need more love, more tenderness, more sex, more
intimacy, more attention, more understanding, or more companionship.

The mall had become Marie's major source of the kind of emotional nourishment that most people get from their love relationships and friendships. Marie, like many compulsive debtors, was using shopping to try to assuage her loneliness and fulfill her need for more. But in the long run, passing acquaintances cannot fill our need for love partners, and chance conversations with strangers cannot substitute for friendships; emotional fulfillment cannot be bought.

The emotional high of compulsive spending was a powerful payoff for Marie, but it was temporary at best. It did nothing to ameliorate her core loneliness, unhappiness, and sense of disconnectedness.

Escaping an Unhappy Relationship

In addition to helping Marie briefly avoid her loneliness, her latest spending spree put her once more in the red, throwing her back into the cycle of compulsive debting that she had just dug herself out of. Though the amount of money may not have been disastrous, it was enough to create new conflict at home and to push her back into her pattern of overworking.

MARIE

I would see a dress and I'd think, "How can I spend that kind of money, owing what I owe?" And then I'd think, "Well, all I have to do is make one more jacket a week for three months, and I'll have it paid off." And when you're working seventy-hour weeks, you've got no life anyway, so what's another four hours?

Marie's spending had always been compulsive—she had always gone shopping when she felt unhappy or lonely and had bought things that she didn't need, couldn't afford, and often didn't even want. But before her marriage, she had always managed to curb her spending to keep her debts within her means.

When her marriage began to deteriorate, however, her debting began to escalate out of control. And because of her increasing debts, she felt obligated to put in longer and longer hours.

No matter how hard she worked, she could never catch up—but that, too, was a payoff for Marie. It was no coincidence that Marie's self-imposed need to work long and late kept her out of the house for extended periods of time. As long as she could work ten hours a day, come home exhausted, and use her debt as an excuse to continue, she could avoid spending time with a husband she got no joy from being with, and in a home she characterized as feeling "like a morgue."

This was another payoff for Marie: Instead of dealing directly with the problems in her relationship, she could avoid the enormous discomfort of emotional confrontation and, at the same time, escape her unhappy home life.

A Substitute for Lost Dreams

Some women spend compulsively in an attempt to substitute for fantasies they've had to give up. Many women who played music, painted, danced, wrote, acted, or showed promise in some other art form when they were younger, or who once had professional aspirations, have had to give up their art or aspirations for marriage, family, or financial reasons. These women often feel cheated or robbed of the life they once dreamed of.

Though compulsive spending is no substitute for their dreams, it *is* a way for these women to act out some of the frustration and resentment they feel.

Just as Marie was able to avoid having to deal with her unhappy marriage, women who use spending as a substitute for creativity or accomplishment enjoy the momentary payoff of being able to avoid the feelings of boredom and emptiness that so often permeate their lives.

Relationship Work

No matter how compulisve debting pays off for the debtor, it rarely offers benefits to her partner. Until the debting behavior stops, bitter and continual money fights are virtually guaranteed. And in that kind of charged atmosphere, it is almost impossible to work on improving a relationship.

Before Carol started therapy and DA, she and Chris had been fighting almost every night. His attempts to control her debting behavior had turned him into a virtual financial policeman. This was clearly a formula for disaster. Carol resented being told what to do, while Chris resented having to act like the heavy.

All that resentment began to dissipate when Carol started budgeting for herself in DA. In taking personal responsibility for a change, she began to feel less like a child in her relationship. She and Chris could begin to let go of the unhealthy parent–child dynamics that had been causing so much friction in their marriage.

It was a lengthy process, but Carol began to discover that being a grown-up wasn't such a bad thing after all. And this freed her up to interact with Chris in new and exciting ways— as an equal.

Facing the Truth

Marie's relationship problems were more complicated than Carol's. Marie's marriage would probably have been a shambles even if she were *not* a compulsive debtor. Despite the fact that I insisted that Marie go to DA—as I had with Carol—her problems with Joseph clearly went beyond her self-imposed financial troubles. As a result, while her work in DA was effective in curbing her spending, it did little to improve her love relationship. So her marriage became the focus of our work in therapy.

One of the first things we had to do was to address Marie's

workaholism. By working out various ways for Marie to cut back on her schedule, she was able to free up more time for herself. She was hoping to spend much of this time at home with Joseph, now that her boys were teenagers and off with their friends so much of the time. But the more time she freed up, the more demanding *his* work seemed to become.

So Marie ended up spending much of this "found" time renewing old friendships. And the more time she spent with friends, the more she grew aware of how unfulfilling her marriage had become.

Like Father, Like Husband

Without the spending sprees and late hours to distract her from her emotional dissatisfaction, Marie's feelings of resentment toward Joseph came bubbling to the surface.

MARIE

It's getting worse every day. Like last week. We were having breakfast, and he goes to get a spoon, and all of a sudden he's yelling at me. "What the hell is this? You call this clean? I call this disgusting! Can't you even wash a lousy spoon? The dog could have *licked* it cleaner than this! You are such a waste, you are such an incompetent, you can't do anything right," and on and on and on. And the funny thing was, it was just a water spot, you know? The spoon was clean, it just had a water spot from the dishwasher. But he keeps ranting and raving . . . he throws the spoon on the floor. . . . And then he starts going through the silverware drawer and picking out every knife, every fork, every spoon with a water spot on it and throwing it on the floor. And all the time I'm just standing there feeling like a total incompetent. Even though it wasn't my fault, I felt like a moron, like a bad girl, like I couldn't do anything right.

Certainly Marie's compulsive debting had created an enormous amount of uproar in her relationship, but that was no excuse for Joseph's inappropriate, disrespectful overreaction to something as trivial as a spotted spoon.

There is a big difference between your partner expressing his anger at your behavior and his insulting your character with demeaning, degrading remarks. Joseph was obviously not expressing honest feelings about water spots; he was using them as an excuse to verbally abuse Marie.

But Marie was used to verbal abuse.

MARIE

Whenever I did anything good, my father would always find a way to make it seem like nothing. He had this need to put me down all the time, as if anything that made me look good made him look bad or something, as if he were the only one who could do anything. So he was always calling me stupid, or telling me I was doing things wrong, or saying how my clothes made me look fat. . . . I couldn't even try to open a jar without him grabbing it out of my hands and doing it himself—as if I couldn't be trusted to open it without breaking it or spilling it or something. And if I did spill anything, he'd just stand there staring over me while I cleaned it up, like some sort of sanitation cop. It made me feel so afraid all the time, so insecure— how could he treat me like that.

At this point, Marie began to cry softly. I asked her what was going on with her at that moment. She replied that she was realizing, for the first time, how similar her father's degrading treatment was to the way Joseph was treating her now. She was getting the same constant criticism, the same disrespect, the same emotional coldness. Joseph's harangues were making her feel like a worthless child, just as her father's always had.

Few adult relationships escape the shadow of the past. We all relive certain aspects of our childhoods in our love relationships, and if our childhoods were marred by hurt, pain, and confusion, than we will come to associate these feelings with love. Not only do we bring a distorted understanding of love into our adult relationships, but we often choose partners whose distortions about love are similar to our own.

Familiar Territory

You might think that Marie, having suffered as she had from her father's tirades as a child, would go out of her way as an adult to find a kind, loving man who was as different as possible from her father. But instead, she gravitated toward Joseph, who in many respects was a carbon copy of her father.

It's difficult to understand why someone who grew up hating the pain or turmoil of a toxic childhood would be driven to seek out similar pain or turmoil in adulthood. But for many adults, unhealthy love is the only love they understand.

We all gravitate toward what we know. When we tread familiar territory, we know what to expect, we know what is expected of us, and we know how we should feel. Even if the feelings are unpleasant, they still carry with them the security of predictability. The familiar is almost always comforting, if not comfortable, especially when the alternative is unknown—a situation that usually produces anxiety.

Drawing the Line

Marie's familiar territory was an unhappy place. If there were any hope of salvaging her relationship, it was clear that Joseph's tirades had to stop. But Marie couldn't just sit around and hope that Joseph would magically come to his senses. If she wanted change, she had to take the initiative. Her most promising course was to change the ways in which she responded to his abuse. If she could stop being his doormat, he would be forced to stop treading on her.

Many women, whether money-reckless or not, deal with a verbally abusive partner's anger by doing nothing. Some believe that passivity is the most effective way of defusing a man's anger. Other are virtually paralyzed by their partner's rage or by their own feelings of helplessness or fear. All of this was true for Marie.

Her response to Joseph's abuse was to stand there and take whatever Joseph cared to dish out, as if she had no options. This was a way of dealing with abuse that she had learned in childhood. The only behavior her father had ever tolerated from her was passive acceptance. And now she was responding in the same way with Joseph.

By submitting quietly to Joseph's outbursts, Marie was, in effect, giving him permission to continue them. But all the while, she was burning with resentment and hurt. These were the emotions that were triggering her compulsive behavior.

I asked Marie to bring Joseph in to see me for an evaluation to help us determine whether there was anything left to salvage in their marriage. Unfortunately, he refused—always a bad sign. Marie was feeling pretty discouraged about the possibility of any future with Joseph.

She acknowledged that if he were to stop his criticizing, his belittling, and his haranguing, she would be willing to hang in there with him to see if things would get better. But if he did nothing to alter his verbally abusive behavior, she agreed that as far as she was concerned, the relationship was over.

I encouraged Marie to explore one more option before giving up entirely on her marriage—a technique I call Drawing the Line. This technique involves clearly delineating the hurtful attacks on your self-respect, your intelligence, and your character that you are *no longer willing to tolerate* from your partner.

The most effective way to do this is to use "nondefensive responses" whenever you start to feel verbally assaulted. These responses can work wonders to empower women in battle-torn relationships. With these nondefensive techniques, women can maintain their dignity in firm, effective, yet nonaggressive ways in the face of verbal or psychological abuse.

We all have a natural tendency to respond to attack by becoming defensive. It is a primitive response that harks back to our animal roots. When attacked, cats scratch, dogs bite, and people counterattack, whether the assault is physical or verbal. As counterattacks ping-pong back and forth between partners, they fall into a pattern of escalating belligerence.

Nondefensive responses can bring this cycle to a grinding halt. It's hard to argue with someone who refuses to argue back.

To demonstrate what I was talking about, I asked Marie to do a little role-playing with me in which she would play Joseph and I would play Marie. She was to repeat some of the more devastating things that he had ever said to her, and I would show her some alternative responses that she could have used.

We moved our chairs closer together and I asked her to begin.

MARIE *(as Joseph)*
You are such a stupid, selfish, lying bitch.

SUSAN *(as Marie)*
I'm not willing to listen to you insult me. I know you're angry, but I won't talk about it unless you treat me with respect.

MARIE *(as Joseph)*
Why should I treat you with respect when you're selfish, self-indulgent, and crazy and you've done nothing but wreck our lives?

SUSAN *(as Marie)*
Because those are my terms. And if you don't stop calling me names and tell me what you're really angry about, we have nothing to talk about.

At this point, Marie broke out of character.

MARIE

Why can't I just say, "Because I'm working so hard to change. I'm going to DA, I'm in therapy, I'm doing everything I can."

SUSAN

Once you start trying to explain or justify or rationalize, you open yourself up to more criticism. He can tell you he doesn't believe you're really trying, or he doesn't think it'll do any good, or he thinks you're doing the wrong thing, and the two of you will be off and running again. This technique is about setting limits, not trying to get him to understand or accept you.

MARIE

What if I just tell him to go screw himself?

SUSAN

That'd be fine—if you want to make him even more hostile and defensive. But if you really want to get him to cool down and try to work things out, you've got to get him to put down his weapon.

MARIE

Well, what if he tells *me* to go screw myself?

SUSAN

Just say, "I'm sorry you feel that way," and leave it at that. You'll be amazed at the effect that will have on him. It's just not satisfying to keep insulting someone when it doesn't get a rise out of them. It's like throwing cold water on the fire when he's expecting gasoline.

Nondefensive responses like these are not going to put an end to money fights overnight. And they're certainly not going to perform miracles on a badly disintegrated relationship. But if you begin to use them on a regular basis, and both you and your partner are motivated to make your relationship work, you'll discover that your money fights will evolve from pitched battles to more rational discussions; your aim will shift from blaming to problem-solving.

Here are the Five Don'ts that I use as building blocks for effective nondefensive responses:

1. *Don't* try to make excuses for your behavior—verbal abusers are adept at using your own explanations, rationalizations, and justifications as weapons against you.

2. *Don't* try to top your partner's accusations, insults, or attacks—you'll just get drawn into the kind of unproductive one-upmanship game that is often referred to as a "pissing contest."

3. *Don't* confuse nondefensiveness with wimping out or backing down—there's nothing more empowering than refusing to let him initiate a shouting match.

4. *Don't* be afraid to repeat yourself several times if need be—sometimes the "broken record" approach is the only way to get heard by a man who's not accustomed to listening.

5. *Don't* be afraid to disengage if he refuses to honor the limits you've set—for example, if he continues to yell at you after you've told him that you won't listen to him anymore, simply leave the room. You've got nothing to gain and a lot to lose by enduring a tirade after you've made it clear that you're no longer willing to do so.

Here are a few examples of some nondefensive responses that have worked very well for me in my own life as well as for many of my clients.

I'm genuinely sorry for what I've done.

I understand you're angry, but I can't change the past.

Can you help me understand what it is that you want me to do?

You're entitled to your opinion, but I disagree.

I'm not willing to talk about this until you calm down.

I'm sorry you feel the need to talk to me that way. It really upsets me.

I'm taking responsibility for what I've done. So there's nothing constructive that can come of your yelling at me.

Don't be surprised if these sorts of responses feel unnatural to you. Human instincts mitigate against them—when you feel cornered, your first impulse is to lash out. But once you get used to nondefensive techniques, you'll find yourself feeling a lot calmer and more powerful in the midst of conflict than you ever have before.

The Point of No Return

For Marie, nondefensive responses came too late to make a meaningful difference in her relationship. Though the technique significantly reduced her anxiety and panic during Joseph's verbal assaults, it did nothing to encourage him to change. Without the heat in their exchanges, however, Marie was able to see her relationship from a new, more realistic perspective, and this gave her the strength to make some overdue changes in her life.

After a brief attempt at marriage counseling, Marie and Joseph both realized that neither one of them was committed anymore to making the relationship work. At first, Marie blamed herself, believing that her debting had driven Joseph away. But on closer reflection, she saw that Joseph's anger and emotional distance were things he had brought with him into the relationship. In fact, he had once told her that his first wife complained about the same things. So Marie and Joseph separated and eventually divorced.

Even if Joseph had been more open emotionally, Marie had waited so long to get help that there was probably too much water under the bridge to save her relationship. This is typical of couples who struggle with money fights. They commonly come into therapy at the tail end of a lengthy downward cycle of emotional and psychological alienation.

Relationships can be likened to a carton of milk that's been left out on the kitchen table—there is a point at which it can still be returned to the refrigerator without going sour, but once it's been left out too long, it's beyond saving.

For Marie and Joseph, the milk stayed out too long. They had endured so much hurt, anger, and resentment that their relationship had truly reached the point of no return.

Slipping Up

Compulsion doesn't go away overnight. Marie learned this the hard way. She had been making excellent progress in therapy and in DA, and she was feeling more confident about her self-control than she had in years. But on the day that she and Joseph decided to file for divorce, she took herself on a shopping spree that set her back almost four thousand dollars.

The following day when she came in to see me, she was a wreck.

MARIE

I was doing so well. I can't believe I did this again. All that self-control was a facade. I was just deluding myself. The truth is I can't do it. I can't control myself no matter how hard I try.

SUSAN

Don't be so hard on yourself. You can take everything back.

MARIE

What difference does that make? I lost control. That's the point.

SUSAN

The point is, you're only human. We all slip up. That doesn't mean you're a failure.

Marie's experience was disheartening at first, but she didn't let it deter her from continuing to fight. For most women, battling compulsion is a "two steps forward, one step back" process. Control is not a state of being, it is a process that ebbs and flows.

The Point of New Beginnings

Compulsive debtors like Carol and Marie, who are fortunate enough to find a way out of the cycle, invariably discover that the momentary rush that their compulsive behavior provided is no substitute for the satisfaction that comes from gaining control over their lives.

Today, Marie continues to go to DA twice a week, plays golf almost as often, and is actively dating. Her spending patterns seem to be under control, despite an occasional minor lapse. Though Marie would like to be in a relationship, she reports that her life now is considerably more fulfilling than it was during her marriage.

MARIE

I have confidence in myself now that I'm going to be able to take care of myself financially. It's made me really creative about ways to do things. Like your car breaks down and you're not sure you have the money to get it fixed, you start thinking, "What are my options?" And then you go, "Well, I can ride the bus. I could ask someone for a ride. I could ride my bike. I could walk." It's made me see that there are a lot of other options in life. Everywhere I look, I'm all of a sudden finding new choices, new ways of looking at things. I've learned to find things to do that I don't have to spend money on but still enjoy. I'm working toward getting out of debt now, and for the first time in years, I feel like I'm in the driver's seat. It's a great feeling.

Once Marie started talking about options, I knew that she was well on her way. Her compulsion had made her feel that she *had* to spend money, as if it were her fate. She was robbed of the freedom to pursue alternatives because she didn't believe she had any. But once she found alternatives to her debting patterns, she turned that belief on its head.

Options are the enemies of compulsion because deliberation kills impulse. Once you start to consider your behavior and its consequences, and once you begin to take steps to change that behavior, you sap the energy from the payoffs of compulsion. And when you do that, nothing remains to drive it anymore.

Self-Help Strategies

Jamming the Trigger

To interrupt the cycle of compulsive debting, you must heighten your awareness of your impulse to spend money you don't have for something you don't need, and turn this impulse into a trigger for new behaviors. Make a list of what these behaviors might be, and carry it with you in your purse or wallet. List any hobbies, cultural, social, or spiritual activities and types of exercise that can divert you. Also list any friends or relatives who have the time, the energy, and the inclination to give you active support.

Regardless of what the feelings or events may have been that triggered your debting impulse, when you feel the urge to spend, take out your list and use it to find something else to do.

Money Autobiography

The questions in the Money Autobiography (see page 115) were designed to help you start to think about how money was used in your family, how it affected your family system, and how it affected you. Certainly there are many, many more questions that you could ask yourself. The questions in this chapter are only suggestions to get you started.

Once you've written your Money Autobiography, comb it for clues to those attitudes, perceptions, and behaviors around money that you might have absorbed in childhood. Look for the kinds of things you observed as a child that you might be repeating in your adult patterns of spending and debting. The simple awareness of repeated patterns will give you more perspective and open you to change.

The Rewriting Exercise

The Rewriting exercise is designed to help you reduce your tendency to identify with or emulate a destructive or irresponsible parent. The key to this exercise is to take a psychological step back from your relationship with a parent who you know has been financially or emotionally unstable, in order to see more clearly how he or she might have affected your attitudes and behaviors toward spending and debting.

From your Money Autobiography it should be clear which parent acted most irresponsibly with money. This does not have to be limited to spending and debting; it could also include unreasonable hoarding or habitual pie-in-the-sky investing. If neither parent fits this mold, you might look at whether one or the other of them might have created an uproar in your life in other ways—perhaps through alcoholism, drug abuse, violence, or depression.

If you find yourself repeating patterns that resemble or parallel destructive parental patterns, it is more than likely that you have found an unconscious way to idealize that parent. In that case, the Rewriting exercise will help you cut through your distortions to get to the truth.

Even if you don't actually have a child to visualize for this exercise, use an imaginary child or a friend or relative you care about. Use an empty chair or a photograph to symbolize the person to whom you're expressing your concerns. Though this may feel artificial at first, you will discover that it is quite liberating to allow yourself to articulate the more negative aspects of your destructive parent's behavior. You will be hearing truths that you have always known but have rarely, if ever, been able to fully face.

By drawing a clearer portrait of your negative role model, it will be much more difficult in the future for you to emulate that parent without setting off your internal alarm bells.

Drawing the Line

In Drawing the Line, remember that just because your partner's words are unnecessarily cruel does not mean that his anger is unjustified. You are not trying to avoid taking personal responsibility for what you've done or to blame your partner for overreacting. Instead, you are trying to drain the heat from your conflict so that you can seek solutions to your problems instead of intensifying them.

Nondefensive responses are limited only by your imagination. You can memorize the responses on page 138, or you can make up others that are more appropriate to your situation. Once you have a list of responses that feel comfortable to you, practice them in front of a mirror, in the shower, when you're driving in your car—any time will do. You can ask a friend to simulate an argument so that you can try them out in a "real" situation. Remember, these techniques are not natural for any of us. Rehearsal helps you internalize them so that you can draw on them in the heat of conflict.

These responses can be effective for everyone, not just for compulsive debtors. As long as you use the Five Don'ts as building blocks, you'll discover that these techniques can be extremely effective not only in your love relationship, but in your interactions with friends, relatives, co-workers, acquaintances, and even strangers.

5

Compulsive Gambling

It's not like you can avoid it—it's everywhere you go. It's in the office, you got office pools; it's on TV, in the papers, with the races and the ball games; it's everywhere. You walk into a mall, and there they are, rows of lottery tickets, just spread out for you to pick, or the 7-Eleven, or even the grocery store.

—*L.R., age 45*

The worst part is the lying. I'll get home late from the card clubs, and he'll wake up and be really sweet and sympathetic because he thinks I've been up working my buns off for fourteen hours straight on last-minute trial depositions. And the more understanding he is, the guiltier I feel. So I just lie there kind of stewing in my guilt, feeling like the scum of the earth.

—*L.G., age 28*

It got to the point where money became totally meaningless to me. I wish I'd gotten paid in toilet paper instead of cash—then, at least I could have gotten some use out of it.

—*B.B., age 34*

What image comes to your mind when you hear the phrase *compulsive gambler?* Most people flash on a stereotype: the slick-haired Vegas hustler leaning nervously over the craps table knocking back free drinks; the manicured gangster at the back-room poker table in shirt-sleeves and suspenders, chomping on a cigar; the nervous racetrack tout with plaid polyester pants and white patent leather shoes sweating over a fistful of betting slips. Whatever image arises for you, it's probably male.

Few of us think of women as compulsive gamblers. And indeed, men *do* make up the majority. But the available evidence suggests that there are close to a million American women who struggle with this compulsion.

I'm not talking about the "social gambler" who spends an occasional day at the track or a weekend in Atlantic City. I'm talking about women whose lives are dominated by gambling, who repeatedly lose all their money (then go into debt) on cards, dice, office pools, lotteries, gambling junkets, horse races, or some combination of these. To their partners, friends, family, and co-workers who are not gamblers, these women appear bent on their own destruction—unless they manage the unlikely feat of keeping their gambling a secret.

A compulsive gambler is someone whose life becomes dominated by an irresistible, obsessive urge to play games of chance for money.

Compulsive gambling increasingly eats away at the gambler's time and energy, causing continuing and growing problems and crises in her life. Yet no matter how many times she loses, she always returns for more, confident that *this* time she will win. Nowhere else in life is the frustration of repeated defeat so easily overcome.

A Different Standard for Women

Gambling men cut dashing figures in our culture. In the 1950s, America's favorite western heroes were not cowboys but professional gamblers—Brett and Bart Maverick. Cary Grant owned a gambling boat in the movie *Mr. Lucky,* which was later transformed into a popular TV show. From *Showboat* to *The Gambler,* betting men have been romanticized and lionized.

But not so betting women. For the most part, women gamblers are viewed severely. In popular entertainment, they are usually portrayed as fallen, immoral, usually alcoholic women. The exceptions are women who must "stoop" to gambling to save their man—or their ranch.

In real life, women who struggle with compulsive gambling often go to great lengths to hide the fact, hoping to avoid the harsh, humiliating judgments of partners, friends, or family. I once had a client whose husband discovered one of her gambling IOUs and yelled, "I'd rather you were a whore! At least then you'd be bringing *in* money!"

This moral double standard is a great source of shame for women gamblers. It causes them not only to feel degraded and unworthy but to shy away from seeking help, even from organizations like Gamblers Anonymous, which are *designed* to foster acceptance and understanding.

A Matter of Life and Death

Rachel stared at her image in the bathroom mirror. Her hair was a mess of limp, stringy clumps. She thought it looked as if it had been soaked in her tears, but the unseasonably muggy weather was the true culprit.

Her eyes shifted to her hand. The sweat from her palm was beginning to soften the handful of sleeping capsules. The dye that stained her skin was the same color as the hundred-dollar chips she remembered from her last fling—the fling that had started it all. Or should she say, ended it all.

She smiled at her gallows humor as she thought back on that night—what she could remember of it. It seemed such a blur now, a pastiche of whirling images—dice flying, cocktails flowing, people cheering, adrenaline pumping, chips, IOUs, grinning men, heady sensations, big bets, big wins, big losses, and then the end of the ride, when the casino finally turned her down for more credit.

How was she ever going to pay off her IOUs if they wouldn't give her a chance to win it back?

"I'm afraid we'll have to call your husband to approve any more credit," Danny, the assistant manager, had said. This really hurt. She thought Danny liked her. Of course her credit was based on her husband's money—that is, her ex-husband's money. Danny didn't know that she and Martin had been divorced for two years, and if he found out, she could kiss her casino credit good-bye.

If Martin even knew she was back in Vegas, he'd have a fit. Maybe even take her to custody court. God forbid he should ever find out that she'd used his name to get the casino to extend her forty thousand dollars.

She had pleaded with Danny for just one more ten-thousand-dollar stake without bothering Martin. After all, she was his friend, not Martin. Martin didn't even know Danny. But Danny was under orders. Period.

The deep green dye from the capsules was now coloring a tiny trickle of sweat that dripped onto the counter. She continued to stare at the capsules, bouncing back and forth between the poles of her decision.

She felt so frustrated, so stupid, so helpless, so guilty. If it weren't for the kids, she'd do it. She would. But the thought of what this would do to her seventeen-year-old twin boys . . . she just couldn't scar them for the rest of their lives like this. One by one, she let the pills fall back into the bottle.

She had only one choice left—to ask Martin for help. She'd never quite understood why he'd left. Sure, she'd lied to him about her gambling and racked up some sizable debts, but she'd sworn to stop that time. She'd even gone to a psychiatrist. Martin had left anyway.

The thought of begging him for money was so humiliating . . . tears filled her eyes.

He still didn't trust her, even though she hadn't gambled in two years. She'd never lost hope that he'd see how she'd changed. After all, he still loved their two children, and she was sure he still loved her, too.

But then the kids had gone off to Europe for a six-week high school senior exchange program—both gone at once for the first time since her divorce—and the loneliness had hit Rachel hard. She'd called Martin on some pretext just to hear his voice, and a woman had answered, obviously just waking up.

After two days of depression, Rachel had taken off for Vegas. Another two days, and she was forty thousand dollars in debt.

To pay off the casino, Rachel had had to take a second mortgage out on the house Martin had given her in the divorce settlement. Plus she'd pulled out another twenty thousand dollars to fix the roof, catch up on her credit card bills, and pay the balance of her kids' vacation expenses that the child support didn't cover. Now it was six months later, and she was so far behind on her mortgage payments that the bank was threatening to foreclose.

She never thought she'd find herself so desperate for a lousy five hundred dollars a month. But even with Martin's child support on top of her salary—she was a librarian at a major university—she was still barely making ends meet. And this damned second mortgage was pushing her over the edge.

She walked into the bedroom and punched one of the three numbers she had programmed into her phone—Martin's number. After three rings, an answering machine picked up: "Hi, this is Martin and Bonnie, we're not home right now. . . ." Rachel banged the phone down. Her entire body trembled from the pain.

This time, her better judgment lost out to her emotions. She ran into the bathroom and grabbed the sleeping pills.

I met Rachel five days later at the private psychiatric hospital where I was working at the time. She still looked pale and weak from her suicide attempt, but that didn't stop her from acting defiant. She was still angry at the friend who had found her unconscious and called the paramedics.

Her admitting psychiatrist had been able to obtain a fourteen-day involuntary commitment for her, and she was furious about that, too. This was a good sign, because anger is an antidote to depression. But her psychiatrist was taking no chances—Rachel was a compulsive gambler, and the tragic truth is that compulsive gamblers have an extraordinarily high suicide rate.

In fact, research indicates that one out of every five compulsive gamblers has attempted suicide. Devastating financial and emotional losses are such an integral part of the compulsive gambler's life that this should come as no surprise. And this statistic is probably conservative—we don't know how many gambling-related suicides or attempts have gone unreported.

Compulsive gambling truly can be a matter of life and death.

The Cycle of Compulsive Gambling

The compulsive debtors we met in the last chapter went into debt because they couldn't control their spending on clothing, jewelry, and other nonessentials. Compulsive gamblers, on the other hand, lose their money by *chasing* money.

The compulsive spender never expects to get out of the hole by spending more, but the compulsive gambler *does* believe that she can get out of debt with one big score. The more she loses, the more she gambles. This inevitably leads to emotional and relationship havoc.

Compulsive gambling, like compulsive debting, follows a predictable cycle. In fact, the twin cycles of compulsive gambling and debting are almost identical:

Compulsive Gambling	*Compulsive Debting*
1. The triggering feelings	1. The triggering feelings
2. Impulsive gambling	2. Impulsive spending
3. Gambler's remorse	3. Debtor's remorse
4. Futile promises	4. Futile promises

The major difference between the two cycles is in how the compulsion is acted out. The triggers can be the same, the rush can be the same, the remorse can be the same, and the fervent promises to partners, relatives, and friends can be the same. It is only the *method* of acting out through money that changes.

Denying the Awful Truth

In the hospital, Rachel refused to accept that she was still a danger to herself and seemed unlikely to sign an extended voluntary commitment after her two weeks were up. She was so eager to get home before her children returned from Europe. Her admitting psychiatrist was having a tough time gaining her trust, so he asked me to talk to her, thinking she might be more receptive to a woman therapist. His hope was that I might get her to agree to join one of my outpatient groups or to attend Gamblers Anonymous after her release.

When I first entered her room, Rachel seemed guarded and defiant. She told me she had no interest in talking to "another shrink." I suggested that as long as she was stuck in the hospital, she might as well take advantage of our time together because her insurance was paying for it anyway. She reluctantly agreed to talk, not because my argument was particularly persuasive, but because, as she put it, "it beats making potholders in OT"—occupational therapy.

Rachel's most recent gambling spree and its tragic aftermath wasn't easy for her to talk about, but with a little prodding and a lot of empathy, I finally got her to begin to open up.

As Rachel told me her story, my heart went out to her. Despite her defensiveness, she was clearly in a great deal of pain and a great deal of trouble.

I asked her whether she had ever sought help for her compulsive behavior. As soon as I mentioned her gambling, she raised a shield of anger and sarcasm once again.

RACHEL

Some shrink asking about my potty training isn't going to get my house back.

SUSAN

I was thinking more along the lines of—and please don't bite my head off—Gamblers Anonymous.

RACHEL

God, you sound just like my ex-husband. That's just what I need. A bunch of bozos sitting around trying to outdo each other for the loser of the year award! What's the point? I'm not like them—I can stop gambling anytime I want to.

Here it was—the motto of all compulsions: "I can stop anytime I want to."

Rachel truly believed that she could voluntarily control her gambling, despite the clear evidence that her gambling was controlling her. It had sunk her into debt, threatened her home, and played a major role in destroying her marriage—a series of events that had induced her to attempt suicide. She was clearly in a state of denial.

A Defensive Camouflage

Denial is an unconscious defense mechanism that protects us from the acknowledgment of certain painful truths that would make us feel uncomfortably fearful, anxious, or inadequate. It is like a screen that filters out certain information that we aren't willing or ready to face or to deal with.

We all use denial to some extent in our lives. Up to a certain point it can help preserve our peace of mind. But when denial camouflages compulsive gambling, it prevents a woman from recognizing the downward spiral she's in. And without that recognition, she won't do anything to get out of that spiral.

Compulsion is the expression of a pain crying to be addressed, and denial is the soundproofing that prevents us from hearing our own cries for help.

As with compulsive debtors, the most effective way for compulsive gamblers to overcome this particularly insidious defense is to immerse themselves in a recovery group. The experiences of other compulsive gamblers make denial in their midst extremely difficult.

Obviously, there's a catch-22 here: How do you persuade someone in denial to join a group she refuses to admit she needs? In fact, most compulsive gamblers attend only twelve-step programs because they have bottomed out so badly that recovery is their last resort.

The Twenty Questions

Recognizing how powerful an enemy denial can be, Gamblers Anonymous, the largest recovery group for compulsive gamblers, has a list of Twenty Questions that they use to open the eyes of first-timers, many of whom are ambivalent about being there in the first place.

The questions are:

1. Did you ever lose time from work due to gambling?
2. Has gambling ever made your home life unhappy?
3. Did gambling affect your reputation?
4. Have you ever felt remorse after gambling?
5. Did you ever gamble to get money with which to pay debts or otherwise solve financial difficulties?
6. Did gambling cause a decrease in your ambition or efficiency?
7. After losing, did you feel you must return as soon as possible and win back your losses?
8. After a win, did you have a strong urge to return and win more?
9. Did you often gamble until your last dollar was gone?
10. Did you ever borrow to finance your gambling?
11. Have you ever sold anything to finance gambling?
12. Were you reluctant to use gambling money for normal expenditures?
13. Did gambling make you careless of yourself or your family? ·

14. Do you ever gamble longer than you had planned?

15. Do you ever gamble to escape worry and trouble?

16. Have you ever committed or considered committing an illegal act to finance gambling?

17. Does gambling cause you to have difficulty in sleeping?

18. Do arguments, disappointments, or frustrations cause you to gamble?

19. Do you have an urge to celebrate any good fortune by a few hours of gambling?

20. Have you ever considered self-destruction as a result of your gambling?

According to GA, if you are a compulsive gambler, you will answer yes to at least seven of these questions. Though any one of these *yes*es alone may not be sufficient to warrant the label "compulsive gambler," when they add up, their combined weight can be very persuasive.

As with most other checklists in this book, the results of this one may be painful to face. But this pain is part of the process, not part of the problem. There can be no solution to your compulsive gambling unless you first acknowledge its hold over you.

I made sure to get a copy of the Twenty Questions for Rachel before our next meeting. She was less than ecstatic about the prospect of answering a GA questionnaire—she'd expressed a pretty unflattering view of the organization in our first meeting. But she agreed to answer it to indulge me. By the time she was finished, she had toted up seventeen *yes*es.

This simple list wasn't enough to magically conquer her denial, but she was clearly unnerved by how many questions had applied to her.

Someone to Rescue Me

By the time Rachel was discharged from the hospital, she was in a much better emotional place than she had been on that first day we met.

Rachel's psychiatrist and I had become reasonably sure that her suicide attempt was a one-time event, a behavioral fluke brought on by the confluence of too much emotional loss, too much humiliation, too many financial pressures, and the sudden deprivation of her children—her primary emotional support.

This was not just cockeyed optimism on our part. For one thing, the impending return of her children made her highly motivated to get back on her feet. She was also feeling very guilty over not having been deterred by the potential impact of her suicide on her children.

For another thing, while Rachel was in the hospital, Martin had come to visit. This had been a big boost not only to her morale but to her financial situation. Though Martin was not interested in rekindling their relationship, he was still deeply concerned about Rachel's well-being and insisted on taking the financial pressure off her shoulders.

This was nothing new for Martin. While he and Rachel were married, he had quite often had to pay off her gambling debts. This inevitably led to fights between them, but it also made Rachel feel cared for and safe.

Martin shared Rachel's love of gambling, but he had no trouble walking away from a table when he'd lost his limit. Rachel's uncontrolled gambling was something he just couldn't understand, and her repetitive debts had finally precipitated his exit.

Yet here he was, two years after their divorce, bailing her out again. In part, he was motivated by his feelings of responsibility for his teenage children, but he was also responding to his own guilt over having left Rachel to fend for herself after so many years of marriage.

As I worked with Rachel, it became increasingly clear that she had a powerful need to maintain as much of a relationship with Martin as she could, no matter how tenuous. And her children's support was her only remaining link to him—her excuse to call him, her excuse to see him.

When her children had gone off to Europe together, she was overwhelmed by the knowledge that they would soon be leaving the nest and their child support would end. This meant that the money connection—the last tie that bound Martin to her— would finally be severed. So her money demons jumped into action, prompting her to seek the comfort she had sought so often before—the comfort of Vegas.

RACHEL

When I left the casino that night with that debt hanging over my head, I just kept thinking about Martin and how furious he'd be. But another part of me knew that he'd have to help me out. That's just the way he is. He'd never let the kids and me go down the tubes.

When Rachel's feelings of loneliness and helplessness overwhelmed her, the inviting environment of the casino was too comforting an old friend for her to turn down.

But there was a secondary gain for Rachel, as well. By getting into a financial crisis, she was pushing the same buttons she'd been pushing in Martin for years—his rescue button.

Though Martin did not pay her debts outright as he had in the past, nor even give her a loan to pay off her debts, he *did* agree to buy the house back from her to keep it out of foreclosure. This was the only way he could insure that she could not borrow against the house again.

He paid a price that was considerably below the market value, but in exchange, he agreed to let her continue living there rent free until their children moved out.

In essence, because of her gambling Rachel had lost her home. She was now living there on Martin's generosity. But there *was* an up side for her, at least on an unconscious level: She had found a way to keep Martin enmeshed in her life. She had added a new layer of complication to a divorce that was much more legal than emotional as far as she was concerned.

For now, Martin was not only her ex-husband and the father of her children but her landlord as well.

The Illusion of Being in Control

Despite the fact that Rachel's immediate crisis seemed under control, she still needed to work on the issues that had driven her to attempt suicide in the first place.

I asked her if she would be willing to try one of my outpatient groups. I assured her that I never ask about potty training. Instead, I would ask her to use her most overtly destructive behavior—her compulsive gambling—as a signpost to direct us through the dimly lit roads of her unconscious, back to the source of her money demons.

RACHEL

What do I need therapy for? My life's back on track now. I'm out of debt. I'm feeling good. I've got some breathing space. My kids are coming home. . . .

SUSAN

I know you've accomplished a lot in the last few weeks. And I'm really proud of you for that. But those changes are all external—you haven't done any work on the inside. And that's where this crisis really started.

RACHEL

This crisis started with my gambling. I'm in control of that now.

SUSAN

Didn't you feel as if you were in control before?

Rachel considered this unhappily. After two weeks of intensive therapy in the hospital, and after solving her immediate financial crisis, she was not in the mood to look back at what she had done. After all, she was feeling so much better than she had when she was admitted that she assumed she was no longer in danger of losing control.

But maintaining control means more than simply being out of crisis. It means gaining the psychological wherewithal to prevent new emotional stresses from *creating* crisis.

A Flight into Health

Rachel's erroneous assumption that she now had a handle on her problems was what psychologists call "a flight into health." This is a fairly common phenomenon: A person feels such enormous relief after a few sessions of therapy that she believes her problems are solved.

When someone's problems are as complex and deep-seated as Rachel's, a few sessions of therapy can indeed be cathartic and illuminating. But it takes more intensive work to dig far enough beneath the surface to effect changes that won't crumble under pressure.

An easy trap to fall into, a flight into health is always an illusion, one of the more subtle facets of denial. Denial can either bolster the belief that "there is no problem," or it can be more insidious, as it was in Rachel's case, and promote the idea that "there is a problem, but I can handle it."

But even though Rachel continued to insist that she could control her gambling, the Twenty Questions and my prodding weakened her denial enough to make her more open to some psychological and emotional work, especially in regard to her relationship with her ex-husband. She ultimately agreed to join one of my groups.

The Great Escape

To compulsive gamblers, racetracks, casinos, card clubs, and betting parlors are more than just gaming places. They are alternative realities, sanctuaries from everyday life.

Compulsive gambling is so engrossing, so preoccupying, that it leaves virtually no room for thinking about day-to-day problems, no matter how overwhelming those problems are. Compulsive gambling is a curtain that blacks out the light of painful reality. It is an escape.

For my client Lisa, this kind of escapism was a habitual pattern whose beginning she could trace back to one specific afternoon during her adolescence.

LISA

It was a really beautiful day, and I just couldn't handle going home because my folks had been drinking for about two days, and they were in their crying and screaming mode. So I went over to a girlfriend's house, and her older brother and a friend of his taught us how to play five-card stud. I remember looking up from the table, realizing it was dark, and thinking how amazing it was that I'd been playing for almost three hours and it had felt like ten minutes. It was the first time in months that I'd actually had a good time without constantly worrying about what was going to happen when I got home. Of course when I realized what time it was, I almost died because I was supposed to be home cooking dinner. But it didn't even matter, you know? Because I'd actually enjoyed myself, which was something I'd pretty much given up on at the time.

With that first poker game, Lisa had discovered an oasis from her feelings of unhappiness and helplessness, as if she were on an emotional vacation.

Lisa began to play poker whenever she could. It was her special activity, her special skill—something that was hers and hers alone, untainted by the turbulence of her family.

Neglecting Other Options

As an adolescent, Lisa had few options for dealing with the erratic and often frightening behavior of her alcoholic parents.

Escape seemed to be her only possible strategy for emotional survival, and gambling was the escape that seemed to work best for her. As she grew into adulthood, this strategy became automatic. Whenever she felt unhappy or tense, she would gamble.

Lisa married her high school boyfriend Gary six years after they graduated, when she accidentally got pregnant with their son Jason. Neither she nor Gary had really wanted to get married, and they both felt cheated of their youth, but they decided to "do the right thing" for Jason's sake.

Gary's childhood had not been much more stable than Lisa's. His father was verbally abusive to both Gary and his mother. With this marriage to serve as his relationship model, Gary—like Lisa—grew up having very confused ideas about how to act loving or intimate.

This was hardly a promising foundation on which to build a marriage.

Gary tried to be good to Lisa. He worked hard to build a small drywalling business, while Lisa worked on and off as a waitress. When she was employed, she always worked lunchtime shifts because Gary didn't like her working nights. This gave her the opportunity to go to the track in the late afternoons on those days when her son was in child-care programs at their church.

Sometimes she would win, sometimes she would lose, but at first this wasn't a major problem because she controlled her betting, never risking more than her tip money. Though it put a strain on their household finances when she lost, she always managed to find an excuse for the shortfall—often a mythical chronic plumbing problem.

Then, about seven years into their marriage, Gary's business suffered a blow—one of his primary contractors went bankrupt. He began to take his frustrations out on Lisa by throwing tantrums and becoming verbally abusive.

LISA

I'd worry about my marriage—whether I should leave him, whether I was happy, whether he was happy—it drove me nuts. Sometimes I hated him, sometimes I didn't, but mostly I just hated my life. So I spent my free time trying to distract myself. I'd watch soap operas, or I'd get my hair done, or I'd read women's magazines, but there was only one thing that really took my mind off him—going to the track. Of course, it was only open for racing a few months a year, but even going down there for off-track betting made me feel better.

Lisa's adult options for dealing with her unhappiness were far greater than they had been when she was an adolescent. As a teenager, she could only try to survive. But now that she was grown up, she had at least three options:

- to accept the relationship as it was
- to negotiate for change
- to leave

By going to the track, Lisa was effectively choosing the first option, the path of avoidance.

Instead of considering her alternatives, Lisa gave herself up to the unhealthy dance of her relationship.

Here were her dance steps:

—Gary, frustrated about work, became emotionally abusive at home.
—Lisa, unwilling to confront Gary, stuffed her feelings and became depressed.
—Lisa tried to escape her depression by going to the track.
—Lisa lied about her gambling and her losses because she was afraid of setting Gary off on another tirade.
—Lisa felt guilty and anxious about lying, and Gary picked up on her tension, putting even greater stress on their relationship.

— As a result of the added stress, Gary's tirades heated up.
— The more Gary vented his anger, the harder it became for Lisa to stuff her feelings, making her even more eager to escape to the track.

All the tension, anger, and depression were detrimental not only to the relationship but to Lisa's self-esteem as well. When Gary was unhappy, she had a tendency to blame herself for being inadequate, just as she had blamed herself as a child for the unhappiness of her alcoholic parents. This belief that she was somehow at fault no matter what went wrong is one of the most common legacies that alcoholic parents hand down to their children. All these elements combined to render Lisa even less likely to muster the strength and courage required to consider new options, even if she were aware that she had them.

A Mood-Altering Drug

Painful feelings have an energy all their own. They don't just go away because they get stuffed into a dark corner. Instead, they get acted out in unexpected ways—compulsions, aggressive behavior, or even physical symptoms. But for women, most often, painful feelings that go unexpressed force their way to the surface in the form of depression.

Gambling is one way for women with compulsive tendencies to fight depression. And if this strategy provides relief, it can easily become habit-forming. Horse racing became Lisa's pain-killer of choice.

LISA

When I'm not at the track, I'm depressed. When I am, I'm happy. Even when I'm losing, I'm still only happy when I'm there. The yelling, the energy, the people—I love that feeling. I just want to be at the track . . . all the time. No matter where I am, that's where I want to go. When I'm not there, I'm restless, I'm bored, I've got no energy.

When I am there, I'm up, I'm happy. It's as simple as that. I just love that constant tense-up and release, tense-up and release. . . . Like good sex—there's just nothing else like it. And when your horse comes in, it's like an orgasm.

As with most compulsive gamblers, it didn't matter to Lisa whether she won or lost, as long as she could be part of the action. The excitement, the suspense, and even the sexual energy of the racetrack combined to act like a drug, swinging Lisa's mood out of its customary rut, if only for a few hours. At the track she felt alive, electric.

Though gambling is not a drug in the sense that heroin and alcohol are—it is not ingested, and it has no physically addictive qualities—it can still have a profound physiological effect on depression. The excitement of gambling can elevate the body's adrenaline levels to fight the apathy of depression. It can also release endorphins—natural brain chemicals that create feelings of pleasure.

Anything that creates feelings of intense, instantaneous stimulation and relief has the potential to be psychologically addicting. Compulsive gambling is a quick fix for depression.

A Brief Euphoria

Compulsive gamblers keep gambling as long as their money lasts. Though losing doesn't discourage them, there is no doubt that it is the feeling of winning that keeps their blood at a boil.

As Rachel explained during her first group therapy session, she was strongly attracted to the environment of the casino, but it wasn't until she began to win that she fully gave in to the seduction.

RACHEL
I guess I always liked to gamble. Even as a kid, I loved to pitch pennies. Then at school there were poker games . . . but it was always pretty penny-ante stuff until I discovered

Vegas. This was just before I met Martin. I was living with a man at the time, and I was pretty sure he was sleeping with another girl. It was really upsetting me . . . crying in the bathroom, feeling depressed all the time . . . but I couldn't bring myself to break up. I was just too scared to be alone. So my best friend asked me to go away for a weekend with her, just to cheer me up. She found this junket, one of those weekend deals for $39.95 for a room, all your meals, free drinks, and twenty dollars in chips. I wasn't too keen on going, but the second we walked into the Tropicana . . . the lights, the sounds, the excitement— it was a rush before I even laid down a bet. . . . And when I got on a roll—that's when I knew I'd found my thing. It was like I was a movie star. Everybody was telling me how beautiful I was and how I should never stop and how I was lucky for everybody. . . . I didn't leave that table for eighteen hours, I just couldn't lose. It was like an angel was sitting on my shoulder.

Rachel had discovered Las Vegas in a big way. It was a match made in heaven—or hell. Vegas was a fairyland that swooped her up and carried her away. Just as the track was for Lisa, the casino was more than just a place for Rachel to bet—it was a whole panoply of sensual and emotional pleasures.

Feeling powerless in the face of her failing relationship, Rachel had found a place where she could turn her mood around. In the fleeting euphoria of winning she found omnipotence.

Of course, she was destined by the odds to lose eventually, but the euphoria of the moment blinded her to that inevitable destiny.

A Fantasy World

Gambling is about dreams and yearnings above all else. When I met Lisa, she was working in an elegant hotel restaurant in

Beverly Hills. Waiting on people of wealth and power reinforced her fantasies of what she wanted for her own life—
fantasies of being a "somebody," which, to her, meant having
an important job, a beautiful home in an upscale neighborhood,
and enough money to be respected and admired. Lisa's dream
was that money would fill the holes left over from her emotionally and materially impoverished childhood.

But Lisa was doing nothing constructive to pursue her
dreams. Instead, she was depending on the daily double to
whisk her away from the daily grind.

Fantasy dominates the thinking of compulsive gamblers.
When they're not dreaming about what they can buy with their
winnings, they're working out complex systems to beat mathe-
matically unbeatable odds.

LISA

I'd dream about the same numbers almost every night, and
I'd wake up with this feeling that my life was about to
change for the better. Like it was a sign—my providence,
my fate, my oracle, my genie. I knew these numbers were
coming to me for a reason, so I kept trying to figure out
why. I'd go to the track and try to figure out if I was supposed to use them to pick the horses. Or I'd buy a couple
hundred lotto tickets with every combination of those
numbers I could think of. And when I'd lose, I'd just figure
that I hadn't worked the system right. I knew there was
gold in those numbers if I could just decode them. And
then one afternoon, I hit the exacta. It was incredible. I'd
finally aced the system. It was based on a combination of
bloodlines, track records and post position. Of course, it
never worked again, but that didn't stop me from betting
that system religiously for a couple of years.

It's typical for compulsive gamblers to think this way—
increase their bets in a certain numerological sequence, pick
their horses through some arcane handicapping scheme based

on Egyptian mythology, or work out lotto numbers with astrological charts, believing that these "systems" can improve the odds in their favor. Others use more seemingly scientific methods based on trigonometry, or physics, or probability theory. But these systems are just as fantasy-based as their more mystical counterparts.

Fantasy Friendships

Visions of big wins and lavish spending are not the only fantasies that keep compulsive gamblers hooked. There is also the seductive fantasy of belonging.

Gambling can be a highly social activity. Unless you only place bets on the phone with a bookie, you're most probably at a gaming table with other gamblers, or you're rooting for horses with other gamblers, or you're playing cards with other gamblers. If one of the things that drives you to gamble is a need to belong, a need to feel included, a need for companionship, the social aspect of gambling can be a powerful payoff.

RACHEL
It was people shouting and cheering and all in this thing together, like some kind of big extended family. And here I was feeling lonely when I walked up to the table, and within ten minutes I was part of them, I was one of them, they were *my* extended family. For those few seconds when the dice were rolling, we were all focused on the same thing, we were all praying for the same thing, we were all, like . . . one.

It didn't dawn on Rachel that she was projecting her own yearnings to be loved on a bunch of strangers. In reality, her new "extended family" was made up of "friends" who didn't know her and really didn't care about her. She was just another face in the crowd, another hand to throw the dice. Compulsive gamblers are so preoccupied with their next bet that any significant emotional connection among them is unlikely. But of course, Rachel's own preoccupation with gambling blinded her to this fact.

In the casino, Rachel found new friends in other gamblers, but they were friends in fantasy only. Sadly, these fantasy friendships would eventually displace many of the real friendships in her life.

The Need for Self-Punishment

When someone gambles to the point of destroying her life, it is safe to assume that—in addition to the motives we've already discussed—she has some unconscious reason to want to punish herself. This was certainly true for Rachel. Everything I knew about her screamed "self-hatred, self-hatred." Her gambling ruined her marriage, it drove her into debt, it caused her to lose her house, and it ultimately led her to try to kill herself.

Women who repeatedly behave in self-punishing ways usually have some serious trauma in their past. The exceptions are women who suffer from repeated depressions or anxiety because of imbalances in their brain chemistry or hormone levels. But Rachel's psychiatrist had already ruled out that possibility before she left the hospital.

Rachel had revealed to me nothing from her past that seemed emotionally painful enough to explain the depth of her compulsion. Still, I became increasingly convinced that she was holding something back.

Shamebusting

When a client holds something back from a therapist, more often than not it is because she is ashamed. In addition, many compulsions are shame-based. I wondered whether some hidden shame might be the key to Rachel's compulsion.

Quite often, especially with victims of childhood sexual or physical abuse, the source of the shame is repressed in the unconscious, inaccessible to the woman whose life is being so negatively influenced by it. But in many other cases, the shame is fully conscious and the decision to keep it secret is conscious as well.

I thought it was time to give Rachel a little nudge, so I asked the group to do a short sentence-completion exercise I call Shamebusting.

I passed out sheets of paper that had typed on them:

Something happened to me that's harder for me to talk about than anything else. That thing is _____ .

I instructed them to fill in the blank with a short, concise answer, preferably not to exceed one line. This would not be an essay contest but a starting point for self-revelation.

For the veterans of the group, this exercise was no big deal. Most of them had already dealt with their innermost secrets, ranging from giving up a baby for adoption to being a chronic shoplifter. But for Rachel, the newest member, this exercise felt threatening. Long after everyone else had finished, Rachel was still staring at her blank line. Finally, she jotted something down.

A lot of people find it easier to write down something they have difficulty saying than to just come out and say it. Even if they then read aloud what they've written, it is easier than talking about it off the cuff. Breaking the task into two parts—writing and reading—makes each part less of a commitment. It's like taking small steps when it's too scary to leap.

I asked for a volunteer to read what she'd written. One by one, we went around the circle. The women in the group read their most painful secrets with varying degrees of ease, but each seemed relieved after she had finally done it. Watching this, Rachel seemed to become less and less resistant.

Finally, Rachel was the only one left. She slowly unfolded the paper and almost whispered three words: "I was raped."

With the group's support, Rachel haltingly revealed how she had been raped on her way home from school when she was sixteen years old. She had run home crying to her mother, who decided not to go to the police because she didn't want to submit her daughter to what she believed would be a humiliating interrogation, or even worse, a public trial.

Instead, Rachel's mother drove her to the doctor for an examination. All the way there, she urged her daughter not to tell anyone else what had happened to her. "Rape is an ugly thing," her mother had said. "No one wants to hear about it."

Rachel had taken her mother's advice to heart. Her mother may have believed she was protecting her daughter, but in fact, she unwittingly encouraged Rachel to believe she was shameful because of the shameful things that had happened to her.

One emotional outcome of rape (and all other forms of sexual abuse) is that the victim feels somehow permanently soiled and damaged, as if she had been responsible for the horrendous act. When Rachel's mother urged her to keep the rape a secret, she was only fueling Rachel's self-loathing.

Because Rachel had never subsequently spoken about the rape to anyone, her psychological wounds were left untreated and her shame was left to fester for almost thirty years. As an adult, this shame translated into a powerful money demon. And her way of acting out that demon was to punish herself through the chaos of gambling.

Over the next several months, Rachel and I worked hard together to begin reversing the terrible psychological damage of rape. As her shame diminished, so did her need for self-punishment. This, in turn, helped her to gain some control over her addictive behavior and to rebuild her damaged self-image.

But Rachel still had a lot of work to do on her relationship with Martin. More than two years after their divorce, her need to remain enmeshed with him still bordered on the obsessive.

Until she accepted that her marriage was over, it was almost impossible for her to gain some independence and get on with her life. So that was our next focus in therapy.

In addition to this psychological work, I sent Rachel to a vocational counselor who helped her identify her areas of strength and competence with the ultimate goal of finding a job and rejoining the real world.

Escalating Chaos

All compulsions escalate. Escalation is part of the program. That's why so many people use the language of addiction to describe compulsions.

Like every addictive drug, compulsive gambling keeps demanding more—more time, more money, more action. Lisa started out one day a week at the track making two-dollar bets, but she soon found herself disrupting her life to get there more often, jeopardizing her family savings to make larger bets.

LISA

I'd go as often as I could. And as time went on, that wasn't enough. I'd start finding ways to get out there more. I'd call in sick to work, I'd go evenings when Gary had to work late, I'd get a baby-sitter and tell Gary I was going to visit my sister. Then I'd talk her into meeting me at the track—whatever I could work out, just so I could be there. The more I went, the more I lost. And the more I lost, the more I had to bet, because that was the only way I could win it back. Before I knew it, my two-dollar bets were two-hundred-dollar bets, which was more than a week's salary if you don't count tips.

As Lisa's gambling behavior escalated, she wound up doing what compulsive gamblers call "chasing"—continuing to increase your bets to try to recoup your losses. The more you

lose, the more you bet, and the more you bet, the faster you
lose. It's a geometric progression that takes you on an emotional ride from the initial excitement of the chase to the ultimate desperation and depression of a hole too big to climb out
of.

And that hole isn't only financial.

The Never-Ending Cover-Up

As the gambler's losses escalate, so does her need for deception.
She sees no alternative but to lie in order to escape the fights
and the tirades that she knows await her if her partner should
discover the truth.

Deception is a way of life for compulsive gamblers, even
though it often compounds the enormous shame and guilt they
already feel. Gamblers often lie about where they've been, what
they've been doing, who they've been out with, why they need
money, how much they've lost, how much they've borrowed,
and how much they've liquidated. And these lies can be extraordinarily intricate, bold, and creative.

LISA

I remember one night I went out with a girlfriend to some
romantic movie that Gary didn't want to see. He was
asleep by the time I got home, and I still had a lot of energy, so I decided to drive down to Gardena and play a
little poker. I ended up playing all night. When I realized
what time it was, I jumped in the car and tried to race the
sunrise home. The light always wakes him in the morning,
and I was terrified that he'd be up waiting for me. I got
home just at the crack of dawn, and thank God he was still
asleep. I managed to sneak in without the dog barking or
anything, and I sat down to take off my shoes. I had just
gotten the first one halfway off when he woke up. I just
froze. It took him a second to focus, and then he asked me

what I was doing. I felt totally panicked, but this lie just came to my lips like magic, like I didn't even think it up, it just came out—I slipped my shoe back on and told him I'd gotten up early and felt like taking the dog out for a walk. He rolled over and went right back to sleep, and I just sat there feeling like the scum of the earth.

Lisa had become so adept at lying that the process seemed to be self-sustaining—an automatic survival instinct. This was not all that surprising, considering her childhood.

Coming from an alcoholic and abusive family, Lisa had been raised on lies and deceit. Children of severely dysfunctional families learn early, from their parents' example, that truth is the enemy and that only lies can protect the fragile illusion of normalcy. They are taught to lie to anyone outside the family about what goes on within it. They learn to lie to each other about how bad things are. They learn to lie to their alcoholic parents to avoid incurring their wrath.

As an adult, Lisa's pattern of deception, although painful, was familiar to her. It was much easier to lie than to face Gary with the truth about her gambling, which she knew would enrage him. Even worse, she knew that he would take steps to stop her from gambling—a fate worse than death.

Truth and Consequences

When a compulsive gambler's partner catches her lying to him—even if he is no angel himself—he understandably feels outraged and hurt. These feelings eat away at their relationship like a powerful acid.

On the other hand, I would be less than candid if I did not say that the truth has its consequences, too. It is certainly possible that if a woman tells her partner she's gambled away their joint life's savings, he will walk out for good.

However, lies offer no permanent solutions. Until the veil of secrecy falls, there can be no common healing between the compulsive gambler and her partner. Confronting the truth, at the very least, offers the possibility of rebuilding their relationship and their financial stability.

Facing the Fear of His Rage

Most people panic when faced with having to tell a truth that they know will enrage, and perhaps even alienate, a loved one. Lisa lived in a continual state of fear. She was terrified that Gary would find out how severely her compulsive gambling had depleted their savings.

When Lisa first came into therapy, her desperation was palpable.

LISA

There's no money in the account, and we've got to pay our property taxes in two weeks. I'm such a nervous wreck. . . . There's no way I can hide it from Gary anymore. I've borrowed as much as I can from my mother, and there's no one else I can ask. He's going to kill me, I just know it. I've ruined everybody's lives—not just Gary's, but Jason's. I don't know what to do.

Lisa had an obvious course of action, but her fears were paralyzing her. I suggested that she tell Gary the truth and let the chips fall where they may.

LISA

What am I supposed to say? "Oh, by the way, Gary, I blew our life's savings"? He'll be furious!

SUSAN

Of course he will. You would be, too. I'm not saying it's going to be easy. But what's your alternative? To keep living in terror?

I wasn't telling Lisa anything she didn't already know, but like most of us, she was reluctant to adopt a course of action that she knew would be painful. Clearly, she had to overcome her fear of Gary's anger, but she had no idea how to do it. I suggested she try an exercise I call Throwing Off the Burden.

Throwing Off the Burden

There is an old saying in sports: "Keep your eye on the prize." It means, if you anticipate doing something difficult or painful, keep your focus on your reason for doing it, on the positive outcome you expect.

To help Lisa do this, I asked her to close her eyes and focus on the fear and anxiety that her secret was causing her.

SUSAN

Imagine that your fear is a backpack . . . a backpack stuffed full of heavy rocks. It's so heavy, you can't walk, you can't lift your legs, you can barely stand. The straps eat into your shoulders, your back feels like it's going to break. You're so squeezed by the weight that you can hardly breathe. Can you feel it?

Lisa nodded. Her brow seemed furrowed in pain.

SUSAN

All right. Now I want you to shrug the pack off. Let those painful straps off your shoulders. Just let the pack crash to the ground.

A smile came over Lisa's face.

SUSAN

You can finally breathe. Let yourself relax. Take a deep breath and pull the relief into your body. How do you feel?

Lighter, freer . . . relieved.

That's the feeling you've got to focus on. That's the kind of relief you can feel when you get this deception off your back and out of your life.

Visualizations like this one are powerful motivators because they provide an opportunity to experience the positive feelings that await you when you're finally willing to cast off the burden of dishonesty.

This visualization did not make Lisa's anxiety disappear like magic. But it did help her to imagine getting past it. She now had a specific goal—the feelings of freedom and relief that she had experienced through her visualization. And for the first time, she saw a real possibility of achieving that goal.

Before she did this exercise, Lisa had considered telling the truth to be the lesser of two evils—better than being found out, but not by much. This was not a very powerful motivator. But now she believed that she had something positive to gain from telling the truth, that she might actually feel better, and that she might actually begin to disentangle herself from the web she'd woven.

Telling the Truth

I told Lisa she needed to commit herself to a specific time and a place to talk to Gary. Without this commitment, it would be all too easy for her to wait for "the perfect moment." When faced with a difficult emotional task like this one, procrastination comes easily.

Lisa also needed to think through exactly what she was going to tell Gary, so that when the time came, her anxiety wouldn't tie her tongue or prompt her to tell half-truths to get herself temporarily off the hook.

I urged her to use these three steps as a guideline:

1. Get him to agree beforehand to let her finish what she has to say without interrupting, no matter how angry her words might make him feel.
2. Take full responsibility and express remorse for her behavior and for the financial losses she has incurred.
3. Express her hope that despite his anger, he will hang in there with her and work toward rebuilding a healthier, more honest relationship.

These steps help avoid the trap of self-denigration. For many compulsive gamblers, telling the truth about their behavior becomes a humiliating exercise in confession, begging forgiveness, blaming and attacking others, making excuses, or beating up on themselves. This only serves to erode whatever self-respect they may have left after the battering their dignity has already suffered at the hands of compulsion.

Lisa took the three steps to heart, going so far as to write down what she planned to say to Gary so that she could practice before her actual confrontation. She knew from experience that the anxiety of a fight often left her grasping for words. The preparation helped to make her feel more secure and in control.

I told Lisa to expect Gary to explode, especially in light of his history of dumping on her when he got frustrated. I asked her to think back on all the fights she'd ever had with Gary and to tell me honestly whether she had ever felt in physical danger with him. She assured me that no matter how upset he had ever become, she had never been afraid that he might lose control and hit her.

To further diminish the threat of an unexpected physical reaction from Gary, Lisa and I practiced some of the nondefensive communication techniques in the last chapter. These would help diffuse the heat that her confession was sure to spark.

When Gary got home from work the next day, Lisa told him she had something important to discuss with him. She turned off the ring on the phone and turned down the volume on the answering machine so they would not be interrupted by any calls. Then she told him what she had to say.

LISA

I was so nervous I couldn't stop shaking. I felt like there was an earthquake inside me. But I knew I had to do it, so I forced myself. He got really upset, but I was ready for it, so it wasn't as bad as I expected it to be. I mean, he started screaming and yelling, but I just hung in there and eventually it was over.

Lisa's nondefensive responses were very helpful in keeping the situation from getting out of hand, but it was difficult for her nonetheless.

Gary slept on the couch that night, but by the next morning he had cooled down enough for them to talk together about what all this meant to their future. Lisa discovered—as so many of my clients have over the years—that her anxieties leading up to her confrontation were worse than the reality of it.

Today, a year later, Lisa and Gary are still together. She goes to Gamblers Anonymous twice a week, and he goes sporadically to Gamanon, a support group for the loved ones of compulsive gamblers. In addition, Gary is working on using intensive physical exercise to help relieve the work-related stresses and frustrations he used to take out on Lisa.

Despite occasional urges, Lisa has not been back to the track in over a year.

While I can't guarantee that telling the truth will always save your relationship, I can promise that it will make you feel significantly better about yourself. When you know you don't have the courage to tell the truth, when you know that your fears are in control of your life, there's no way your self-respect can survive.

No matter how frightening and painful it is to be honest

about your gambling (or any other self-destructive behavior you feel compelled to conceal), telling the truth is the one gamble I always urge women to take.

Self-Help Strategies

Every compulsive gambler should attend regular meetings of Gamblers Anonymous. Period. This is the first step toward gaining control of this particular compulsion.

Shamebusting

Most compulsive gamblers can use GA as their forum for this exercise, if their shameful secret is a conscious one. If you don't have a chapter of GA in your area, I strongly advise that you consider seeking out some kind of support group to tell your secret to. The telling of powerful emotional secrets is one of the best ways to stir up strong, perhaps unexpected feelings and bring them to light.

If you are without the support of a therapist or a group, you can still begin the process of releasing yourself from the power of this demon by reading (or just telling) your secret to another person. Be sure to choose a person you feel safe with, preferably someone with whom you have a long history and who you know will not be judgmental.

Throwing Off the Burden

This visualization is not only useful for helping you deal with the fear of your partner's anger, it can be effective in dealing with any kind of emotional burden.

You need to tune into the physical sensations that your anxiety is creating. Some people feel the tension in their neck muscles or lower back; others feel a tightness in their chest; still others get headaches. If you have a specific physical sensation like this, use it to create a visualization that speaks to you. If the image of the backpack does not suit you, make up one that works better. Try a boulder on your chest, or a chainmail coat, or a wrecking ball around your neck, or a straitjacket.

The key is to really *experience* how oppressive your negative emotions are, and then to experience what it could feel like to free yourself of these emotions. Once you've done this, you have something specific to shoot for.

Telling the Truth

The key to telling the truth is preparation. If you are afraid to tell your partner about your gambling, you will be fighting a lot of anxiety when you try to do it. The more you've rehearsed what you have to say, the easier it will be to say it. Follow the three steps (page 176) and review the nondefensive responses we explored in Chapter 4.

There is no way to predict how a partner will react to a painful truth. If you believe your partner may become physically violent, telling him about your gambling becomes more complicated, but you still must find a way to do it. You may want to invite a close friend or relative to be present when you tell him. Alternatively, I strongly advise that you seek professional counseling to deal with the fact that you are living with a man who frightens you. Then you can tell him in the presence of your counselor. Whatever decision you make, I urge you to take the threat of physical violence very seriously and to reevaluate whether this is a relationship you really ought to remain in. Under no circumstances should you allow guilt over gambling losses to justify violence against you.

If you have *no* reason to believe your partner has a potential for physical violence, you should still be prepared to weather a verbal storm. Remember, the shocking nature of the truth you have to tell can easily cause your partner to say some very cruel things that he may not really mean and later will probably come to regret.

6

When You Make More Than He Does

I really love him, and I know he loves me, but it's so hard sometimes. . . . We go out with friends, and I see all these women with successful husbands, and I can't help it. . . . I just sit there and stew in my own envy.

—M.M., age 33

We fight about the bills all the time—he doesn't pay his share. I know he would if he could, he just can't. But we fight anyway. It scares the hell out of me. . . . I'm afraid it's going to tear us apart.

—R.O., age 26

Every time my mother asks how he's doing, I can see the disappointment in her face.

—W.F., age 42

In the traditional marriage relationship, the man was expected to bring home the money. It wasn't so long ago that a woman rarely joined the work force by choice, but almost always by tragic necessity. If a man's wife worked, tongues would wag: "Isn't it a shame? The poor fellow can't support his family—the wife has to work."

And if a woman chose to work when she didn't *have* to, she could only maintain her social standing by treating her job as a hobby and her income as a disposable frill.

But in the last several decades, as two-income families have become common and women have made great strides in the workplace, our cultural attitudes about women and money have undergone some dramatic shifts—at least on the surface. Women are actively pursuing careers, sharing responsibility for family income, and slowly but surely catching up to (and in some cases surpassing) men as family wage-earners.

Today, in fact, there are hundreds of thousands of American women who earn significantly more money than their partners. Yet the impact of this financial imbalance on relationships has gone largely unexplored.

While our society has slowly come to accept women's increasing independence, the flip side of this acceptance has been slower to develop: We have yet to come to terms with how a woman's financial achievements reflect on a less successful partner. If a woman makes more than her partner, people wonder: Is he after her money? Is she really that desperate? Is he really that good in bed?

If the situation is reversed and the man makes more than the woman, no one thinks twice about it. Those men who take primary financial responsibility for their families are fulfilling a traditional role that can be a great source of pride. There is very little of that same gratification for women. They are not fulfilling a time-honored role. And when they earn the greater part of the family income, they often experience very little of the social approval that cushions the burden for men.

Even in relatively healthy relationships, a disparity in income can create enormous and surprisingly complex tensions and conflicts.

I'm not talking here about women in relationships with men who are financially reckless or destructive. Such men constitute another story altogether, which we will look at in depth in

Chapter 7. The men in the couples we will meet in this chapter are generally productive, financially responsible partners—they simply don't earn as much as their wives or lovers.

What Will People Think?

Nancy felt like a million dollars as she and Bob walked into the ball-room. Her sexy new Valentino gown made her look ten years younger, and Bob could have stepped out of the pages of GQ in the Armani tux she'd bought him that morning.

Bob hitched his shoulders uncomfortably. It wasn't so much the fit of the tux as the idea that irked him. It was such a waste of money. He could have just rented. But Nancy had insisted: "It's my money to waste, so don't give me an argument." So he hadn't. Instead, he'd just backed down, feeling like a powerless child.

With mixed feelings, he thought back on their last class reunion, the twentieth, where he'd run into Nancy for the first time since college. They'd originally met in their senior year and had been immediately attracted to one another. But they'd both been involved with other people at the time.

Two decades later, when he'd remet her at the reunion, they were both divorced and unattached. It had taken just one dance to rekindle the old flame.

Now, five years after that, they were going to another reunion as husband and wife. As Bob straightened his jacket, he wondered whether their marriage would last.

Nancy's freshman roommate Gloria was the first to see them. She rushed over and threw her arms around both of them at once.

"Don't you two ever age? You look great!" she said. "Can you believe it's been five years? What are you up to?"

Bob felt his stomach contract as if anticipating a blow.

"Still practicing law," Nancy replied. "Malpractice litigation, mostly."

"*Raking it in, no doubt.*" *Gloria laughed.* "*What about you, Bob?*"

Nancy felt a wave of panic that propelled her to cut Bob off before he could answer. It was an automatic reaction, a reflex: "*He's in management . . . health clubs. Isn't that great?*"

Bob felt the hair bristle on the back of his neck, but he said nothing. Gloria smiled and went on to tell them about herself.

On the way home, Bob drove in silence. Nancy knew what was bothering him, but she played dumb. "*Is something wrong?*"

"*You did it again.*"

"*What?*"

"*Why are you so ashamed of what I do?*"

"*I'm not ashamed of—*"

"*I'm not in management,*" *he interrupted,* "*and I don't work at a goddamned health club! I coach kids at the Y, all right? Get used to it. I know it's not glamorous, but I happen to like it.*"

"*You're making a big thing out of nothing.*"

"*You just can't get over the fact that I only bring home twenty-four grand a year, can you?*"

"*That's ridiculous. You know that doesn't matter to me.*"

"*If it didn't matter, you wouldn't have bought me this goddamned monkey suit.*"

"*Can we not start in on the tux again, please?*"

"*It's a waste of money.*"

"*It's my money, all right?*"

"*No! It's not all right! And I'd appreciate it if you'd stop rubbing it in!*"

Nancy and Bob's fight was part of an ongoing pattern that had begun when they first decided to live together three years earlier. Bob had moved into Nancy's house at the time, and though they had decided to share their daily living expenses equally, they agreed that she would continue to pay the mortgage by herself. He simply did not make enough to share that expense, and besides (she reasoned), it was her house.

Bob was apprehensive about how he would fit into Nancy's life because she was accustomed to spending much more money on entertainment and social events than his income allowed. But at first this was not an issue—in the bloom of new love, they preferred to spend most of their evenings alone at home anyway.

Nancy had assured Bob that his income was not a problem for her. They had had long discussions about their financial disparities, and by coming to an amicable solution about sharing expenses, they believed that they had dealt with the problem.

But the incident at the reunion was just one of many that revealed that Nancy was much less comfortable with the imbalance in their relative earning power than she claimed to be.

Giving Him Double Messages

Nancy was an interesting client because she was relatively symptom free when she first came in to see me. She wasn't depressed; she wasn't a substance abuser; she wasn't experiencing any anxiety; and there had been no major traumas in her life.

But she was insightful enough to realize that she needed to resolve her ambivalence about the disparity between her income and Bob's.

One the one hand, Nancy was reassuring Bob that she didn't care about how much money he made. But on the other, her obvious discomfort with his employment situation was telling him just the opposite.

Ambivalence is almost impossible to hide from your partner, no matter how loving and reassuring you try to be. And despite your best intentions, ambivalence has a natural tendency to express itself in confusing ways.

NANCY

I don't understand why I keep doing this. I do it to him all the time, not just at parties but when we're alone. Things just slip out. I say these things about how I wish he made more money or cared about it more. What is it inside me that makes me keep hurting him like this? Why can't I just keep my big mouth shut?

I told Nancy that I didn't think learning to keep her mouth shut was the ideal solution. Although that might prevent her from hurting Bob's feelings, it would also clamp a tighter lid on her own feelings, which were clearly trying to get out. This would be a temporary solution at best. Ultimately, her unconscious would find some way to act out her ambivalent feelings.

Nancy's double messages revealed a conflict between what she thought she believed (that she really didn't care how much money Bob made) and what she felt in the pit of her stomach (that she wished he were more successful). And unfortunately, when she acted out this internal conflict, it hurt and angered Bob, threatening what was basically an otherwise solid and satisfying relationship.

Defining Your *Worth by* His *Income*

When your partner makes less than you do, you are in a relationship that does not conform to social norms. And no matter how well-matched you and your partner may be, when the discrepancy in your incomes is apparent to others, they may very well disapprove—whether openly, secretly, or unconsciously—of your match.

We internalize the judgments of others, rightly or wrongly. We soak up biases and opinions about how the financial balance in a relationship "ought" to be through our schooling, our religious training, our friends, our relatives, our co-workers, our role models, and the media we're exposed to.

Our society still tends to judge a man by his professional and financial success. No matter how much Nancy loved Bob, it was hard for her to ignore that part of herself that was molded by her culture. She assured that others would share her hidden beliefs and think less of Bob if they knew how little he earned, so she tried to make Bob's job sound more important than it was.

NANCY

He's okay with what he does—why can't *I* be? I feel so damned guilty that I can't just accept him for who he is. I walk into a party and see some woman with a doctor or a lawyer, and I can't get it out of my mind. I just can't. I mean, I love him, I really do. He makes me laugh, he makes me feel loved, he makes my house feel like a home—what is my problem? I *know* it's not important how much money he makes. He's doing something meaningful, he's working with kids. And he gets a lot of fulfillment out of it. So why is it so embarrassing to me?

Nancy's confusion was understandable—embarrassment is a confusing emotion. She thought she was embarrassed for Bob, but in fact, she *couldn't* have been. Embarrassment, by definition, is "a state of self-conscious distress"—with the emphasis on *self*. Nancy was embarrassed for herself.

We often feel *badly* for someone else, or we feel *pity* because we empathize with someone *else's* embarrassment. But when *we* feel embarrassed, it is because of what we fear other people are thinking about *us*.

Despite the fact that Nancy was a successful professional, despite the fact that Bob was a loving man committed to his work for reasons that many would consider more important than money, Nancy still felt diminished by Bob's job. No matter how much she tried to convince herself to the contrary, she could not shake the buried belief that Bob's lack of financial drive was a measure of *her* inability to attract a successful man.

Sadly, in our culture women are still often judged, at least in part, by how good a "catch" they make. It's not a very enlightened way to look at relationships, but it's still a fact of life for all too many women.

The opinions of others about untraditional relationships are often mirrored by our own deep-seated fears and conflicting beliefs about ourselves and our partner.

The Disapprovers

Even if you are reasonably comfortable with the fact that your partner makes less than you do, if a few people around you keep grousing about it, their opinions have a nasty tendency to lodge in your thoughts like an itch that refuses to be scratched away. This can wreak havoc on your confidence in your choice of partner.

My friend Molly is a case in point.

Molly met Ron one afternoon when her car broke down. She got towed into a gas station, and he was the mechanic on duty. As he fixed her car, they talked, and she was surprised to discover that he was an extremely intelligent, sensitive, cultured man. Ron's work was a means to a paycheck, but he also wrote poetry and sculpted in bronze.

In Molly's job as a branch manager of a large bank, most of the men with whom she came in contact were businessmen or bankers—men driven by career aspirations. Ron was decidedly different, not only because of his "day job," but more important, because he seemed to be unusually introspective, emotionally accessible, and caring.

Molly found herself fascinated by Ron, and she accepted his invitation to see some of his sculpture the following weekend. Within a month, they were seeing each other exclusively, and about six months later, he moved into her house.

Though Molly's income was significantly greater than Ron's, he insisted on paying his share of their living expenses. Molly had expected that the difference in their income might create tension between them, but it never did.

However, soon after Ron moved in, a problem arose from an unanticipated source.

MOLLY

Everything'd be great if it weren't for my family—especially my sister. She and I have always been real close, but this thing of hers is so infuriating—she is absolutely convinced that Ron is just out for a free ride, and there's nothing I can say to change her mind. She just can't understand how a man can be so unambitious about money and career and all that. And my mother—well, at least she keeps it to herself, but when we're over there, she's like a black cloud. And my dad keeps making these "friendly" suggestions about what kind of other work Ron might look into. . . . Ron keeps telling him he's happy doing what he's doing, he can always find work, and the pay's livable. But my dad just doesn't get it. It's very uncomfortable for both of us, and I always feel like I'm in the middle of this tug-of-war, like I'm being torn apart. I wish it didn't matter so much to me, but I'm very family oriented . . . it's important to me. So I keep dragging him with me to family stuff, hoping they'll finally see him for the incredible person he is. But it's always the same. By the time we get home, we're both upset, and if I try to defend my parents, he accuses me of deep down agreeing with them that he's some kind of failure. And the worst part is, after one of these fights, I'll lie awake at night and wonder if we can really make this work in the long run.

After telling me her story over lunch one day, Molly asked me what I would do in her situation. I told her that I'd probably feel as upset as she did, but I would certainly not keep turning family meals into emotional proving grounds by pushing Ron to attend against his will. If he didn't want to go, she shouldn't insist that he accompany her when she went to visit her parents or her sister. This solution might not be perfect, but would it be any worse than the fights she and Ron were having? It's healthy for couples to have separate activities, and in Molly's relationship, visits to her family seemed like an ideal place to start.

Molly liked this idea, but she was concerned that it would not be enough. Even if she left Ron at home, her sister or her father would still drop verbal grenades like "you can do better," "he's a loser," or—worst of all—"he's only in it for your money," and Molly would still get upset.

I assured her that there was an easy solution to this: Insist that her family not talk about Ron unless they let go of their unfair biases.

Molly didn't think she could lay down the law like that—she was afraid she'd back down if she tried to tell her parents what to do.

I suggested that she try using nondefensive communication techniques (see Chapter 4), and I gave her a few examples of the sorts of things she might say to her parents and her sister:

We disagree. That doesn't mean that we can't still love each other, it just means that we don't have the same opinion.

You've obviously made your mind up about Ron, and no amount of talking is going to change that. So let's just talk about something else.

I'm sorry you feel that way. It hurts me that you can't accept the man I love.

It's your right to disapprove of Ron, but that doesn't give you the right to badmouth him. If you keep doing it, I'll leave.

None of us wants to allow spoken or unspoken judgments from friends or relatives to control or even affect our love relationships, but it is sometimes hard to avoid. You can, however, control it, as Molly was to discover.

Phrases like the ones I taught Molly can take a lot of the sting out of family or peer group disapproval by disarming the emotional conflict.

It's a waste of breath to try to get them to change their minds about your partner—only time and experience can do that. Instead, make it clear that the subject of your partner's financial situation is off limits to discussion, and reinforce that position with nondefensive responses.

The Battle of the Beliefs

If you and your partner love each other but the disparity in your incomes keeps getting in the way, it's likely that your discomfort is arising from beliefs that you may not even be aware of.

We all have two kinds of beliefs. I call the first kind *overt*— beliefs we easily espouse, are readily aware of, and generally identify with. Overt beliefs are the ones we think we ought to live by, beliefs we think are "right."

The other type, *covert* beliefs, are trickier. Covert beliefs are at least partially hidden and often contradict our overt beliefs. Covert beliefs are somehow shameful to admit, not only to others but to ourselves.

Nancy's ongoing ambivalence about Bob's financial situation indicated that her overt and covert beliefs were at odds. This conflict was damaging her relationship, but there was no way she could stop her beliefs from clashing if she didn't even know what her covert beliefs were. But before she could resolve her inner conflict, she had to identify the combatants.

Disarming Your Beliefs

To help Nancy get a line on her covert beliefs, I introduced an exercise called Disarming Your Beliefs. The premise was simple. I asked her first to write down some of the things she believed about relationships in which women make more money than their partners. These were overt beliefs—beliefs she was aware of, beliefs she had been expressing to Bob to reassure him (and herself) about her feelings for him.

Once her list was complete, I asked her to take it home and try to come up with a covert belief to contradict each overt belief. Even if the covert beliefs didn't necessarily seem true for her, they would still give her some jumping-off points to explore her inner conflicts.

The following week, Nancy brought in her assignment:

Overt belief: It doesn't matter how much a man makes as long as he contributes what he can.
Covert belief: Bob should contribute as much as I do.

Overt belief: A man should be judged by who he is, not by how much he makes.
Covert belief: There's something wrong with Bob because he isn't successful.

Overt belief: I don't care what other people think. I only care about how my partner and I feel about each other.
Covert belief: Bob's inadequate, and everybody knows it.

Overt belief: It doesn't bother me that my partner is less successful than I am.
Covert belief: Men are supposed to make enough to take care of their wives.

Not surprisingly, Nancy felt uneasy about the covert beliefs she'd come up with because they were so demeaning to Bob. They seemed to contradict both her feelings for him and her values. I assured her that she had nothing to be ashamed of. We all find ourselves torn at times between our thoughts, feelings, or desires and the values with which we were raised.

Like so many covert beliefs, Nancy's were generally traditional, often judgmental, and sometimes based on stereotypes rather than facts. Her overt beliefs were more contemporary, reflecting some of the newer, more enlightened, empathetic social trends in our society. But old programming dies hard. Nancy's covert beliefs were deeply engrained by our culture, our society, and many of the relationships that served as role models when she was younger.

She was raised in a family where her father—a well-known psychiatrist—was the sole provider. Her mother was active in charity work and volunteer politics. Most of her parents' friends had traditional marriages, and those women who worked seemed to do so by choice, not necessity. Though Nancy grew up being encouraged to be independent, to go to college and later to law school, she still developed deep-rooted beliefs based on the relationship patterns she saw in most of the couples she knew as a child. Her expectation was that her partner should be able to support her, whether she needed it or not. This covert belief was contaminating her feelings for Bob.

I explained to Nancy that by bringing her covert beliefs into the open, she could begin to disempower them. Awareness is a powerful weapon against the kinds of belief-driven demons that were pushing her to do things like embellishing Bob's job in public or making unintentionally hurtful remarks to him in private.

Whenever she felt embarrassed, she needed to remind herself that her embarrassment was coming from old beliefs that were damaging her relationship. In this way, her new awareness might short-circuit her impulse to act in self-defeating ways. I suggested that the next time she felt the urge to act as Bob's public relations representative in a social situation, she take a deep breath and say something to herself like:

> I'm only embarrassed because these old beliefs are trying to undermine my love and my confidence in Bob. The truth is, he's responsible, he's loving, and he's strong. I've got nothing to be embarrassed about.

Nancy was accomplishing two things by repeating this affirmation to herself. First, she was preventing herself from answering for Bob. By the time she'd finished saying her affirmation, Bob would already be answering for himself. And second, she was beginning to chip away at her discomfort by focusing on Bob's good qualities instead of allowing her embarrassment to control her.

This affirmation may seem simple, but it was an important starting point for Nancy. The beliefs that she had grown up with were her money demons, and by making them conscious and then consciously denouncing them, she could begin to make real changes in her attitude toward Bob.

Nancy began to go down to the Y once a week to watch Bob work, and this gave her a renewed appreciation for the social value of his work. It was obvious to her that the kids respected him, and she was impressed with his ability to motivate them to do their best. As her own opinion changed, so did her concern about the attitudes of others.

As Nancy made these changes, Bob grew increasingly secure about her opinion of him. This is turn allowed him to accept gifts from her—like the tuxedo or the occasional expensive meal—without feeling that she was making a statement about his adequacy. As she became increasingly comfortable with his work, they both became less defensive about money issues, and they found themselves fighting much less often.

The Resentment Factor

A woman who goes into a relationship with a man who makes less than she does generally believes that it doesn't matter which one of them brings in the most money as long as their relationship is a loving one. But she often discovers, to her dismay, that it matters *to her* a lot more than she thought it would. The income disparity often puts a much heavier financial strain on her than she had anticipated, and this can lead to a great deal of resentment.

Resentment comes in a variety of shapes and sizes. Some women resent having to pay more than their partner to sustain their joint lifestyle. Others resent having to work overtime because their partner doesn't bring in enough money. And still others resent having to abandon their expectations for a traditional marriage.

In a perfect world, all money matters in a relationship would be decided upon jointly. But few of us achieve this ideal in real life. More often, money decisions lead to power struggles. Does the woman get to make most of the decisions because she makes most of the money? Or does the man decide because traditionally he's been taught to handle financial matters? If he used to bring in more money and made most of the decisions, does that responsibility shift to her if their relative income should shift? Or does he continue to make financial decisions as before? All these issues can raise resentments.

And resentment almost always finds expression through a familiar but destructive behavior: blame.

The Blame Game

Blame is a style of communication that focuses on what you believe someone else has done or is doing to hurt you. It is a behavior steeped in anger and frustration that rarely accomplishes anything other than to drive people apart.

When you consistently blame your partner for situations that arise out of the financial imbalance in your relationship, you make him feel attacked, which naturally leads him to act defensively. He'll stop listening, he'll stop trying to be understanding, and he'll stop trying to compromise. Blame is a game that beats down its players and leaves no victors.

This is the dead-end game that Shelly and Marc were playing. They had been married for four years when they came in to see me. They both looked emotionally exhausted—their continuing money fights had taken their toll.

Two nights earlier, Shelly and Marc had had a fight about how much they could afford to spend on an upcoming vacation. Marc had stormed out and a few minutes later rear-ended a truck at a stop sign. He had been so upset and distracted that he hadn't even seen it. This experience shook both of them so badly that they decided to seek therapy together.

Marc was an independent systems analyst and Shelly was a human resources director for a midsize telecommunications company. They first met when Shelly's company hired Marc to do a three-month study. The two of them found themselves working long hours together, and as their friendship developed, Marc's already shaky marriage fell apart. Shelly was a supportive friend during the breakup, and a few months later they began to date.

A year after that, they married and Marc moved in with Shelly and her thirteen-year-old daughter.

Though Marc's income was lower than Shelly's, it was only slightly so. However, he had come into their marriage with extremely heavy obligations to his ex-wife—so heavy, in fact, that they cut his net income almost in half.

Though Shelly had gone into the marriage fully aware of Marc's financial situation, she still found herself feeling resentful about it.

SHELLY

We fight about it constantly. I mean, sure he's got to take care of his kids—but why her? He gave her everything—the house, the savings, *everything!* On top of which he *volunteered* to assume more than sixteen thousand dollars in joint credit card debts. And she didn't even ask for it! That's why I'm so angry. She's got a boyfriend. Why doesn't she marry him? Because the alimony'll stop, that's way.

MARC

I'm just taking care of my family. That's all I want to do. And if I have to go without in order to do it, that's what I have to do.

SHELLY

Our whole marriage has been about paying the price of
that marriage—

MARC

And you never let me forget it.

SHELLY

Well, I've worked really hard. . . . I'm tired and I'm burned
out, and I start thinking about my future and realize there
will never be a time—at least that I can see—when I can fall
back in your arms and let you take care of *me* for a change.
And I resent that. It isn't fair. Why do *I* have to hold up
the fort all the time? Consciously, I know love isn't
money, but deep down inside there's a little voice that says,
"If you loved me, you'd support me, you'd take care of
me."

MARC

What was I supposed to do? It was a fourteen-year marriage—that's a long time. I had a lot of issues about the
morality of caring for my ex-wife and kids, notwithstand-
ing the advice of my divorce lawyer.

SHELLY

Admit it. You felt guilty. So you let her walk all over you.

MARC

All right, I felt guilty! Is there anything wrong with that?
I was leaving *them,* not the other way around. So I made a
divorce settlement that put me in the position of having to
struggle for a few years. . . .

SHELLY

More than a few—we've been together four years, and
we're still paying off the debts of that marriage.
(turning to me)
Marc is an absolute child about money. He came from a

family that never seemed to have money problems, so it just doesn't bother him that we're not able to save, that we've got to tighten our budget—and there's a lot of resentment there, too. *I'm* the one who always has to worry about it. *I'm* the one—if he can't come up with the money, I have to. And I resent that. I'm sick of it. When is it going to end? When is the ghost of that marriage not going to be part of ours? When can we get even so we can start our financial solvency together and not just have a hole from the past?

I'm sure that many of you can identify with Shelly's anger. It's perfectly natural for a second (or third or fourth) wife to resent the fact that her husband is still financially enmeshed with his ex-wife, especially if this causes financial hardship. No woman wants to feel unfairly deprived because her husband sends off money to a former wife.

You might also identify with Shelly's yearning to be taken care of. All of us have these yearnings to one degree or another, but many women (and men) still find the desire for dependence shameful because it implies that we want to regress to a child-like state of helplessness, that we don't want to be self-reliant. Yet it is very human to want someone else to solve our problems and free us from responsibilities. Almost all of us share this yearning once in a while, and when it is constantly frustrated, resentment builds.

But blaming behavior does not get rid of resentment. In fact, blame feeds resentment. Blame locks people into antagonistic positions. Instead of opening doors to possible solutions, blame slams those doors shut.

In Shelly and Marc's case, they made a habit of slamming the door. There was something almost ritualistic in the way she blamed him for the financial burden of his divorce settlement and he then withdrew into a defensive shell of rationalizations and justifications.

The Resentment/Guilt Cycle

As Shelly talked to me about her feelings, it became increasingly clear that resentment was not the only emotion she was struggling with.

SHELLY

I know he can't do anything about the alimony—it's a done deal. But I still find myself nagging him about it—I just can't help myself. And then he gets upset, and we fight. I hate myself when I hurt him like that, and then I turn around and resent him more for making me feel so guilty.

It is almost impossible to resent a man you love without feeling guilty about it. Resentment can make you feel both unsympathetic and unloving, especially if you are acting resentful toward a man whose worst crime is that he does not make as much money as you do. Such undeserved resentment can create an enormous amount of guilt. And if you're dumping on him, the guilt just multiplies. Then you turn around and resent him even more because he appears to be making you feel guilty. It can be an endless cycle.

Shelly was baffled by her inability to stop badgering Marc. The pattern went something like this: She would feel stressed out, worried about the future, and overburdened by having to carry so much of the financial load. This led her into a cycle of resentment and guilt. The result was an accelerating buildup of distress and tension. And the only way she seemed to be able to relieve those uncomfortable feelings was to take them out on Marc.

Marc, as the dump*ee,* took the brunt of Shelly's resentment, which intensified his already uncomfortable feelings of inadequacy, foolishness, and guilt.

MARC

I understand what she's going through. I went through it myself in my last marriage. I remember wishing I had

someone to take care of me. But I'll tell you, I'd give anything to have that pressure back again, because the alternative is a pisser. I mean, I love Shelly's independence, and I
love her accomplishments, but I wish I could be there, too.
I don't know where I am in this picture anymore. My
whole training and background from youth through my
first marriage was that I was going to be the one who provided, just as my father did when I was growing up. But
I'm not doing that in this family, and I feel bad about it
already. So it really jangles my raw nerves when Shelly
keeps harping on it.

Marc was defining his self-worth by his financial worth, as
so many men are raised to do. And because he was failing to
meet both his own and Shelly's standards, his confidence and
sense of personal worth were taking a serious beating.

Marc had come from a traditional family. His mother took
care of the house and the kids; his father was the provider. And
Marc stepped easily into this same role in his first marriage.

But when he married Shelly, everything turned around. Not
only was Shelly not dependent on Marc, but she was the primary provider. This was a difficult adjustment for Marc to
make, going against everything that he had grown up believing. And Shelly's expressions of resentment only reinforced his
feelings of shame and inadequacy.

I told Marc and Shelly that they needed to interrupt their
ritualistic cycle of resentment and blame if they were going to
have the kind of relationship that they both claimed to want.
But I did not want to see them as a couple. In my experience
the most effective way to interrupt and change destructive relationship patterns is for each person to do therapeutic work sep-
arately. While this was not what Marc and Shelly were expecting, they were receptive to the idea. Marc agreed to work with
one of my associates on his personal issues while I would continue to work with Shelly. I wanted to help her focus more on

those things that Marc did that *were* supportive, things that might not have a monetary value but were valuable to her nonetheless.

Love Deficits

While Shelly's resentment stemmed, to a great extent, from the financial pressure she was feeling, my client Willa's came from a different sort of trigger, a sadly common one—her husband's emotional limitations.

Willa's husband Stuart made less than she did because of a streak of unhappy circumstances. These had culminated in his being forced to resign from a high-pressure chemical engineering position on his doctor's orders after suffering from bleeding ulcers. He was now working as a free-lance consultant. He was having trouble getting his business going in a tough economic climate but was working hard at it nonetheless.

Willa, on the other hand, had a solid middle-management job with a giant multinational corporation. And during the time Stuart had been struggling, she had been prospering.

Stuart's struggle had become increasingly frustrating for him, and he responded to this frustration by becoming more self-absorbed. He became preoccupied with speculative work and seemed to have less and less interest in spending time with Willa.

Slowly but surely, Stuart lost the penchant for playfulness and romance that had so delighted Willa in the first few years of their marriage. As a result, despite Willa's sympathy for what Stuart was going through, she found herself becoming increasingly bitter about feeling shut out and rejected.

During this period Willa and Stuart were in the process of remodeling their house. They began to fight more and more about how much money to put into the remodel and what specifically to spend it on.

WILLA

He kept making all these decisions about cabinetry and car-
pets and colors, and I wasn't being involved with my opinion. I felt taken advantage of because it was mostly the
money I was making that was contributing to being able
to do it in the first place. That was a cause of a lot of resentment and a lot of fighting, too, because I kept thinking,
"We need to fix our marriage before we fix our house."

I asked Willa whether she had ever expressed this thought to
Stuart or talked to him about how emotionally unfulfilled she
was feeling. She told me that she didn't want to burden him
with it because he was having such a hard time as it was. I
pointed out to her that by leaving her feelings unspoken, she
was stuffing a lot of her hurt and frustration. Instead of exposing her feelings to the light so that she could do something
about them, she was hiding them behind money fights and not
dealing with them at all. It was time for that pattern to change.

The Resentment Journal

To help Willa dig beneath the surface of her conflicts with Stuart, I suggested that she start a Resentment Journal, making an
entry every time she was aware of feeling hurt or resentful and
including in her entry what she did in response to those feelings. Through this journal, we would be able to get a clearer
picture of the cause-and-effect relationship between her feelings
of resentment and her behavior.

Here are a few entries from the Resentment Journal she began
that week.

What happened: I wanted to make love, but Stuart said he was
too tired and rolled over with his back to me.
How I reacted: I felt really rejected and hurt, but I didn't want
to push it, so I just rolled over and went to sleep.

What happened: Stuart bought himself some expensive glasses.

How I reacted: I felt upset and angry and picked a fight with him for using my money to buy something extravagant. I knew I didn't really care about the glasses, it wasn't that much money, but I got really heated up anyway.

What happened: I paid the bills.

How I reacted: I felt resentful about how much more I had to pay than he did. I made a nasty remark to him about it, and we fought again.

What happened: I got a promotion at work, and I came home in the mood to party. Stuart was in a lousy mood all evening and really brought me down.

How I reacted: I really resented the fact that he was depriving me of my celebration, but instead of letting him know it, I spent the evening trying to make *him* feel better.

What happened: Stuart chose a crown molding for the ceiling of the new family room and told the contractor to go ahead with it without consulting me.

How I reacted: I felt ignored and invisible, as if I didn't count. I hated the molding and blew up at him for thinking it was okay to make an expensive decision like that alone, especially since I was the one who was going to end up paying for it.

This was only a partial list. As Willa continued her journal over the next few weeks, we began to identify certain patterns. It became apparent that whenever she felt resentful over money issues—as she did when Stuart bought the glasses or ordered the molding—she blew up at him.

However, whenever she felt resentful (or hurt or angry) over emotional issues—when he didn't want to make love to her or when he threw cold water on her celebration—she stuffed her feelings and remained silent.

Willa admitted that many of her money fights—like the one about the glasses—were about things that weren't particularly important to her. When confronted with this fact, it became obvious to her that in her money fights, she was responding in part to her unexpressed resentments over emotional issues.

When you transcribe events from your emotional life onto paper, the square pegs begin to find the square holes. First of all, if you are unaware of how repetitious certain of your behaviors are, the written page will make those patterns jump out at you. A clarity emerges on paper that may not be apparent in conversation. Writing engages the left hemisphere of your brain, the part that thinks in a step-by-step logical manner. Through your journal entries, you can take a step back and get some distance from behavior patterns that may have been previously obscured by emotional clutter.

A Convenient Outlet

It took only a few therapy sessions for Willa to realize that the money fights she and Stuart were having were really outlets for the hurts, fears, and frustrations she was feeling from their love relationship.

WILLA

What I'm seeing is that I'd be able to feel more important, and not taken for granted, if I had a lot more emotional support. Then, financially supporting us wouldn't bother me so much. I really truly feel that if we were balanced in other areas of our relationship—less struggle and more love—I could go on for a very long time like this. But somehow it's just a lot easier to fight about money than it is to ask for love when you're not sure it's there.

Willa's realization is true for many women. When we feel lonely in a relationship, when we feel deprived, when we yearn for affection and attention and don't get it, it's scary to put those yearnings into words. If we don't get what we ask for, we face humiliation, embarrassment, feelings of weakness and dependency, and the awful pain of rejection.

So instead of making ourselves vulnerable to these frightening emotions, many of us become resentful of having to ask for what we need in the first place.

As always, the tangible nature of money makes it an easy target for expressions of anger and frustration. And if your partner makes less than you do, his financial situation is a ready scapegoat for all sorts of resentments, including those that have nothing to do with money.

Permission to Tell the Truth

As hard as it was for Willa to share her feelings about her relationship frustrations with Stuart, it was even harder for him to share his with her. Like so many men in our society, Stuart was raised to hold his feelings inside.

The inner world is still a foreign land to most men. When men get together, they rarely talk about feelings, as women so often do. And when a man experiences fear, or depression, or sadness—emotions that can imply some sort of weakness or "femininity"—he tends to become ashamed of his own feelings and to keep them hidden. If his financial situation reinforces this shame, it is doubly difficult for him to share his feelings, especially with the partner in whose eyes he so desperately wants to appear competent.

The self-help, personal growth, and recovery movements have made this male tendency less true now than it used to be. More and more men are learning to embrace their introspective side, and this is giving them the courage to face down their socialization and try to make changes in the way they interact with others and perceive themselves. But Stuart was not among these sensitized men.

I told Willa that a lot of the anger and distancing she was

feeling from Stuart was probably due to the fact that he was sitting on painful feelings he was too ashamed to share.

While it was Stuart's responsibility to find less combative ways to deal with his personal frustrations and anxieties, he probably had no idea how to begin. If Willa planned to bide her time until Stuart decided, on his own, to make changes, she might have a long wait.

On the other hand, if she was willing to take the first step, she might, in essence, be able to model the kind of emotional openness they needed to unite around their common problems instead of being driven apart by them.

Nonoffensive Communication

The first thing Willa needed to do was to let Stuart know about her loneliness, her fears about his withdrawal, and her resentments about how he was treating her. But she had to do this in a nonthreatening way in order to open a dialogue instead of starting a fight. If she could tell Stuart her honest feelings about their marriage without blaming, attacking, or guilt-peddling, Willa just might make him feel safe enough to open up to her.

We've already taken a look at non*defensive* communication— the use of simple responses to maintain your dignity and personal power in the face of an emotional tirade or assault. These techniques can help you avoid the counterproductive pitfall of defensiveness.

But there are many times in your life when the shoe is on the other foot—when the honest communication of your feelings makes your *partner* feel defensive. This is not only true for your angry or resentful feelings, it can also be true for your feelings of hurt and disappointment.

In order to change the counterproductive style of communication that Willa and Stuart were used to, I suggested that she and I do some role-playing to help her learn to express her feelings in more nonthreatening or non*offensive* ways.

I role-played Willa, and she role-played Stuart. Here's how we began:

SUSAN (as Willa)

There are some things I want to talk to you about. Is this a good time for you?

WILLA (as Stuart)

I guess it's as good as any.

SUSAN (as Willa)

I'm really feeling scared about us growing apart. I've been feeling very hurt and lonely lately. I take full responsibility for having been too scared to share those feelings with you. I've been dumping a lot of my resentments on you, instead—especially when we fight about money. But I feel so burdened by all the bills, and sometimes I feel like you take me for granted. But mostly, I feel like we're not connected anymore, and that's what really scares me. The last thing in the world I want is to lose you. You've got to be holding in a lot of feelings, too, just like I've been holding mine in. And I think it's really important for us to talk about them.

WILLA (as Stuart)

Look, I appreciate what you're saying, but this is stuff I just have to work out myself.

SUSAN (as Willa)

I know how hard it is to express feelings that you know I don't want to hear. I'm doing that right now. But when you try to work stuff like this out by yourself, I feel this wall go up between us. I really want our marriage to be a partnership. I want us to be able to help each other through tough times. And I want you to know that it hurts me a lot more to feel shut out than it would if you shared your feelings with me, no matter how painful they are.

WILLA
(breaking out of her role-playing)

God, it's such a different way of thinking. I mean, I would have just gone into this by telling him that I'm pissed off because he's not bringing in his share, and then he would have gotten upset, and before long we would have been at each other's throats.

Willa understood how these very specific ways of expressing herself could make her feelings far less threatening to Stuart, but she confessed to feeling a bit uncomfortable with the specific phrases I chose to use. They just didn't feel natural to her. I assured her that my words were only a demonstration of the method, not a script that she had to follow. I encouraged her to find her own words, but to be sure to follow certain ground rules in order not to trigger a defensive response.

Here are the rules I gave her:

1. Try to make "I contact" as much as possible. This involves using statements that focus on yourself, using the word *I* as the starting point for expressing your feelings. Begin sentences with such phrases as "I want . . . ," "I need . . . ," "I feel . . . ," "I wish . . . ," "I hope . . . ," or "I appreciate. . . ." But be careful to avoid statements like "I feel you are being selfish" or "I need you to change." These kinds of statements are focused on him, not you, and will only work against you.

2. Try not to make inflammatory statements. Don't blame, ridicule, belittle, preach, or psychoanalyze. Most of these tactics are at least veiled attempts to change your partner, which is neither your responsibility nor within your power.

3. Don't get caught up in a chick-and-egg discussion. It doesn't matter who started a particular fight or who did what to whom first. If his position is "If you weren't such a nag, I wouldn't be so distant," and your position is "If you weren't so distant, I wouldn't be such a nag," you could argue in circles forever. The need to assess blame never leads to resolution.

As with any communications guidelines, these nonoffensive ground rules will not necessarily change your relationship overnight. Nobody gets these techniques down the first time around, or the second or the third. In fact, even if these techniques become second nature to you, you'll still find yourself backsliding once in a while, especially in the heat of an argument. I know I do.

Nonoffensive techniques can feel unnatural; they contradict our animal instincts to fight or flee when threatened. But with practice and patience, they will become increasingly comfortable to you. Believe me, it's well worth the effort—these techniques really do make a difference.

Willa went home and, despite some anxiety, sat Stuart down that same night for a talk. Following the nonoffensive guidelines, she told him about her frustrations, her fears, and her resentments about their relationship. They wound up talking well into the night, and though much work remained to be done, she felt closer to him than she ever had before.

Six weeks later Willa described their progress:

WILLA

I think what's really helping us is that now, when we have money fights, we don't just talk about the money, 'cause that's the smokescreen. Now we try to talk about what's really going on. Like, if I'm feeling afraid, or if I'm not trusting, that's where it's coming from. And if he's feeling inadequate, or feeling that he's not good enough, you know, instead of yelling at me, he shares that vulnerable feeling with me. When you just fight about money, there's never any closure. I never walked away from a money fight feeling that it was settled. But now—at least most of the time—we really seem to be able to work things out.

Displacing Anger

If an angry child is afraid to talk back, he or she is likely to break something, kick the dog, or pick a fight with a classmate.

If you're angry at your boss, instead of saying something that might get you fired, you might yell at your secretary. If you're angry about getting a traffic ticket, instead of saying something that might get you arrested, you might snap at a supermarket cashier.

The person we attack is not always the person we're *actually* angry with. Sometimes we "displace" our anger by making one person the target of our anger at another. We do this because we don't feel safe either physically or emotionally expressing our anger toward the appropriate person. This unconscious defense mechanism is called *displacement*.

The most common target of displaced anger—especially childhood anger—is a love partner. And I suspected that this was the explanation for Shelly's intense resentment of Marc's divorce settlement.

There was a clear contradiction between her feelings and her behavior: On the one hand, from everything Shelly told me and from what I was able to observe, Marc was a terrific guy. He was responsible, caring, and honest, and he adored Shelly. The last thing in the world Shelly wanted was to hurt him or to undermine their marriage.

Yet Shelly kept lashing out at Marc about money. Granted that Marc's financial commitment to his ex-wife was a strain on his and Shelly's resources, there was nothing he could do about it now. No matter how unfair Shelly felt her situation was, nothing positive could come of her repetitive blaming and dredging up events from the past. Shelly's blaming solved nothing, resolved nothing, changed nothing for the better, and made both her and Marc miserable.

Displacement seemed to be the only likely explanation.

Hidden Anger

At my suggestion, Shelly tried a few behavioral techniques to interrupt her angry impulses, but nothing she tried seemed to work. Clearly there were some powerful money demons driving her self-defeating behavior patterns, and before she could change, those demons had to be unearthed.

The first place we dug was the most likely—Shelly's childhood.

SHELLY

My mother was an awful woman. She was always yelling at us kids, and she was even worse to my father. She was this bitch on wheels twenty-four hours a day, and my father used to just sit there and take it. I remember how furious I used to get at him for not standing up to her, but he would just say, "What good would it do? She'll just get madder." So he'd sit there and soak up her abuse like a sponge. To this day, I'm sure that's what killed him. He died of a heart attack when he was only fifty-six because he just took it and took it and took it until it ate him up.

SUSAN

And you feel like Marc did the same thing with his ex-wife—let her walk all over him.

Shelly had never considered that her anger and disappointment toward Marc might be a reenactment of feelings she had for her father. But neither man had stood up for himself, and as a result, Shelly had suffered—in her father's case, both from his failure to protect her as a child and from his death, and in Marc's case, from his financial sacrifices.

Though this connection seemed apparent to me, Shelly had trouble believing it.

SHELLY

It sounds great, but it's just not true. I'm not mad at my father—he was the only one who ever loved me. My mother I'm furious at, but not my father.

I explained to Shelly that we're often as angry or even angrier at a parent who fails to protect us from another parent's abuse than we are at the abuser. There is nothing benign or loving about permitting verbal abuse (or any other kind) to go unchallenged, and when a parent does this, the child invariably experiences this passivity as betrayal.

But since the abusive parent's transgressions are so blatant, the passive parent's negligence is often lost in the shadows. Because of this, most children in this situation grow up unaware of the enormous anger they harbor toward their passive parent.

Every time Marc wrote out an alimony check, Shelly was reminded of how he had allowed himself to be victimized, just as her father had. Every time they came up short of funds because of Marc's obligations, she was reminded that Marc would not be there to protect her if she needed him, just as her father never had been.

As I explained this to Shelly, the pieces finally began to fall into place for her. Certainly, she was still angry with her mother, but this was anger that she had vented openly and was well aware of. Her anger toward her father was more difficult for her to deal with because not only was she out of touch with it, but it threatened a belief that was central to her self-image—the belief that she had had at least *one* loving parent.

Even though the circumstances were vastly different, in Shelly's unconscious Marc had become a stand-in for her father—a receptacle for all the long-buried anger, frustration, hurt, and disappointment that she had never been able to express.

But neither Shelly nor anyone else can finish unfinished business by using a stand-in. Anger, like justice, is effectively discharged only if it is directed at the responsible party.

The Overdue Letter

As I explored in detail in *Toxic Parents,* the best way to resolve childhood anger toward a parent is to confront that parent directly, in a nonthreatening but truthful way. This "confrontation" process takes a good deal of preparation in terms of working out, ahead of time, what you're going to say and what you can realistically expect in response—as opposed to the response you're hoping for.

This was what I suggested Shelly do, even though her father had been dead for several years. Many people mistakenly assume that a parent's death precludes the possibility of confrontation. But the key to a successful confrontation is what *you* are able to express and release—not how your parent responds to that release. Because of that, a parent need not be alive for confrontation to be effective.

I told Shelly that I wanted her to write a letter to her father telling him how she felt when her mother screamed, threatened, and humiliated her in his presence and he did nothing to stop it.

If she wanted to balance her pain with expressions of appreciation for the good things her father had done for her, she was welcome to, as long as she didn't hold back in telling the truth about her painful feelings.

The next week Shelly brought in a photograph of her father, as I had asked her to do, along with her Overdue Letter. I told Shelly to put the photo on a chair and read the letter out loud to it as if she were reading it to her father.

This was a tough assignment for Shelly. It was far easier for her to be angry at Marc than to face her anger with her father. When you're angry at your partner, you're angry as an adult. When you're angry at a parent, you're dealing with childhood anger that is mixed up with childhood fears, taboos, dependencies, and feelings of helplessness. This is a daunting collection of obstacles.

As Shelly read her Overdue Letter, she fought tears:

SHELLY

"Dear Daddy,

"It really hurts me to tell you this because I know how

much you loved me, and I loved you a lot, too, but the truth is, you really let me down. You let Mom scream and yell at us all she wanted without saying a word. Why didn't you do anything? Why did you let her treat us like that? When I needed you to be my strong daddy, you were a total wimp. You were never there for me when I needed you, and now I have a really hard time trusting anyone to be there for me. This has been really hard on my marriage, and it's been really hard on me. So I just wanted you to hear this and know how I feel. I still love you, but I've been carrying this around for most of my life and it's time I got it off my chest.

> "Love,
>   "Shelly"

As is usually the case when a person reveals painful childhood experiences to a parent—whether living or dead—Shelly's letter was long overdue. After Shelly finished reading it, she finally let her tears flow.

SHELLY

I feel so guilty about taking all this out on Marc. He really doesn't deserve it.

SUSAN

Don't be too hard on yourself. You're not responsible for your unconscious. And besides, you should give yourself some credit for having done something about your problems. You've come a long way in a short time. And now that the big mystery's solved, you're ready to do some healing.

As Shelly and Marc lay in bed that night, she told him about her experience with the letter. He asked if he could read it, and she let him. When he finished, she told him how sorry she was for having treated him so unfairly. She realized how her focus on his inability to take care of her financially had overshadowed the fact that he was always there to take care of her emotionally.

He reassured her that he loved her and that while they had some repair work to do on their relationship, he was still in for the long haul. The rest of the evening, as Shelly put it, "was X-rated."

The hard part about dealing with displaced anger is that when we displace our anger onto our partner, we nearly always do so under a very convincing pretext. That makes it pretty hard to spot. For women who make more money than their partners, this pretext is often a money fight—a fight that cannot be resolved because the source of the anger is not being addressed.

But as Shelly discovered, there *can* be resolution if you follow the trail of your money demons back to their source.

Walking on Eggs

Men who make less than their partners are often extremely touchy about being reminded of this discrepancy. If your partner's earning power is less than yours, he may be hypersensitive not only to money disagreements but to just about anything else you say or do.

Your partner may misinterpret your most innocent behavior as a put-down. If you try to be generous, he may feel that you are patronizing or pitying him. If you try to assert your opinion, he may feel that you are trying to use your monetary advantage to control him. When a man's self-image is threatened, any behavior can be fair game for distortion.

My client Andrea came to see me because she was becoming frustrated with her boyfriend Paul's hypersensitivity. In fact, she was contemplating ending the relationship. It had gotten to the point where Paul could experience even a selfless gesture of generosity as a blow to his ego.

ANDREA

He was waiting tables when we met, waiting for his big
break in Hollywood. . . . I'm a partner in the restaurant.
We went out a few times and it just clicked. But there was
always this thing about him being the underling dating the
big cheese. Even when we moved in together, there was
always this—this thing. He jokes about it a lot—he calls me
"boss" and stuff—but there's always this sort of uncomfortable pointedness about it. Like the other day, I saw a
shirt and I thought it would look so perfect on him that I
bought it for him. It wasn't even that expensive. But when
I gave it to him, he got really upset and accused me of trying to rub his nose in the fact that he doesn't make much
money. All I did was try to buy him a present. So what
else is new? I spend half my life biting my tongue because
I don't want to say something that'll make him feel like I'm
lording it over him.

Andrea spent a great deal of time censoring herself to insure
that she did not do anything that Paul might misconstrue as a
comment on his adequacy. But with a partner as overreactive
as he, Andrea was in a no-win situation.

ANDREA

I'm afraid to say anything. I can't just talk to him, I have to
go over everything in my head first to make sure there are
no hidden potholes. And even then, it's not enough. Like
the other night—he wanted to go out to this Chinese restaurant, and I told him I was really in the mood for Italian.
Do you hear anything inflammatory in that? But he went
off about how I can't ever let him make a decision, and one
thing led to another, and we got into a fight, and sure
enough it came back down to how I can't let him forget
that I bring in most of the money.

I asked Andrea why she felt the need to take responsibility
for Paul's self-worth, for that was exactly what she was doing.

In order to protect his ego, she was making an enormous sacrifice. By walking on eggs, she was preventing herself from *being* herself. She could not express her feelings, she could not express her thoughts, she could not share her fears, she couldn't even relax with her own lover. She felt a great deal of tension whenever she was with him, which didn't sound like much of a relationship to me.

Putting Your Foot Down

I pointed out to Andrea that she needed to stop catering to Paul's emotional overreactions and tell him how unhappy it made her to have to hide so much of herself from him.

If talking to him and changing *her* behavior didn't do the trick within a few weeks, her next step would be to warn Paul that if he wasn't willing to do something to help himself—like go into a men's support group or seek out some kind of counseling—she would have no choice but to end the relationship. She was already miserable—there was no reason to prolong the agony if he wasn't willing to change.

Unfortunately, Paul proved unresponsive to anything Andrea suggested, so she did, in fact, leave him. As she put it:

ANDREA

Obviously his self-esteem is in the toilet, and I still feel lousy about that. But I can't keep playing Joan of Arc when he's not willing to help himself.

When you're with a man who can't handle the fact that you make more money than he does, his feelings of inadequacy may manifest themselves in a number of ways, besides those we've already seen. He may start having sexual problems or lose interest in sex altogether. He may flirt openly with other women to try to pressure you or to reassure himself of his desirability. Or he may become irrationally jealous of you to assert his personal power.

By trying to protect his ego, you are only enabling him to continue to avoid doing anything about his own frustrations and fears. As long as he can blame you for his shaky self-image, he doesn't have to take responsibility for it himself.

There is nothing inherently unnatural about a woman making more money than a man, but there *is* something unusual about it in our culture, albeit less and less so. And in a society that is slow to change, you'll probably find yourself confronted by obstacles. But none of them are insurmountable.

Self-Help Strategies

At the beginning of this chapter, I told you that the men we met here would be basically responsible and productive. The exercises in this chapter are based on the assumption that your partner fits this description. If you are with a man who is taking financial advantage of you or being reckless with your joint assets, these exercises may not be appropriate for you. We will explore relationships with these types of men in the next chapter.

Disarming Your Beliefs

When you list your overt and covert beliefs, remember that the covert ones might be uncomfortable for you to acknowledge because they can easily make you feel insensitive, shallow, or greedy. I urge you not to allow your discomfort to get in the way of your discovery process. Discomfort is perfectly normal and shared by most women who find themselves in similar relationships. If there weren't any guilt attached to these covert beliefs, your mind would have no reason to conceal them in the first place.

Feel free to find your own words for the affirmation with

which you battle your covert beliefs. The important thing is to
focus on your partner's positive qualities and to counter the
covert beliefs that have been clouding those qualities.

The Resentment Journal

You can use this same technique to keep a Depression Journal,
an Anxiety Journal, or a Guilt Journal. The more you learn
about what triggers your negative feelings and behaviors and
how you characteristically respond to them, the more empow-
ered you become to combat them. If you can even partially
understand your own psychological processes, you can significantly increase your ability to manage them.

Nonoffensive Communication

Using this technique is like playing a musical instrument—it
takes practice, practice, practice. Don't be frustrated if you
don't bat a thousand; the key to nonoffensive communication
lies in continuing to refine your technique. Nobody does it perfectly every time, but if you observe the ground rules as best
you can, you'll find that this kind of communication can work
for any conflict, not just those we saw in this chapter.

The Overdue Letter

Shelly's father was not living when she did this exercise but, of
course, it can be just as effective if your parent is still alive.
Once you write your letter, you can mail it to your parent if
you are afraid to present it in person. But if you are willing to
do the hard work and preparation that should precede a face-
to-face confrontation (see *Toxic Parents*), I've seen extraordinary
healing results in clients who either read their letter out loud or
recited it from memory to their parent(s).

7

Enabling a Money-Reckless Man

He was a blind date, which made me pretty nervous, so you can imagine my relief when I opened the door and laid eyes on the handsomest man I'd ever seen. I'd been told that he was from a wealthy family, that he had recently been a candidate in a congressional primary (which he lost), and that he was a bold entrepreneur. But I never expected him to be so gorgeous. My heart started pounding. It was a warm summer night, and he whisked me off in a bright red convertible with the top down. It was magical. He was warm, he was bright, he was funny. . . . By the time we pulled up at one of the most elegant restaurants in town, I was in seventh heaven. He was all grace and charm as he ushered me inside. The maître d' came rushing up to greet us, clearly recognizing him. And then the bubble burst—the maître d' asked us to leave. I felt like I was taking an emotional nosedive, I was so startled, so humiliated. It seemed that my heartthrob had an enormous outstanding bill that was long overdue.

No, this is not a client's story, but the story of my first date with my ex-husband. I went on to marry him four months later, knowing he had no steady income, knowing he couldn't get credit, knowing he was in debt, knowing he was driving a borrowed car, and knowing he wasn't able to pay his child support. But I didn't care—I was madly in love.

Just as he had a good excuse for what happened on that first date (he said that the restaurant had made a bookkeeping error, charging someone else's tab to his account), he had good explanations for all those other things as well. He seemed full of potential, constantly running off to meetings in which he was pulling together the biggest deal of his life. His favorite refrain was, "When we're rich, honey-baby . . ."

In the meantime, I was making a decent living as a television actress and was able to keep us afloat. I believed with all my heart that if I just stood by him long enough and loved him strongly enough, he'd get back on his feet. If I had only known then what I know now about money-reckless men.

Money-Reckless Men

A money-reckless man will drive you crazy. His behavior around money will spark continual money fights, erode your emotional well-being, cause you so much anxiety that you may experience physical symptoms, and of course, create serious financial problems not only for himself but for you.

As you read on, you may notice that I seem harder on money-reckless men than I was on the money-reckless women we met in Chapters 4 and 5. I may even appear to have a double standard, seeming to be more sympathetic to money-reckless women than to men. But there is a reason for this apparent bias, and it has nothing to do with gender. Every money-reckless woman we met was aware that she had a problem and had *chosen to do something about it.* The same cannot be said of the men here. Without exception, the men in this chapter refuse even to admit to a problem, let alone do anything about it.

Different Men, Different Styles

Money-reckless men come in a variety of packages. They generally fall into five categories:

1. The Dreamer is often a self-styled artist, inventor, or entrepreneur. He is typically unrealistic about his prospects and does nothing effective about trying to alter them. He feels entitled to fame and fortune by dint of the talent and potential he believes he possesses, and he considers any alternative work beneath him. He may have sporadic spurts of success, but he always spends far more money than he makes.

2. The Dropout is a man without ambitions or dreams. He may stubbornly refuse to work, or he may lose every job he manages to get. He sabotages every opportunity that comes his way, yet he always sees himself as an innocent victim of an unreasonable boss, a greedy ex-wife, a traumatic childhood, or a crass, money-grubbing society.

3. The Wheeler-Dealer is a grandiose man who thrives on financial drama. He is a crisis junkie who seems to need financial jeopardy to make himself feel alive. Whether he's trying to pull together a multimillion-dollar shopping mall on Tonga or buying two hundred dollars' worth of tube socks to sell door-to-door, his plans are usually ill-fated. He has an ambivalent relationship to money. On the one hand, he covets it; on the other, he can't get rid of it fast enough. If one of his schemes should happen to hit, he will inevitably find a way to lose the proceeds, either through reckless spending or by reinvesting it in yet another improbable deal. He may spend a lot of time in court, either suing someone or, more often, being sued. He is a born salesman whose enthusiasm, confidence, and charisma are extremely seductive.

4. The Gambler is propelled by unconscious drives that he seems unable to control. Of the five types of money-reckless men, the gambler's way of acting out is the only behavior among these types that is generally recognized as being compulsive, though any of these behaviors can be.

5. The Con Man brings us into the darkest realm of financially irresponsible men—the compulsive liar and cheat who makes a conscious decision to live off of or steal from his lover.

He is remarkably free from the burdens of conscience, guilt, or remorse. He is often an exciting, charming man who has an uncanny ability to win the blind love and devotion of the women he exploits.

There is frequently a lot of overlap among these types. Some money-reckless men may be defined by only one category, but most can be described only by a combination.

A Disturbing Realization

You may wonder why, in a book written for and about women, I am focusing so extensively on the behavior of men in this chapter. The fact is, the women who gravitate toward men like these live in a state of almost total denial. By taking a closer look at money-reckless men, you may very well see a reflection of your own partner and, if so, begin the process of removing your emotional blinders.

If you are with a man like this, you are, at the very least, reluctant to acknowledge the possibility not merely that he is unlucky with money but that there is something embedded in his character that *drives* him to be financially irresponsible, inadequate, reckless, or even malevolent.

You are probably resistant to the unpleasant notion that your partner might be orchestrating his own disasters, that he might have emotional problems that are causing him to bring down the financial roof on his own head—not to mention yours. But if your partner fits into one or more of the categories above, you must know, on *some* level, that you are living with a money-reckless man.

You may have great faith in the man you love or in his potential. You may even believe his dreams of glory or his elaborate schemes. You may try hard to believe his continual excuses about the various people who are sabotaging his jobs or blaming him for things he didn't do. Your heart may ache for the pain you know he is suffering or for the humiliation you know he has endured.

However, if your partner *consistently* behaves in money-reckless ways, his problems are more than monetary—they are psychological.

This is a disturbing realization. I know how painful it is to think of your partner as someone who is psychologically troubled—as opposed to someone who merely needs a loan or a break. But until you acknowledge the source of the problem, you can't hope to find a solution.

A Different Kind of Enabler

When the partner of an alcoholic, a substance abuser, or a compulsive gambler repeatedly endures his destructive behavior, bails him out of trouble, does whatever she can to cover up for him, and denies the seriousness of her situation, she is called an *enabler*.

If you deal with your partner's money-recklessness in these ways, you may very well be what I call a *financial enabler*.

You may be thinking this has nothing to do with you, especially if you are familiar with the term *enabler* or its similar but less precise cousin, *codependent*. Some aspects of financial enabling don't necessarily conform to the standard definitions of enabling behavior.

For example, classic enablers are attracted to men who obviously need rescuing and caretaking. Yet you may have been initially attracted to the confidence, charisma, and apparent success of your partner. Though many money-reckless men are in desperate financial straits, they frequently avoid revealing their financial troubles when they first begin dating a woman. In fact, they will often go to great lengths to appear successful, spending lavishly with money they don't have or weaving convincing stories to explain why they are "temporarily cash poor."

In addition, though the majority of financial enablers come from alcoholic or abusive households, a surprising number do not. In fact, you may have had a relatively happy childhood. Many financial enablers do *not* learn in childhood to be rescuers by having to take care of inadequate parents; they are *not* reliving their traumatic childhoods through their adult relationships. A "toxic parent" background is not necessarily the source of every overdeveloped sense of responsibility.

But regardless of your background, the bottom line is: When you repeatedly bail out, make excuses for, or support a man who routinely runs up debts, wastes money on grandiose schemes, makes bad investments, gambles, or loses jobs, you may be as much an enabler as the woman who buys wine for her alcoholic husband in hopes of keeping him out of bars.

Are You a Financial Enabler?

Do you suspect that you might be unknowingly encouraging your partner to continue money-reckless patterns? This checklist can help you clarify the issues and arrive at a better understanding of your true role in your relationship:

Do you . . .

- consistently pay off your partner's debts or bounced checks?
- regularly turn your paychecks or earnings over to him, even though you know he has a history of debt or reckless spending?
- have property or assets that you've transferred to his name in order to prove how much you trust him, to make him feel better about himself, or because of some rationale of his that never quite made sense to you?

- lie to family and friends about how he's doing financially, whether you're supporting him, or how much you're spending on him?
- regularly stuff the anger caused by his irresponsible spending or financial inadequacy?
- borrow from family or friends to cover the financial problems he's created?
- go along with his schemes, even though you know they probably won't work out?
- avoid confronting him on his behavior for fear of angering him, humiliating him, or losing him?
- feel financially used or cheated by him?
- believe that if you rescue him financially, you will secure his love?
- seem much worse off financially now, because of this man, than you were before you became involved with him?

If you answered yes to two or more of these questions, you are, indeed, struggling with financial enabling. This does not mean that you have a deep character flaw or that your parents did something irreversible to you as a child; it is just a characterization of your behavior. Financial enabling is something you can change relatively quickly, and in this chapter I'll show you how.

You'd be amazed at how many women are unknowingly doing many of the same self-defeating things in the name of love that you are. If I had taken this test fifteen years ago, I would have answered yes to every one of these questions. You are definitely not alone.

The Payoffs of Financial Enabling

Like any other self-defeating behavior, financial enabling has its payoffs. No one does something against her best interests without getting some psychological reward out of it. When a woman takes on the responsibility of saving a man who is drowning financially, she often feels extraordinarily powerful, in control, adequate, indispensable, worthy, and noble. These payoffs can be especially rewarding for a woman who has felt powerless in the financial arena, in her relationships, or in both.

There is another common payoff that is a little more subtle and more difficult to grasp. Many women who have been deprived of feeling loved or protected, especially as children, try to make up for this by treating someone else in the ways they've yearned to be treated themselves. Going into the relationship, they identified with their lover's pain, and now, through enabling him, they identify with his rescue. As convoluted as it may seem, this vicarious means of getting dependency needs met can be a powerful payoff.

When you admit to being an enabler, you put your payoffs at risk. This, of course, makes it all the more difficult to face the truth.

The first question you may ask is: What's so destructive about supporting someone you love or lending him money when he's in a bind? Your conscious motives may be sterling, your actions may seem totally selfless, and your alternatives may seem nonexistent. The problem lies not in coming to his rescue but in coming to his rescue *again and again*. If you're doing all the financial giving and he's doing all the taking, or if you're being financially responsible and he's not, you'll almost certainly find yourself exhausted from the daily struggle against debt. Your relationship will suffer from continual fights about money, and you'll end up terrified of falling off the financial highwire that you're constantly forced to walk.

When First Impressions Are Deceptive

Money-reckless men are extremely hard to identify on first meeting. They don't wear signs. You can almost never tell what their financial patterns have been in the past from the situation you find them in when you meet them. And some money-reckless men actually make quite a bit of money—at least once in a while.

What characterizes these men as money-reckless is not how much or how little they make but their inappropriate financial priorities, their irresponsible spending habits, and their unwillingness to take responsibility for their debts and obligations.

But this kind of behavior can be extremely difficult to gauge when you're caught up in the excitement and passion of a new relationship. Passion and romance are forgiving filters through which perceptions rarely pass without being transformed or at least softened. When you're in love, it is only natural to push aside any evidence that might contradict your romantic hopes.

The Illusion of Financial Success

When my friend Laurel first met her husband Sean, he was not only making a good living, he was making it steadily. She had no reason, at first, to suspect him of being money-reckless, and by the time she found a reason, she was married to him.

LAUREL
I had been doing fairly well selling real estate, but then the bottom fell out of the market, so I started selling cars. Sean was my sales manager—a nice Irish guy from New York. We worked really well together—I made the pitch, and he closed the sales. He was a really good closer . . . in fact, I never made so much money in my life. He seemed very secure financially. I mean, I *knew* how much money he was making, and it was a lot. When he started asking me out, I said no because I didn't want to screw up the work thing, but there *was* something about him . . . he really made me laugh—a lot. So I finally said yes, and things just started rolling from there. Two weeks later, we went to Vegas and got married. I told you he was a good closer.

Most women know far less about a new husband's finances than Laurel knew about Sean's. Because of the nature of their professional relationship, Laurel had a very accurate measure of his income. Unfortunately for her, the money he had coming *in* was only half the equation.

LAUREL

The first thing that happened was, he had this parrot—a nasty, nasty bird. You'd walk past it, and it would reach out to bite you. So I took it to the pet shop where he bought it and asked the lady what I could do to train it. She took one look at it and said, "That's not your bird. It was never paid for." She went into the back and brought out a copy of a bounced check with his name on it. I told her I had just married Sean and I didn't know anything about it, but I was so embarrassed that I wrote a check for $350 right there and paid for the stupid bird.

This episode, in and of itself, would not be enough to label Sean a money-reckless man. Anyone can inadvertently overdraw a checking account. Laurel's first reaction—to cover for him—was understandable. Since she knew he was making good money, she believed this was a fluke. Besides, they were married, and their money was now commingled. And more important than any financial consideration was the fact that she loved him.

But by writing this first check, Laurel was stepping into a financial tar pit.

LAUREL

When I told him about the pet store, he kind of shrugged it off. But then a little while down the road, I get a call from our dry cleaner. Before we got married, Sean had bought his daughter an old car from this guy. So the cleaner calls and says to me that the car had never been paid for. And he keeps saying, "Your husband, every morning he said, 'I'll stop by and give you the money. . . . I'll stop by.' And he never did." One more time, I was so embarrassed that I went right over to the dry cleaner and set up a payment schedule, and then I paid the whole thing off. It was all so confusing—I mean, he seemed like such a winner to me, but he was stiffing people. He always had some kind of explanation, but I was starting to get really paranoid. . . . It was like, "What's next"?

As the episodes of Sean's financial malfeasance mounted, it became increasingly difficult for Laurel to excuse them as accidental oversights. His fiscal habits were causing her anxiety and embarrassment, yet Laurel continued to cover up for Sean instead of holding him accountable. She loved him, and because of that she was willing to make his irresponsible behavior *her* problem.

When the Illusion Crumbles

Laurel went into her marriage with a rosy perception of Sean's financial stability, but that perception began to deteriorate in the face of escalating evidence to the contrary.

LAUREL

I could never figure out why he didn't have any money. I knew he was making six or seven thousand dollars a month, but he was always out of cash. And he didn't have any credit cards either because he'd lost them in a personal bankruptcy—which he didn't bother to tell me until after we were married. And then one day the pieces all came together. I got a call from the company that managed our building, and this woman said our rent was two months overdue. Sean had told me he'd taken care of it, so I figured it was a bookkeeping mistake. I told her I'd find the canceled check and send her a copy. So I went into the bedroom and opened the drawer where he kept his papers, and

there was this rat's nest of bills and summonses and overdue notices just staring me in the face. The state and the
federal government were both garnisheeing his wages.
That's why he had no money. There were notices from the
marshal for him to appear in court, there were bills from
three different credit cards that he didn't even have anymore. It was a nightmare. Collection agencies, all kinds of
stuff. I just sat and leafed through these things, feeling like
I was being sucked further and further into some black
hole.

Even though Laurel had dealt with a few incidents that
suggested Sean had problems dealing with his financial
responsibilities, she was not prepared for the enormity of the
problems she found in that drawer. The successful sales manager who had swept her off her feet had a dark side, and she
was staring at the results. She was now faced with indisputable
proof that Sean was not only financially irresponsible but had a
clear pattern of intentional avoidance and deception. Yet she still
refused to let the full impact of the evidence register.

LAUREL

All along, he'd been telling me that he'd been taking care
of these bills, when he hadn't even been trying to. But I
still couldn't believe it because it didn't make any sense to
me that an intelligent person could do something like this.
I couldn't imagine how he could have thought he was going to get away with it. I could only figure that he just must
be under *enormous* pressure, like pressure so bad that he
couldn't even think straight. So when I found the bills, I
decided that I had to think straight for both of us. I set up
payment schedules with all his creditors and set up a budget for us that he *swore* to me he was going to stick to. I
was going to fix everything, and he was going to get back
on his feet. I knew he would. I mean, he was the best sales-

man I'd ever seen. All I had to do was get his spending under control, and we'd be on top of the world.

Laurel had now gone beyond writing a few checks to cover Sean's unpaid debts. She had taken responsibility for his entire financial mess. She had such a strong need to hold on to her first impression of him as a stable, rational, successful man that she took his word that he would adhere to her new budget, despite the fact that she knew he had been lying to her about his financial situation from the beginning. But to acknowledge that he was a liar would have shattered her hopes.

Lying is almost second nature for the money-reckless man. "The check is in the mail" is a favorite refrain. He'll make unrealistic promises to creditors, collectors, and ex-wives. He'll answer the phone and pretend that he's someone else to avoid having to answer for his financial negligence. He'll make up conflicts to justify his refusal to pay.

And he'll inevitably lie to his partner. He'll claim that a reckless purchase cost much less than it actually did. He'll pretend that his debt is much smaller than it is. He'll swear that he's paid bills he hasn't. This makes it that much harder for enablers to see their partner in the harsh light of reality.

But Laurel herself did all she could to see Sean as the man she wanted him to be instead of as the man he was. To see him otherwise would have been to acknowledge that she had made a terrible mistake. By perpetuating her fantasy, she could avoid the painful and difficult possibility of having to end her marriage.

An Answer for Everything

When Laurel met Sean, he was making good money—she had every reason to assume he was financially responsible. But when my client Diane met Vic he was on a financial downswing. She might have taken this as a sign of trouble, but instead, she accepted his explanation that his money problems were purely temporary. Her first impressions were based not on what she saw but on what he said. Money-reckless men can be very persuasive.

Diane is an obstetrician in a small public clinic in a beach community near Los Angeles.

DIANE

I met Vic jogging on the beach. I really had no thoughts about getting involved with him, but we started jogging together sometimes and it just sort of grew from there. He was very articulate, very charismatic. He'd been vice-president of a clothing company. Then he'd gotten a degree in kinesiology. Then he'd had his own exercise show on TV in the east. When we met, he was working as a personal trainer, and from the way he talked, I thought he was doing pretty well—until I saw his place. He was living in a tiny apartment with paint peeling off the walls . . . no door on the bathroom . . . no bed, just a piece of foam or something. And he was driving a car that looked like it came from the dump. It wasn't even his car—it was somebody else's. He had five shirts and two pairs of pants in his closet, and that was it.

I asked Diane why she hadn't been concerned at the discrepancy between Vic's apparent financial situation and what he was telling her about his background. She replied that he had had what seemed to be a perfectly reasonable explanation for everything:

What she saw: A rundown apartment.
What he said: He had finalized his divorce a few months earlier and was taking a financial beating because the court had forced him to support his ex-wife in a fancy apartment in Beverly Hills. But it was only for another year.

What she saw: Peeling paint, no door on the bathroom.

What he said: He had discovered termites in the door and had to get it out of the apartment before they infested the whole place. He wasn't replacing the door on principle: It was his landlord's responsibility, and Vic was taking the man to small claims court to force him to replace the door and paint the place.

What she saw: He had no bed.

What he said: There's nothing like sleeping on a pad on the floor to keep your back straight and healthy. He advised all his clients to do it.

What she saw: He was driving a borrowed wreck of a car.

What he said: His own car had been totaled in an accident, and his insurance settlement was being held up by a dispute over whose fault it was and how much the car was worth.

Because Diane found Vic so charming and attractive, she was willing to give him the benefit of the doubt, especially since she had not yet become seriously involved with him, so she had nothing to lose.

Though a judicious amount of caution is always wise, none of us wants to enter a new relationship with a backpack filled with suspicions to weigh us down. And when a man is as adept as Vic at finding creative explanations for his money troubles, he is easy to believe.

It's Always Someone Else's Fault

Vic blamed others for much of the sorry state in which he was living. His wife was bleeding him dry, his landlord was negligent, and his insurance company was trying to avoid payment.

DIANE

He had two exes and he was always complaining about how much alimony he was paying out. Whenever he had

an overdue bill, it was because his alimony had tapped him
out. It broke my heart to watch him suffer over this every
month. He called it his "cross to bear." What I didn't
know at the time was that he was stiffing them both. He
never paid out a penny.

Greedy ex-wives and needy children are favorite excuses for
money-reckless men. Other frequent targets of blame are un-
scrupulous business partners, heartless bankers, bloodthirsty
creditors, and deadbeats to whom he's made loans.

Like Vic, Laurel's husband Sean was a maestro of finger-
pointing.

LAUREL

With the parrot, it was, "I bounced a check? I never knew.
Why didn't she call me? She knew where I lived. She could
have gotten ahold of me . . . she could have, she could have,
she could have." He transferred all the blame to this poor
lady who sold him this stupid bird. He did the same thing
with the dry cleaner. The car was a lemon or something,
and it was the dry cleaner's fault. And the drawer full of
bills—he was planning to pay them with his tax refund,
but his accountant screwed him so he never got one. It was
as if everybody in the world had either let him down or
knifed him in the back.

Both Vic and Sean saw themselves as victims of other people's deception, inadequacy, and greed. Their convenient explanations always seemed to afford them the opportunity to
avoid taking personal responsibility for their own role in their
financial problems.

A Master of Embellishment

The easiest way for a money-reckless man to persuade you that
his problems are merely a blip on an otherwise fast track to

success is for him to paint a glowing picture of his past successes. If these autobiographical vignettes are not outright fabrications, they are almost always gross exaggerations of the truth.

Such embellishment is not necessarily an indication of deceit, though deceit is surely second nature to *some* of these men. Many of us exaggerate the truth a little bit to make ourselves more attractive to a prospective love interest. Even a financially *responsible* man will often stretch the truth about temporary financial problems to avoid scaring off a woman he's attracted to.

But money-reckless men tend to embellish more than a little. Their embellishments serve not only to aggrandize themselves but to obscure the destructive financial patterns of their past.

DIANE

I had no way of knowing it then, but Vic's whole life was an embroidery. It took me about a year to figure this out. If he said he had a TV show, he probably went on some show once or twice as a guest. But in his mind, he had his own TV show. Or if he was vice-president of the company, that probably meant he worked there selling clothes for a month. But he had an incredibly charismatic personality and was very certain of himself in the way he expressed himself. So he seemed, at least, believable. He was very smart, very talented, very articulate. He showed me poems he had written, and stories. He was very good. So I thought, "It must be true. He *is* talented." I really thought it was just a matter of time before he had his own TV show again.

Even if Diane had known in the beginning that Vic's descriptions of his past were overstated, she might just as easily have found them endearing as troublesome. When a man needs to build himself up by overstating his accomplishments, enablers have a tendency to sense that he has feelings of inadequacy and to sympathize with him. The financial enabler will inevitably rationalize his embellishments as touching manifestations of his vulnerability, a trait that will almost always draw her closer to him.

When His Problems Become Your Problems

As you begin the never-ending process of rescuing a money-reckless man, the emotional boundaries between the two of you blur as surely as the financial ones.

When you love a man, you can't help but empathize with him. When he hurts, you hurt. When he suffers, you suffer. It is only natural to want to help him solve his problems—not only for his peace of mind, but for your own.

You may invest in one of his schemes. You may loan him money to pay off his debts. You may move him into your home. You may buy him a car, bail him out of jail, or even pay his back alimony. But no matter how you become enmeshed in his financial matters, your compassion and desire to help are likely to lead you deeper and deeper into a morass of problems until your financial situation is as chaotic as his.

Tough Times, Great Expectations

If a money-reckless man lacks the resources to put on a show of prosperity, he can still exude enormous self-confidence and charm. Some money-reckless men generate a wonderfully grandiose facade, an aura of excitement and drama that can really get your adrenaline flowing.

When my client Mary met Sam, he was, like Vic, having lean times. But Sam had lofty plans that seemed so imminent, so plausible, that Mary found herself easily swept away by his optimism.

MARY

We met at a party. He told me he'd quit his job to pursue
his dream of starting his own import-export business, and
he'd just gotten back from this trip to Argentina—which
had pretty much eaten up all his savings, it turned out. But
he had this deal all set up to ship waterbeds from Berkeley
to Buenos Aires. He knew it sounded crazy, but this Ar-
gentine marketing guy had done all this research, and it
was going to be the next big fad. Sam had it all figured
out—he'd make about two hundred thousand dollars the
first year, twice that the second year, and on and on. . . .
It all sounded so exciting to me because he was going after
his dreams. I'd always been one of these people who would
never leave a job till I was absolutely in another job. My life
was very slow, very deliberate. So Sam's plans seemed really exciting to me, really different, really daring.

Sam had the palpable aura of a mover and shaker. With his
entrepreneurial lifestyle, so filled with the promise of riches and
foreign travel, Sam appealed to that part of Mary that yearned
to break out of a routine existence.

Many women are in awe of what they perceive as their partner's financial wizardry. Women often assume that they're incapable of understanding the monetary alchemy that seems so
clear to so many men. International exchange, futures options
contracts, public offerings—the more complex the concept, the
more impressive it seems. But the alchemy of the money-reckless man, which promises to turn lead into gold, invariably
works the other way around.

Mary had no way of knowing that Sam's dazzling grasp of
the import-export business was all talk and no knowledge. Sam
was a wheeler-dealer—an addict of the "big deal" that would
propel him into the financial stratosphere. Like all wheeler-
dealers, Sam was adept at persuading others to buy into his
financial fantasies—but his fantasies rarely came true.

Crossing the Line

About six months after Mary began dating Sam, he ran out of
money. He told her he had sunk everything he owned into his
waterbed deal, and he asked if he could move in with her until
the profits came in from his first shipment. Sam was raising the
stakes, and if Mary wanted to stay in the game, she would have
to feed the pot.

MARY

I was really in love with this man. And I knew in my gut
that it was only a matter of time before he got it together—
he had success written all over him. But it wasn't like I was
making that much money, and he was totally broke. So I
wasn't exactly ecstatic about the prospect of supporting
him. Besides, we'd only known each other about six
months. Still, he was so depressed about all this . . . and I
kept thinking, "Why am I not willing to do this for him?
He'd do it for me. He's not asking for so much—he just
needs me to get him through this for a couple of months."
So I moved him in.

As Mary's emotional stakes grew, she became increasingly
motivated to believe in Sam. And as a true believer, she saw it
as her duty to help him achieve the success she was so sure
he deserved.

It never occurred to her that it might be Sam's responsibility
to take care of himself. Because of her inability to distinguish
between her own responsibilities and his, she became a hostage
to his money-recklessness. Now, every time he ran out of
money, she was left holding the bag for their joint living expenses.

Like Laurel, Mary had crossed a critical line, the line that all
financial enablers eventually cross—the line that had separated
her problems from his.

The Big Spender

Mary had taken on more than she bargained for when she moved Sam in. Wheeler-dealers don't just live—they live *big*. They have an enormous need to impress others, sometimes under the guise of promoting their schemes, but sometimes merely to appear more successful than they are. They will typically host big dinners at restaurants, give away expensive tickets to cultural or sporting events, or lease lavish homes, offices, or cars they can ill afford. Image is everything.

Sam jumped out of the car and ran around to open the door for Mary. She smiled at the gesture. Chivalry was not dead.

"You look so beautiful tonight," he said. "Birthdays become you."

"Thank you."

As they walked toward the restaurant, he offered his arm. She snaked hers around his forearm.

"Why don't you give me your credit card?" he said. "I know that you're paying for us tonight, but—you know—with all our friends there—it'd just look better when the check comes. I mean, there's enough talk as it is."

She agreed. Her girlfriends had been giving her a rough time about Sam, about how she had virtually supported him for three months now.

As she fished her credit card out of her purse, she suppressed a sigh of resignation, wishing that her boyfriend could pull his weight like the other men who were going to be there tonight. But her thoughts went unexpressed, as usual.

Dinner was wonderful—she was with the man she loved, eight of her closest friends, and a salmon filet that melted in her mouth. She was in heaven.

And then the check came.

As the waiter put it down, Sam lunged across the table to grab it, knocking over a glass of water in his zeal.

"Nobody move," he said. "This party's on me."

Mary felt her heart sink.

"Don't be silly, Sam," said one of the other men. "We agreed to split the bill." The others chimed in with similar responses, all of them acutely aware that Sam could hardly afford his portion of the tab, let alone the whole thing.

Mary felt a moment's relief, but then Sam replied, "No way am I going to let another man have the pleasure of treating the woman I love on her birthday. This is her night, and I'm paying."

Mary couldn't afford the six hundred dollars that Sam was about to spend. She wanted to scream at him for blowing her money like this, but instead she said meekly, "Are you sure you can afford this, Sam?"

"Don't you worry, honey. This is your night."

And my money, she thought. "Sam, you really don't have to do this."

But he did it anyway. Mary bottled up her fury. The last thing she wanted to do was cause a scene on her birthday—especially since she knew how tongues would wag the next day if she did.

But as soon as they got in the car, Mary exploded. "How could you do that? That's my money!"

Sam seemed genuinely surprised. "I'm sorry. I thought you'd want me to. After all, we invited them all."

"I hate it when you do this."

"Do what?"

"Can't you just go out and have a good time without showing everybody what a big shot you are?"

"What are you talking about?"

"I'm talking about you using my credit card to show off."

"I'm not showing off."

"No? What about those Laker seats you spent $280 on last week?"

"That was for your parents, for God's sake!"

"It was to impress my father!"

"This is really unfair. I do something nice for you, and what do I get?"

"Not the bill, that's for sure."

"If this is so important to you, why didn't you say something in the restaurant?"

"What was I supposed to say? 'Give me my credit card back'?"

In fact, Mary *should* have demanded her card back, but she didn't because she was protecting Sam's image, accepting responsibility for his ego problems as well as his financial problems.

As Mary told me her story, I felt my stomach tighten. I remembered, all too well, nights out with friends or business associates that ended with my ex-husband almost fighting to grab a check he had no way of paying.

Reckless social spending is a powerful symbol of denial for the wheeler-dealer, a way of pretending that the realities of his financial situation simply don't exist. By acting as if he's rolling in money, he reclaims, for a moment, the power and ego gratification that he has lost to the humiliating reality of unemployment, nagging debt, or business failure.

In addition, the big spender derives much of his self-image from the approval and admiration of others. He basks in being perceived as generous, successful, and lovable. This enables him to see himself as he thinks others see him—the life of the party, a helluva guy.

The only thing that promised even a remote possibility of discouraging Sam's reckless spending was a hard slap of reality. But he didn't get it. Instead, Mary helped cover up his financial troubles—as Laurel did with Sean—making it possible for him to avoid suffering the consequences of his actions. Mary's behavior, as well-meaning as it may have been, merely served to protect Sam from the wakeup call he needed.

The Piggyback Effect

In enabling Sam, Mary was assuming that she needed to provide only short-term relief for a man whose setback was temporary. She didn't know just how repetitive his self-destructive business and spending patterns were.

MARY

He kept promising that as soon as his deal came together he'd pay me back, but something always seemed to get in the way. His waterbed deal *was* a big success, but before the first bed ever landed in Buenos Aires, he'd already committed his profits to importing this weird fish called merlusa to the United States. When *that* deal fell apart, he had to sell his ownership in the waterbeds to pay off his loans. My heart ached for him. He'd poured so much of himself into these deals. . . . It really upset me, but it hardly fazed *him*. He just kept saying how something else was bound to click. But in the meantime, I was taking care of all the household expenses. And I had to start making his car payments to save it from getting repossessed. And then he went out and bought a stereo system on credit, and a new guitar, and I ended up paying for those. I was paying this, I was paying that, and now *my* bills started piling up. There were creditors on the phone all the time—it was really humiliating. Then the next thing I knew, he was all excited about producing a music video with this friend, even though the two of them put together couldn't program a VCR.

Sam's catastrophic loss on the fish scheme didn't stop him. He was already onto his next big deal. In typical money-reckless fashion, he decided to throw himself into "producing" a music video—without know-how, without experience, without financing, without a buyer, without a distributor—in short, without a prayer of success.

At the same time, he was still impulsively spending money on adult toys he couldn't pay for.

Mary was discovering the hard way that Sam had a habit of piggybacking bigger and bigger debts to finance his investments. His deals were like a house of cards—when one of them collapsed, they all did. But none of this seemed to stop him from starting over. In his mind, unbridled optimism was all he needed.

I don't mean to belittle optimism—I believe in it strongly. But when optimism veers away from reality, it can become a runaway train. First of all, Sam was so driven from one deal to the next, he rarely took the time to properly evaluate any of them and, as a result, was often attracted to ill-conceived or poorly planned ventures that had little chance of working out.

In addition, should his plans fall apart, which was likely, Sam had nothing to fall back on—no savings, no job, no contingency plans.

On the surface, Sam and Mary's financial chaos would seem to have stemmed entirely from Sam's money-reckless behavior. But Mary was making a sizable contribution as well.

As she crossed the line to assume his monetary responsibilities, Mary gave Sam a powerful message: He didn't have to worry about drowning financially because she was there to save him. And each time she covered another one of his debts, she renewed confidence in the fact that he could pursue his deals with impunity because he had Mary as his safety net.

The Entitlement Syndrome

If you were to describe a person who never worries about consequences, bases his beliefs on what he wants to be true instead of on facts, acts on impulse, comes up with a lot of plans but then loses interest in their execution when it becomes difficult, needs instant gratification, has no appreciation for the value of money, always finds someone else to blame for his own mistakes, and has little sense of responsibility, you would be describing a child.

You would also be describing a money-reckless man.

Like a child, the money-reckless man sees himself as the focus of the universe. He expects to be taken care of without giving anything in return, and he has little patience with his caretaker when his desires are not fulfilled. Nothing illustrates the money-reckless man's immature thought processes as clearly as this Entitlement Syndrome.

Spending the Money He "Deserves" to Have

Many money-reckless men feel as if, by some celestial mandate, they deserve to have whatever they want. Because of this, they seem to have no qualms about bouncing checks or running up exorbitant house tabs or credit card charges (often on their partner's card)—debts they have no hope of paying off.

Within a few months of meeting Diane on the beach, Vic gave her a vivid demonstration of how reckless he could be when it came to spending money he didn't have.

DIANE

We were getting very close, spending a lot of time together, and one day he just opened up to me about these debts he had. He was trying to work it out by writing this check to cover that check to cover the other check and just getting farther and farther behind. He made it sound so unfair that he should be in this situation because so many people were letting him down, and he deserved better. He used to say, "If I could just get out from under all this stuff, everything would be fine. But I'm always chasing my own tail." So I thought, "If it's going to solve all his problems to lend him five thousand dollars, I should go and give it to him." It seemed logical to me. So I lent him the money, even though it almost tapped me out. He came back that night and gave me this really pretty pearl and gold necklace. For some reason in my mind I didn't actually translate that he had used my money to buy it. I did something different with the information. He also bought himself some clothes. Supposedly he was going to use the rest to pay off these loans, but then he went and bought some kind of classic car that needed a lot of fixing up—instead of buying a little VW, he went out and bought this red convertible. And he was so excited about it . . . like a little kid at the circus.

You'd think that Vic would be worried about Diane becoming angry when she discovered that he'd gone on a shopping spree with money she'd given him to pay his bills. But instead he acted as if he had done something terrific. He didn't try to hide the fact that he'd acted irresponsibly; rather, he reveled in it, even calling attention to it by buying an expensive gift for Diane.

Yet Diane seemed oblivious to any feelings of anger because her denial was so strong. Rather than resenting her lover, she overlooked the depth of irresponsibility that he had demonstrated.

Vic was thumbing his nose at what he obviously saw as a dreary world of obligation and debt. He refused to allow his creditors to set his priorities for him.

At the same time, Diane had her own priorities, and love was at the top of the list. As Vic's love was filling her heart, his reckless spending was draining her pocketbook.

The reckless spender always shortchanges his obligations in order to satisfy his impulses. If he has some money in his pocket, he feels *entitled* to decide how to spend it. And if that means his creditors have to wait a little longer to get paid, so be it. The money-reckless man lives for the moment, and in order to be there with him, his partner usually winds up paying the price.

Too Talented to Work

My client Angela had been living with her boyfriend Cliff for about three years. They had met on the set of a television soap opera in which she had a small but regular role. He was filling in for a vacationing cameraman. Cliff asked her out, and within four weeks they were seeing each other exclusively. A few months later he asked her to move in with him. Deeply in love, she jumped at the chance, not knowing he was two months behind on his rent.

After they started living together, Angela discovered that Cliff was able to find only occasional work. It wasn't long before she found herself having to shoulder all their expenses.

ANGELA

I asked him why he didn't go look for something else if he couldn't find work as a cameraman. He said, "I'm an artist. I'm not going to give up on my art to go work in an office. All these people who work nine to five and forty hours a week are just too afraid to really make their dreams come true." And I think, "Oh?" I'm cooking breakfast and cleaning the kitchen every morning, before rushing out the door to fight an hour's traffic to work ten hours and then an hour's traffic to get home, and I'm supporting him, and then I come home and he's sitting on the couch in the same old pair of shorts watching a movie and ranting about how he could have shot it better. He lives in this rarefied atmosphere. There's just something about him that thinks he's separate, that he's better than everyone else, and that really pisses me off. We get in these huge fights about it.

Even though Cliff wasn't running out spending recklessly or making ill-fated investments, he was still spending money he wasn't earning in the form of his part of their joint living expenses. He made no effort to find alternative ways to pay her back for supporting him. He didn't even try to earn his keep by taking on additional household responsibilities. Instead, he lived off his lover's largesse as if it were his birthright.

This was not an arrangement that Angela had either agreed to or felt comfortable about. She had never signed on as the primary breadwinner, she had entered the relationship hoping to be an equal partner.

But Cliff not only refused to work or look for work, he voiced great disdain for those who *did*. The fact that it was Angela's steady work that supported him did nothing to lessen his scorn—or his feelings of superiority and entitlement. And being an enabler, Angela soon found herself acting as if she believed his feelings were justified.

The Manipulation Dance

The money-reckless man is a master at exploiting his partner's feelings to get what he wants. Even though he often does this unknowingly, he seems to have an uncanny instinct for zeroing in on his partner's emotional Achilles' heel to control her with a battery of promises, pleas, blame, and threats.

For her part, the financial enabler plays into her lover's manipulations, following his lead like a partner in an intricate dance.

Playing on Your Sympathies

One of the most effective skills in the money-reckless man's repertoire is his ability to elicit, to nurture, and to exploit his partner's sympathy. Whether knowingly or unknowingly, many money-reckless men use woeful tales of childhood miseries or adult misfortunes to maneuver their partners into trying to make reparations.

When Vic bought the red convertible and the necklace for Diane, Diane should have had serious misgivings. Instead, she overlooked the significance of his behavior. And later she justified his irresponsibility as a reaction to the enormously painful childhood he had had.

Soon afterward, she agreed to marry him, hoping that by

providing him with an emotional commitment, she could make up for the emotional turmoil of that childhood.

DIANE

He never had the normal things, he never had the normal childhood. He was raised by terrible people. They beat him, he was incested by his stepmother—it was horrible. He had stories about how his father bit his fingers to punish him and he had to wear gloves to school. He felt completely alone, abandoned. It's such a sad story. You know the cartoon *Dondi*? Wasn't he an orphan or something? Anyway, Vic always said he felt like Dondi. He looked like Dondi, too. And he just had this look in his eyes. Still, to this day, when people see him, they want to do something for him. When you meet him, you feel it so deep in him, it's so compelling. You just want to offer him something. It's the strangest feeling. And that was always in my mind . . . like this damaged person. He was beaten, he was this, he was that, and he just needed someone to really love him. So I married him. And I loved him. And I bought him anything he wanted. Anything. I bought him clothes, this humongous home gym, a CD system for his car—he didn't even have to ask, he just knew how to get me to pay for things. I just never was even conscious of resenting it. I really wasn't. It was just amazing. If it made him happy for a little while, I was happy.

If you're familiar with my work, you know I never diminish the difficulties that can arise from the kind of brutal childhood Vic had. But adulthood should be a time for healing childhood wounds, not for using them as excuses to stay stuck. In his relationship with Diane, Vic was milking the traumas of his childhood to avoid personal responsibility for his own financial mess. And Diane, feeling sympathy for the pain he had suffered, felt that getting him back on his feet was the least she could do.

Diane became Vic's self-appointed rescuer. She did not feel responsible for what had happened to him as a child, but he found ways of getting her to try to make up for it nonetheless. His life was one big attempt to compensate for the past, and Diane somehow felt responsible for paying the price.

Diane's rescuing behavior suggested an inner need that is common to almost all enablers, financial and otherwise—the need to be needed. This is a powerful motivation for many women. They derive a great deal of their identity from how much they can do, give, fix, and nurture others. Some of this drive is encoded in our genes—we call this our maternal instinct. And some of it is behavior learned from our families and our society. But regardless of the source, this intense need to be needed often propels us into love relationships where we obtain a great deal of our satisfaction and emotional fulfillment from self-sacrifice.

Rescuing Vic made Diane feel so noble, indispensable, purposeful, and fulfilled that the financial drain seemed almost irrelevant.

The Lure of the Downtrodden Man

A man who seems to be one of life's underdogs can be a seductive magnet for an enabling woman. Many money-reckless men almost brag about their financial troubles. Instead of acting grandiose or temporarily cash poor, they seem to derive their very identity from their struggles.

These men may see themselves as tragic victims of life who must scratch for survival at the bottom of the heap. Some of them are alcoholic or addicted to drugs. Some may have spent time in mental hospitals or jails. Or they may be clinically depressed or unstable men who sporadically wander from job to job without ever settling down.

This was exactly the kind of man who attracted my client Leslie.

LESLIE

I met Bill at the park. He came up and gave my dog water
out of his cup. And that just touched my heart. We ended
up having coffee, and we talked for hours. He had just
come out of a recovery home—like a halfway house for
people who've bottomed out and are trying to get sober—
so he had no money at all. He had nothing. I really felt for
him because I'd been sober five years, and I knew how
hard it was to get through that first push. He was real fam-
ily-oriented, he had five sisters, and he was a real charmer,
very good looking. And he had this great voice—it gave
me goosebumps. But he had this—I mean, he didn't seem
depressed exactly, but he kept making all these jokes about
what a loser he was. He'd had a nervous breakdown when
he was in his twenties, and from that point on he'd gotten
odd jobs now and then, but he'd basically lived by latching
onto different women. Of course I didn't know this at the
time. He was living out of his car, which was weird but he
said it was only for a few days while he was between places.
So I told him he could use my shower. When he came
over, he brought me this little daisy that he'd picked, and I
thought it was so sweet. Three days later, I let him move
in for a couple of weeks. He's still here seven years later.

Aside from the immediate potential danger of inviting a
stranger into her home, the risk was pretty great that a man
living out of his car would spell trouble for any woman who
became romantically involved with him. You would think that
a man with Bill's multitude of problems would have a difficult
time attracting an intelligent, competent woman. Yet Leslie was
a worldly, well-educated, successful businesswoman. She was a
respected specialty soap manufacturer whose business had
grown from a vat in her garage to a factory that employed
twenty-five people. If ever there was an unlikely pair, it was
Leslie and Bill.

Unlike Vic or Sam, Bill didn't try to sugar-coat his past, present, or future. Instead, he bared his soul to Leslie at his first opportunity, painting such a bleak picture of his life that she could not help but hear him silently calling for help. And it was a call that came at a particularly vulnerable time in Leslie's life.

LESLIE

I was always with men who had money. The last man I was with was very wealthy. I was just getting going in my business, and we'd been seeing each other for a while and he'd offered to bankroll me. If I had known about the strings attached I never would have jumped at it, but I did. We moved in together soon after, and he became this total control freak. I felt as if I were living under his thumb twenty-four hours a day. He became this compulsive sexual being. Sex was just expected of me whenever—on demand, no matter what I was feeling. It was a power thing with him—the money, the sex—it was all the same. He told me who I could see, what I could do, and when I could do it. We ate when *he* was hungry. We went to sleep when *he* was tired. We watched what *he* wanted to watch on TV. I could have been set for life with him, but I was miserable. I felt totally used, totally stepped on.

Leslie had lost her self-respect in her previous relationship. She had allowed herself to be dominated in exchange for financial security and opportunity. This is hardly a new situation for many women. In recent years, this kind of unhealthy financial dependency has come to be called *golden handcuffs.*

Leslie was so determined to escape the grip of those handcuffs that she took a chance on Bill, a financially unstable man.

Who's Really in Charge?

If ever a woman had red flags waved in front of her, Leslie did. Bill had a history of alcoholism, mental instability, serial unemployment, and sponging off women. But in many ways this history played into Leslie's unconscious need to be the one in charge.

This is a strong lure for many financial enablers. The unconscious need for power and control is especially compelling in women who come from childhoods in which their needs and feelings were squelched by an overbearing or uncaring parent. But this need can also come from adult experiences with overbearing and uncaring lovers, as Leslie's did.

Leslie rushed headlong into a situation that promised to finally give her the sense of control that she believed would restore her self-respect. Unfortunately, it turned out to be an empty promise.

On the surface it might seem that because an enabler holds the purse strings, she holds the power in the relationship. But paradoxically, when you react to your partner's manipulations by giving in to his demands—whether they are stated or implied—you are *being* controlled. Real power in a relationship resides in the partner who consistently succeeds in getting what he or she wants.

Tapping into Your Guilt

Bill may not have gone into the relationship with any economic strength, but as it turned out, he had his own source of power that made money pale in comparison—guilt. If sympathy was the tool he used to persuade Leslie to move him in with her, guilt was the tool he used to consolidate his position once they were ensconced. And believe me, in skilled hands, guilt can be a real power tool.

LESLIE

One night he didn't come home, and I got really worried. Finally, about two A.M. he called. He was in jail. I asked him what happened, and he told me he was in for parking tickets. I couldn't believe it. He told me he had $798 worth of outstanding parking tickets and a few speeding tickets to boot. I was so furious that he'd let it get out of hand like that that I refused to come bail him out. I was heavy into Alanon at the time so I felt very strongly that he had to deal with his own consequences. So I left him there for a couple of days. But every day he'd call and really lay on the guilt about how dirty it was and how scared he was and how awful the food was and how sorry he was. . . . And I really wanted to stick by my guns but by day three he got me thinking maybe I was this terrible person to do this to him. So I finally went down there and bailed him out. Then, for the next couple months, every time he wanted something, he found a way to bring it up how I'd let him sit in jail and how I really didn't love him, and this guilt would just come welling back up in me and I'd end up backing down again.

When you refuse a money-reckless man something he wants, when you thwart his desires, when you attempt to force him to experience the consequences of his own money-reckless behavior, he will inevitably find a way to use guilt to undermine your resolve.

Leslie tried to take a stand with Bill for one of the few times in their relationship. Bill responded by laying the guilt on so thickly that she buckled under the emotional weight and bailed him out of jail.

But that wasn't the end of it. The jail experience became Bill's store of ammunition to haul out whenever he needed to control Leslie. For months, whenever she tried to protest his spending habits or complain about his apathetic attitude toward finding work, he would lob a salvo like "You've got no right to lecture me about what I 'should' be doing. If it were up to you, I'd still be rotting away in that filthy jail cell."

Despite her experience in Alanon (a support group for partners and family members of alcoholics), which taught her that the most loving thing she could do for both Bill and herself was to set firm limits on his behavior, Leslie found herself falling prey to Bill's manipulations. Logic and wisdom could simply not stand up to the power of guilt under Bill's skilled stewardship.

Using Other Family Members

As an enabler becomes more deeply enmeshed with a money-reckless man, other family members may become enmeshed as well.

I've had clients whose partners used their children as unwitting tools to manipulate grandparents into lending or giving money. Nothing moves a grandparent like the threat that their grandchildren might suffer loss or deprivation.

Siblings, in-laws, other relatives, or friends are prime targets for this sort of manipulation as well. Family relationships become increasingly strained and complicated as the money-reckless man pressures his partner to ask other family members to bail him out of his troubles.

If the financial enabler has been lying and covering up for her partner, she will have to endure the shame of exposing the truth in order to get emergency funds from relatives. If she has been defending and making excuses for her lover in response to family members who have seen through him, she will face added humiliation when her requests for money prove them right.

But perhaps the most powerful manipulation a money-reckless man can use to control an enabler is her own child's fear of losing "Daddy." The threat of putting her child through the pain of family separation can easily bind a woman to the very money-reckless partner whose behavior jeopardizes that child's future.

This was Bill's ultimate weapon against Leslie. Though Leslie and Bill had never married, they had a son—Marcus—about a year after they started living together. During the next several years, Bill managed to land a succession of jobs, but none lasted longer than a few months. By the time Marcus was seven years old, Bill had started drinking again, he was once again unemployed, and he seemed to be making no efforts to find work.

When Bill "borrowed" Leslie's credit card without her permission and ran up several thousand dollars' worth of new debt, she finally reached the end of her rope. That was when she came to see me. She wanted to leave Bill, but she couldn't muster the nerve.

LESLIE

My hook is our son. I don't know what to do about it. I mean, I kicked Bill out once before, and it was murder on Marcus. He went through this abandonment thing, and it took him a year to recover, even though Bill came back after a couple of months. He was really irritable, he started messing up in school, I couldn't leave him alone with anybody—it was horrible. I'm so afraid to rock his boat again, and Bill knows it. So every time I threaten to end it, Bill asks me how I could destroy Marcus's life like that, how I could take his father away. I feel so trapped . . . it tears me apart just thinking about it.

I told Leslie that I knew how painful her dilemma was but that she was kidding herself if she thought she was helping Marcus by submitting to Bill's emotional blackmail. While Bill was getting everything he wanted from Leslie, Marcus was learning about love relationships in a toxic, dysfunctional way. This was far more damaging than seeing his mother take her power and say "I'm not willing to live like this any more."

Besides, what kind of a role model was Bill for Marcus? He was drinking again, he wasn't working, he wasn't paying his way, he was lying to Leslie, he was stealing from her—was this the kind of man she wanted Marcus to grow up emulating?

In the long run, Bill's presence was likely to be more hurtful than his absence, unless he was willing to make some major changes, which didn't seem likely. Yet Leslie was still reluctant to make the decision she knew she wanted to make—the decision to leave him. I asked her if she was prepared to take care of Bill for the rest of her life, because that seemed to be her only realistic alternative.

SUSAN

You've *got* to remember that it's *his* behavior that's causing all this. It's *his* financial irresponsibility, it's *his* reckless spending, it's *his* refusal to work, it's *his* drinking. If anyone should feel guilty, it should be him. *He's* the one who's breaking up the family, not you.

Over the next several weeks, Leslie and I continued to work together on finding ways for her to deal with her fears and her unwarranted guilts. After some tough soul-searching, Leslie finally began to accept the fact that the healthiest thing she could do for her son and for herself was to end her relationship with Bill before it put her either into the poorhouse or into a mental hospital. She slowly grew to feel secure enough to do what she knew she had to do—tell Bill to leave.

In refusing to put up with Bill's irresponsible behavior any longer, Leslie was not only ceasing to move to the music of manipulation, she was walking off the dance floor altogether.

Malicious Manipulations

Most of the manipulations we've seen so far have been at least partially unconscious or driven by financial desperation. But there is a class of money-reckless men whose manipulations are calculated and ruthless—they're outright con artists.

In professional parlance, these men are *sociopaths*. A sociopath is a person who has little or no conscience, who moves through life leaving chaos in his wake without concern for the damage he may be doing to the lives of others.

Though stories of women being literally conned out of their savings may seem extreme, they are sadly quite common. Every day, thousands of women are deliberately fleeced by crooks in lovers' clothing. And it is enabling behavior that gives these men their keys to the vault.

Unfortunately, many sociopaths can be extremely charming and persuasive. Because of this, it is often possible to recognize such men only in retrospect—as Laurel would find out.

LAUREL

Sean would bitch and moan about his ex-wife calling and hollering all the time: "Where's my money? Where's my money?" And he had to pay her two thousand dollars a month, which, of course he didn't have. So he came crying to me for it, saying that she'd have him thrown in jail if he didn't pay it. He said it was just for another four months, and in my mind I thought, "Well, okay, it's only till February," so I told him I'd pay it. Then one night I'm sitting home watching television and the telephone rings, and it's his ex-wife, and she wants to know where her money is. So I told her I'd given him the alimony check last week, and she started laughing. "Alimony?" she says. "Is *that* what he told you? He doesn't pay me alimony—we're still married. We never got divorced." I was totally blown away. So I called him and confronted him with the fact that he's a bigamist, and he says, "Don't move, I'm coming right home." So he comes home and he's, like, surprised that I'm ready to kill him. He says, "I came home, didn't I? I could have just run, but I came home. I could have run," as if I'm supposed to forgive him because of that. And then he says, "I only did it because I loved you too much. I loved you so much, I was willing to break the law." Well, that was it for me. I mean, he's lying and he's stealing, and our marriage isn't even legal, and I'm out tens of thousands of dollars, and he's trying to convince me he did it because he loved me.

Laurel decided she had no choice but to split up with Sean that night. She had had plenty of warning beforehand, but because of her tendency to enable, it took a sledgehammer to drive home the message: Sean was a user, a financial tornado that had touched down in her life—a con man, pure and simple.

When Dependence Breeds Resentment

No matter how much manipulating a money-reckless man does in a relationship, no matter how much power he wields, he often still finds himself dependent on his partner for financial survival. Even though this is usually a situation of his own making, it inevitably sticks in his craw.

Financial dependence is a humiliating state for a man to be in, a state of perpetual vulnerability in which it is extremely difficult for him to feel self-respect. He knows that if his partner were to leave him, he would have a difficult time making it on his own. His dependence is a constant reminder of his inadequacies and failures.

The money-reckless man's financial dependence has just the opposite effect on his enabler. Her partner may be exploiting her, but as long as he needs her, the financial enabler feels safe, believing she is indispensable and irreplaceable in their relationship.

Unfortunately, this sense of security is false. The financial enabler rarely banks on the fact that dependency of this kind almost always makes a man feel resentful. And this resentment can be expressed in any number of unexpected and sometimes traumatic ways.

DIANE

One day I got this call from this woman out of the blue. She said she'd been having an affair with Vic for six months and that he kept promising to leave me for her, but.

he didn't, and she was pissed off about waiting, so that's why she called. I totally lost it—I was stunned. When he got home, I was so upset I could hardly talk. I just started bawling about the phone call. And you know what he said? He said, "What do you expect? You never do anything but bitch to me about how much money I'm spending. I'm tired of being ragged at all the time, I'm tired of your twenty-dollar handouts. I needed someone to look up to me for a change, give me a little respect. Is that too much to ask?"

Vic's angry response was the last thing Diane had expected. He might have been apologetic, he might have seemed humiliated, he might have acted remorseful. But instead, he went on the attack, making Diane the scapegoat for his affair, as if her legitimate complaints somehow justified his inexcusable behavior.

Having an affair is just one of many ways in which a money-reckless man may act out his resentment. He may internalize it by becoming moody or depressed, or he may externalize it by picking fights, belittling his partner, or stepping up his money-reckless behavior.

But turning to another woman is one of the most common ways for a money-reckless man to escape the resentments that grow out of his dependence on his partner. It is like a breath of fresh air for him to be with a woman who has not seen him humiliated by creditors, failing in business, or groveling for cash. He can escape the feelings of being judged or diminished that he might feel with his partner.

At the same time, he can feel as if he's striking a blow for freedom against his partner—the woman upon whom he's become so unbearably dependent.

This may not be the first time he has rebelled against a caretaker upon whom he felt overly dependent (and therefore inadequate). Many money-reckless men unconsciously use their adult love relationships to reenact their adolescent rebellion against their mother or father. Unable to win the struggle to be free as teenagers, they are still fighting the battle as adults.

Once you move into that maternal role, you are in a no-win situation. On the one hand, your partner wants nothing more than for you to allow him to act like a little kid. On the other hand, he resents you for making him feel like one. It is an internal conflict that works against you no matter which side wins.

An End to Enabling

If your story could have been one of the cases in this chapter, and if your relationship is draining you both financially and emotionally, then you must know by now that your relationship cannot continue as it is. Something must change.

I realize that you probably think it's *his* responsibility to do the changing since he's doing all the reckless spending and debting. And it *is* his responsibility. But if he's not willing to do something effective to change his behavior, you can't *force* him to. You can only change your *own* enabling behavior, and when you do, your relationship will have to change by default.

The nature of the changes you need to make depends on the nature of your financial enmeshment with your partner. These changes will vary depending on whether you're married, whether you've commingled your finances, whether your partner brings in any money, whether your partner is regularly employed, and whether you are the sole support of your household.

But no matter what your financial relationship, the most effective way for you to bring an end to the financial chaos and to give your relationship its only chance of surviving is to *set firm limits* on his money-reckless behavior.

Before you do this, you may want to protect yourself from the possibility of an impulsive backlash on his part by doing whatever you can to eliminate or reduce his access to your money or to money that the two of you have in common. This could mean withdrawing cash from your joint accounts and putting it into an account in your own name. It could mean canceling all of your credit cards. And it certainly means refusing to give or lend him any more money.

If you have to enlist his cooperation in dealing with such things as canceling credit cards and closing joint bank accounts where both of your signatures may be required, you need to be firm in your resolve, leaving no doubt that this is his *only* choice if he wants you to remain in the relationship.

Only after your financial resources are beyond his reach can you sit down with him and set some new limits without risking financial sabotage.

Setting Limits

You may believe that you are already doing something about the money issues in your relationship by nagging, or reasoning, or complaining, or screaming, or crying, or making empty threats. Let me assure you that none of these behaviors has any effect on a truly money-reckless man. He will find any number of ways to outmaneuver you in an argument, charm you out of your determination, or make promises to change that, if he keeps them at all, he will keep only as long as it takes to placate you.

If you want to get through to a money-reckless man, instead of haranguing or pleading you need to set limits—clearly and calmly tell him what you are no longer willing to do for him and what you will no longer tolerate from him.

You need to be very explicit about no longer being willing to pay any bills or financial obligations for which you are not personally responsible.

In Angela's case, for example, she told me that she didn't want to keep living with Cliff unless he got a job. She was tired of supporting him, and she was losing respect for him. Yet every time she got up the courage to give him an ultimatum, the intensity of her feelings for him undermined her resolve. Like most enablers, setting limits went against her grain.

ANGELA

I just can't do it. He needs me too much. And I need him. He'll sit and listen to me and talk to me and process with me for hours. I need that. I can't just throw him out on the street. Besides—how will he support himself?

Angela's reluctance wasn't surprising. The notion of caring for others over yourself is deeply embedded in the enabler's personality. I know how difficult it is to do something when the voices within you are screaming "No, no, no!" But as your behavior changes, so will those voices.

I am a firm believer in a process that may seem backward to you—the process of making changes first and feeling "right" about it later. Most people think that they have to feel strong, or courageous, or confident before they can act in those ways. But the truth is, the results of assertive limit-setting will be the same no matter what your inner feelings are. And once your new behavior produces change, you'll be amazed at how much better you feel about it.

I encouraged Angela to pick a quiet time to tell Cliff that she was willing to support him emotionally but not financially. If he couldn't find work that he considered worthy of him, he'd have to make some compromises if he wanted them to be together.

It took Angela several days to muster the courage to confront Cliff with her limits, but she finally did. At first he tried to argue with her and make her feel guilty, calling her unsupportive, unsympathetic, and out of touch with the current job market. But Angela and I had worked out some nondefensive responses to deal with Cliff's reactions. They were different from the responses suggested in Drawing the Line in Chapter 4, because Cliff tended to become self-pitying rather than abusive under pressure. Angela didn't argue with his dire predictions or accuse him of inadequacy. She remained respectful but firm. Here are a few of the statements we practiced together:

I'm sorry things aren't going your way.

I have confidence that you will figure something out.

I'm not going to lend you any more money. Maybe someone else will, but that doesn't solve the problem.

What I've been doing is bad for me and it's bad for you. It's bad for any chance we have of making it together.

Angela's limit-setting didn't seem to make much of an impression on Cliff's behavior at first. But when she refused to pay his car payment at the end of the month, he was forced to either look for a job or lose his car. A week later, he found work.

It's been six months now, and Cliff is still employed, though he complains about it regularly. But he and Angela seem to be fighting a lot less, especially about money.

ANGELA

It wasn't just the money that made me mad before—it was being taken advantage of. I mean, I'd look at him and I'd wonder what kind of a person I was to let him keep doing that to me. But I'm not letting him anymore, and I feel really good about that. Maybe *he* doesn't, but I do. I mean, things aren't perfect, but I *think* they're getting better.

Mary had a similar experience with Sam, except that Sam took Mary's limits seriously from the start. The day after she had her talk with Sam, he went out looking for work. It took him almost a month, but he kept up his search, and he finally landed a decent job as a sales rep for a large importer.

Mary and Sam's relationship, like Angela and Cliff's, still needs work. But both Mary and Sam are quick to admit that things have improved significantly between them.

When you set limits on a money-reckless man, there are no guarantees of how he will respond. He may agree to your terms; he may be reluctant, like Cliff, but then come around; he may dig in his heels and refuse to make any changes; or he may even end the relationship.

If your partner has any capacity to change for the better, limit-setting will set the process in motion. On the other hand, no matter how much you may love your partner, if he is incorrigible, you are better off knowing that now before your financial situation deteriorates any further.

Limit-setting is more than a behavioral technique. It is a critical litmus test of a relationship's real potential.

Taking the Lid Off

Diane had been seeing me for about a month when she found out about Vic's affair. She was extremely upset when she came in that week, yet her initial impulse was to try to salvage her marriage by forgiving him and even by accepting part of the blame.

Diane was clearly stuffing the anger that any woman would have after being treated as Vic had treated her. Between his money-recklessness and his infidelity, she had plenty to be furious about, yet she was neither acknowledging nor expressing her anger. Like most enablers, Diane was an old hand at pretending things are fine when they aren't. And if she didn't get in touch with this anger and deal with it effectively, it would surely find destructive ways to express itself through physical or emotional symptoms.

I pointed to an empty chair and suggested that Diane do some role-playing to gain access to the anger she'd been sitting on, anger that she could then use to motivate herself to start acting in her own best interests—which was long overdue.

She faced the chair and imagined that Vic was sitting there. Tears came to her eyes, she was so overwhelmed by feelings, but anger wasn't one of them.

DIANE

I don't feel angry, I feel sad. . . . I feel hurt. . . . I feel used. . . . But I just don't feel angry.

SUSAN

Of course you feel sad, but right now it's important for you to focus on your anger, because that's what's going to empower you to get unstuck. Close your eyes, and let me draw you a picture. I want you to visualize Vic and his girlfriend in a romantic restaurant, sharing a champagne toast to each other. The bill arrives, and he whips out his wallet to pay—with your credit card.

I could see Diane begin to simmer. She obviously didn't like the images I was suggesting, but neither did those images strike her as unlikely.

SUSAN

Then later, they're lying naked in bed, and he's telling her how much she means to him because *you* just don't understand him. He tells her that you're so smothering that he doesn't even like to be with you anymore. Getting angry yet?

DIANE

I'm getting there.

SUSAN

Well, tell him, don't tell me.

Diane again turned to the empty chair, but this time, after a halting start, she had little trouble coming up with the words.

DIANE

I—I can't believe you—how could you do this to me? After all I did for you! I loved you, I thought you loved me. . . . I trusted you. . . . What a joke. You just stabbed me in the back. I loved you, and you betrayed me, you lied to me, you cheated me, you stole from me, you used up my money, you used up my life, you used me up.

The words poured out of her. It came as no surprise to me that Diane was so full of anger—she had been repeatedly exploited.

Some enablers express their anger on a regular basis, by fighting, nagging, sniping, complaining, or whining—doing more to perpetuate than to resolve the conflicts in their relationships. Others, like Diane, are volcanoes of resentment just waiting to erupt.

But in taking the lid off her feelings, Diane allowed herself to see for the first time that she had been perpetuating an untenable relationship with a man who was making her miserable.

Learning from Your Mistakes

With her real feelings coming to the surface, Diane was finally able to acknowledge the true costs of her relationship with Vic. Once she stopped deceiving herself into believing that everything was okay, she was able to gain the clarity she needed to decide what she really wanted to do about her relationship.

DIANE

I realized that somewhere in my life I learned how to be overly responsible, and that's all I was doing with Vic. We weren't communicating, we weren't friends, I couldn't trust him—and I knew that had to end. I had that moment of clarity where I went, "Holy crud! This isn't what I want. But I'm giving him everything he wants, so why should he change?" I know it's not fair, but what's fair? My concept of fair was "If I love you, you'll love me. If I give to you, you'll give to me." But this concept of fair was "You give to me, and I take." And I've learned that I don't have to fix anything I didn't break. And you know what? I couldn't have gone to school to get that kind of education, even if I spent the kind of money he cost me.

Once Diane gained a clear perspective on her relationship with Vic, she chose to end it. Though this was very painful for her to do, it was a decision that she has never regretted.

Avoiding the Trap of Self-Reproach

Diane's response to her own realization was extremely healthy. She used her new insights to make some difficult but self-affirming decisions about her relationship, and then she looked back on the experience as a vital life lesson. However, other financial enablers use the mistakes they've made in their relationships to flagellate themselves.

It is not unusual for a woman to end a relationship with a money-reckless man and then beat herself up for having allowed him to victimize her. Financial enablers often become preoccupied with the enormous time, energy, emotional resources, and money they believe they've wasted. They use words like *stupid, idiotic, crazy,* or *blind* to describe themselves. They become stuck in self-recrimination instead of using their new insights and clarity to move on.

Remember, you did the best you could with the amount of awareness and information you had. We all did. Even if a part of you knew the truth (which is almost always the case) you probably were afraid to look at it. Women are often moved by passion and the need to be needed to discount the clarity of their inner voices.

In addition, most of us have been programmed not to validate our own perceptions and feelings. When that is combined with fears of being unlovable and not being "enough," we are extremely vulnerable to the seductions of a money-reckless man.

If you make the decision to end your relationship, there's

another kind of self-reproach you might be faced with—remorse over what you've given up. In my own marriage, there were many wonderful times. I went through years of a torturous internal tug-of-war between my love for my husband and the stress of constant financial and emotional chaos. I tried several times to set limits, but he simply refused to take them seriously. I finally came to the realization that leaving him was my only viable option for restoring sanity to my life.

After I made that painful choice, I thought the hardest part was over, even though I knew I had a lot of grieving to do. What I wasn't prepared for was the inner conflict that assailed me. For several months following our separation, I obsessed about whether it had really been as bad as I thought it was, whether it had been worth tearing the family apart, whether I had made the biggest mistake of my life.

I finally dealt with this problem by finding a way to bring myself back to reality whenever I discovered myself sugar-coating the past. There are a thousand ways to do this, but mine was to keep a box of canceled checks that my husband had written over the years. These checks were written to fund one futile, venture after another, using money we needed to live on. Whenever I started to have second thoughts about my decision to leave him, I would open that box and leaf through the checks to evoke vivid memories of the suffering each one had caused us. These repetitive reminders helped me turn my self-recrimination into self-validation for having done something truly healthy for myself and my children.

Repetitive self-reproach can become as self-defeating as enabling. Ending a relationship with a money-reckless man does not, in and of itself, free you completely from the destructiveness of that relationship. You must also release the negative feelings about yourself that it may have left behind.

Ultimately, this chapter is about one single word: *no*. If you learn to use this word wisely, you will take away the crutch that has allowed your partner to avoid taking personal responsibility for his life. Whether or not you are able to save your relationship, you will be ready to begin the sometimes difficult but always empowering process of rebuilding your emotional and financial resources and reclaiming your self-worth.

Self-Help Strategies

It may seem uncharacteristic of me, but I have not explored the childhood issues that shaped the enabling behavior of some of the women you met in this chapter. There is an important reason for this. If a woman's partner is money-reckless, chances are that her financial and emotional life are in crisis, and in order to deal effectively with that crisis she will need all of her adult coping skills and power.

The intense emotional work of uncovering and exploring money demons formed in childhood often evokes old feelings of helplessness, dependency, and powerlessness. These feelings can make it extremely difficult to stay focused and committed to the behavioral changes that a woman needs to make in order to stop enabling.

This doesn't mean that you may not need to do some childhood work in therapy or in a support group anyway. But you're asking too much of yourself if you try to do this when all hell is breaking loose around you. If you wait until your financial fires are at least partially under control, you will be in a much stronger position to deal with your more deep-seated emotional issues. Believe me, there's no hurry—your childhood isn't going anywhere.

Setting Limits

Don't look upon setting limits as being tyrannical, punitive, or degrading. It is an affirmation of your own right to an honest and nonexploitive relationship. Limit-setting is an external control that can be very calming to someone who is out of control internally. Just as consistent rules can be emotionally stabilizing for a child, so can they be for a money-reckless man.

Aside from setting limits on your partner's behavior, you may need to consult a financial adviser, an attorney, or both to find out how you can protect yourself. I've had clients (and friends) who have found themselves liable for debts they didn't even know about—debts that jeopardized savings, automobiles, even homes. If you are married, you may be stuck with some of his debts because of community property laws, but you can still use limit-setting to put the brakes on his spending.

Some of my clients have been quite successful in making their partner's attendance in Debtors Anonymous part of their requirements for staying in the relationship. Some of you may see this as taking responsibility for fixing your partner, but to me it is simply putting the bat in his hands and giving him a chance to step up to the plate. At the very least, you should make sure he is aware of the program.

Taking the Lid Off

When you take the lid off, you release a lot of tension and anxiety. This can be extremely cathartic when you act out against an empty chair. But there is a difference between accessing your anger and dumping it on your partner. Don't confuse personal catharsis with conflict resolution. It is rarely effective and often counterproductive to try to communicate your feelings to your partner when you are emotionally distraught. Angry confrontations have a nasty habit of turning into frustrating shouting contests that only serve to lock both of you into increasingly defensive positions. Unbridle your anger in a safe place when you're by yourself; when you're with your partner, use your anger to gain the strength to stop backing down when he tries to undermine the limits you've set.

Does this mean that you shouldn't tell him how angry you are? Of course not. But you won't get him to hear you by attacking and blaming. The best way to get a money-reckless man to heed your feelings is by expressing your anger with the nonoffensive communications techniques that you learned in Chapter 6.

CODA

There is a twelve-step program that is especially helpful for women who are trying to stop enabling. It is called CODA, which is an acronym for Codependents Anonymous. Like all twelve-step programs, CODA provides a support network, a sense of community, a place to share your experiences in a non-judgmental environment, and a structure that encourages behavioral changes. Though it is not specifically designed for *financial* enablers, many of my clients who are struggling with this issue have found the program extremely helpful.

Epilogue

Living Without Money Demons

I know that many of you, like the women you've met in this book, may be feeling overwhelmed by the financial conflicts in your relationship or by your problems with money and the resulting emotional frenzy. You may spend a lot of time feeling frustrated, hopeless, resentful, powerless, or even victimized.

But let me tell you, as someone who's been there, that even though your financial troubles or money conflicts may seem insurmountable, the painful feelings do not have to dominate your life. If you follow the guidelines in this book and adhere to the self-help tips that are appropriate for you, you *can* prevail over your money demons.

Some authors insist that the solution to money fights is sound financial management. But as we've seen, these conflicts are rarely simply about money.

Financial solutions, as anxiety-reducing as they may be, simply can't deal with the emotional and psychological issues that often lie at the heart of financial problems. It is only by tackling inner issues, as you've begun to do in reading this book, that you can tackle your money conflicts both from within and without. Only in this way can you find solutions that will not just balance your books but go a long way toward helping to stabilize your relationship.

By using the dramatic experiences that the women (and men) in this book have been generous enough to share, and by sharing some of my own experiences as well, I hope that I've helped you illuminate what's really going on not only between you and your partner when you fight about money, but also what's really going on inside of *you*.

No matter whether you are struggling with self-deprivation, self-sabotage, financial compulsions, financial imbalances in your relationship, or enabling behavior, you can put the specific behavioral strategies and exercises that I've given you into practice immediately to help you gain control of your money demons and break many of the money-related patterns that are tripping you up or instigating fights between you and your partner.

Rita—whom we met in Chapter 1—used these techniques to find a new way of being in a relationship.

RITA

One of the things with Stan now—one of the things we're trying to do as a couple—is to find ways that we can share money. Because we've been together seven years, and up until a year and a half ago we didn't own anything together. I was very slow to find ways to share. But I've learned that that wasn't normal. That people that live together—whether they're man and wife or not—they're supposed to share. That always felt so unnatural to me, but it doesn't anymore because I've learned to let myself trust him, and I've learned to let myself trust me. So it's as if we're finally in this together, and it really feels good—it really does.

Whether or not you are currently in a love relationship, you will discover, as Rita did, that the mistakes you've made can be your best teachers. If I have helped you discover how your personal money demons operate, where they may have originated, and ultimately how to manage them, you are well on your way.

Supplemental Reading

BLUMSTEIN, PHILIP, and PEPPER SCHWARTZ. *American Couples: Money, Work, and Sex*. New York: William Morrow, 1983.

FELTON-Collins, VICTORIA. *Couples and Money: Why Money Interferes With Love and What to do About It*. New York: Bantam Books, 1990.

KAUFFMANN, WILLIAM. "Some Emotional Uses of Money." In Ernest Borneman, ed., *The Psychoanalysis of Money*. New York: Urizen Books, 1976.

MATTHEWS, ARLENE MODICA. *If I Think About Money So Much, Why Can't I Figure It Out?* New York: Summit Books, 1991.

MILLMAN, MARSHA. *Warm Hearts and Cold Cash*. New York: Free Press, 1991.

NEEDLEMAN, JACOB. *Money and the Meaning of Life*. New York: Doubleday, 1991.

SIMMEL, GEORG. *The Philosophy of Money*. Translated by Tom Bottomore and David Frisby. London: Routledge and Kegan Paul, 1978.

About the Authors

SUSAN FORWARD, Ph.D., is an internationally acclaimed therapist, lecturer, and author. Her books, which include *Men Who Hate Women & the Women Who Love Them, Toxic Parents, Obsessive Love,* and *Betrayal of Innocence,* have been translated into fifteen languages. She is much in demand as a guest on the major national media. She hosted her own daily ABC Talkradio show for six years.

Dr. Forward maintains offices in Encino and Tustin, California. For further information, call (818) 905-5292 or (714) 838-4444.

CRAIG BUCK, a film and television writer and producer, has written extensively on human behavior for many national magazines and newspapers. He is the co-author of *Toxic Parents, Obsessive Love,* and *Betrayal of Innocence.*

Bantam's informative, easy-to-use business books provide up-to-date advice for today's financial needs

---